KT-439-018

A Natural History of Latin

A Natural History of Latin

TORE JANSON

Translated and adapted into English by
Merethe Damsgård Sørensen *and* Nigel Vincent

OXFORD
UNIVERSITY PRESS

OXFORD
UNIVERSITY PRESS

Great Clarendon Street, Oxford OX2 6DP

Oxford University Press is a department of the University of Oxford.
It furthers the University's objective of excellence in research, scholarship,
and education by publishing worldwide in

Oxford New York

Auckland Cape Town Dar es Salaam Hong Kong Karachi
Kuala Lumpur Madrid Melbourne Mexico City Nairobi
New Delhi Shanghai Taipei Toronto

With offices in

Argentina Austria Brazil Chile Czech Republic France Greece
Guatemala Hungary Italy Japan South Korea Poland Portugal
Singapore Switzerland Thailand Turkey Ukraine Vietnam

Published in the United States
by Oxford University Press Inc., New York

Swedish edition, *Latin; Kulturen, historien, språket,* published by Wahlsröm and
Widstrand, Stockholm © Tore Janson 2002

© Tore Janson 2004

© English translation Merethe Damsgård Sorensen and Nigel Vincent

The moral rights of the author have been asserted
Database right Oxford University Press (maker)

First published 2004

All rights reserved. No part of this publication may be reproduced,
stored in a retrieval system, or transmitted, in any form or by any means,
without the prior permission in writing of Oxford University Press,
or as expressly permitted by law, or under terms agreed with the appropriate
reprographics rights organization. Enquiries concerning reproduction
outside the scope of the above should be sent to the Rights Department,
Oxford University Press, at the address above.

You must not circulate this book in any other binding or cover
and you must impose this same condition on any acquirer.

British Library Cataloguing in Publication Data
Data available

Library of Congress Cataloging in Publication Data
Data available

ISBN 0–19–926309–4

10 9 8 7 6 5 4

Typeset by Newgen Imaging Systems (P) Ltd., Chennai, India
Printed in Great Britain
on acid-free paper by
Biddles Ltd., King's Lynn, Norfolk

CONTENTS

Contents

Part II *Latin and Europe*

Part III *About the Grammar*

FOREWORD

This book is for everyone who wants to know more about Latin, about the language and about its influence on the culture and history of Europe. It covers the basic facts about the pronunciation of Latin, the most common words, and something about the forms of words. It also includes a fair number of well-known phrases and quotations. This is not a textbook in any traditional or modern sense. It is mainly about how and when the language was used, and how it has gradually influenced other languages. You will not need special previous knowledge; everything you need to know will be introduced as you go along. My idea is to communicate to the reader what we know about a language and a culture which has had, and continues to have, a very great influence on us all. Of course, I hope that some readers will become so interested that they will want to acquire a thorough knowledge of Latin for themselves, but to do this they will have to move on to ordinary textbooks. My aim here is simply to offer an overview and an appetizer.

Even so, if you want to know the meaning of individual Latin words and expressions, this book will take you quite a long way. At the back there is a brief grammar and a list of basic vocabulary and a collection of the most common phrases and expressions. There is also an index which will enable the reader to find matters that are discussed in the text. The book can be used as a reference work for people who quickly want to find out something about the Latin language.

Latin was both a spoken and a written language in ancient Rome. It gradually fell out of use as anyone's native language, but for more than a thousand years after the fall of the Roman Empire it was used as a spoken and written language by educated people throughout western Europe. However, the language played a different role in antiquity from the one it came to play later. For this reason the main part of the book falls into two halves, one about Latin and the

Romans in antiquity and one about Latin and Europe thereafter. The written language has in principle remained the same for two thousand years from antiquity until the present day. This book aims to give a portrait of that language.

While working on this book I have benefited from the opinions, advice and suggestions of Magnus Wistrand, Hans Aili, Eva Halldinger, and not least my wife, Christina Westman. The English version is not just a translation, since the text has been revised and adapted in many places, and a couple of sections are entirely new. It has been a great pleasure to cooperate in this work with the translators, Merethe Damsgård Sørensen and Nigel Vincent (who wrote the sections on Latin and German and on the pronunciation of Latin in England), and with John Davey at the Oxford University Press. None of them is to be held responsible for any remaining errors or flaws.

The translators of the English edition would particularly like to acknowledge the help of John Briscoe, Tim Cornell, Roy Gibson, Kersti Börjars, Martin Durrell, and Katy Vincent, not to mention Tore Janson!

Part I
Latin and the Romans

Lingua latina: *a first acquaintance*

Many Latin words are easy to understand. Here is one to start with:

femina

It is easy to guess that this means 'woman'. It's the name of several women's magazines in various countries around the world and is also a brand of perfume. Then there are related words like *feminine, female,* and *feminist*. And it doesn't take a big leap of the imagination to link it with the French word *femme* 'woman'. It's often that way when you study languages, particularly one as widespread as Latin. Latin words are sometimes borrowed unchanged. They also frequently appear as parts of learned or abstract words. English has borrowed large numbers of words from Latin, often via French. And there are even greater similarities with French, Spanish, and Italian, languages which have developed out of Latin.

Anyone who has a large vocabulary in English therefore already knows quite a lot of Latin words, and anyone who speaks Spanish or French knows even more. But it also works the other way round. Anyone who has acquired a basic Latin vocabulary will more easily be able to understand many words in other European languages.

Let's build up a little more Latin:

femina clara

This is a bit harder, even if Claire and Clara are English names and *clear* is a loan from Latin (by way of French). Yet in Latin the word usually meant 'light' or 'bright', as in English *a clear day,* but also 'shining' or 'famous'. So *femina clara* means 'a famous woman'.

This example also shows us that Latin has a different word order from English. An adjective like *clara* usually comes after the word it goes with. The same word order can be seen in the phrase which is in the title of this section: *lingua latina*. One can guess that *lingua* means 'language' from the English word *linguistics,* which means the science of language, or indeed from the word *language* itself or the French word *langue* 'language'. The word *latina* obviously means 'Latin', and so the whole phrase means 'the Latin language'.

One might query this translation on the grounds that there is nothing in the Latin expression which corresponds to the English word *the*, or what is called the definite article. But Latin has no equivalent to *the* or to the indefinite article *a/an*. A Latin phrase like *femina clara* can be translated as 'famous woman', 'a famous woman', or 'the famous woman' depending on the context. This is in fact the way things are in most of the world's languages. The definite and indefinite articles are by and large found in modern western European languages like English, German, and French.

Just a few words in Latin quickly give an idea of what is easy and what is difficult. The words are often already known, or at least you can often connect a Latin word with an English word you already know. But the rules for how you put the words together into phrases or sentences, that is the grammar of the language, are very different from those that apply in a language like English. In this book for the most part I focus on words in the main body of the text, and you can read it without bothering about the word endings or other complications. If you are interested, however, you can find the most important rules in the section entitled 'About the Grammar' at the end of the book.

Latin is written with what we have come to call the Roman alphabet, which English and most other European languages have taken over. Our script was originally created to write down Latin, and so the letters correspond very well to the sounds of that language. The words we have met so far are pronounced more or less as we would expect.

Obviously, there are still some differences. In the Latin of antiquity the letter *c* is only used to represent the sound which we indicate with *k* in words of Anglo-Saxon origin such as *kill* or *king*. Due to French influence, we have retained this value for the letter *c* in words of Latin origin such as *clear* or *castle*, but we pronounce it as [s] when followed by *e* or *i*. What the Romans never did was to use the letter *c* to represent an *s*-sound, so that we pronounce several words that come from Latin in a way that would have surprised the Romans. For example, we say the word *cell* with an initial *s*-sound although it is in fact the English version of the Latin word *cella* 'room' which was pronounced with an initial [k]. It is the same with Latin names like Cicero (which the Romans pronounced approximately *kickerow*), Caesar and Cecilia. In other contexts, the modern pronunciation of Latin in Britain and northern Europe respects the ancient norms and uses the *k*-sound in all words that are spelled with a *c*.

Why there should be these differences requires quite a bit of explaining, and we will deal with the question later in the book. It has to do with the way the pronunciation of Latin changed over the centuries. Here I will just concentrate on how the ancient Romans pronounced their language. There is also a difference between English and Latin as far as the vowels are concerned. Latin had only five vowels, represented by the letters *i, e, a, o,* and *u,* which had more or less the same sounds as these letters do in modern Spanish or Italian, so that for example *Roma,* the name of the city of Rome, must have been said in much the same way by the Romans as it is by the Italians who now live there. Similarly, the Romans would not have much trouble recognizing modern Italian or Spanish words like *casa* 'house', *tu* 'you', and *luna* 'moon', whose pronunciation has changed very little in two thousand years. Although the single vowel letters are never associated with the kind of diphthongal pronunciation of the English *i* in *wine* or *a* in *fate,* there are three sequences of vowel letters which represent diphthongs, namely *ae* pronounced roughly as English *I, oe* as in English *boy,* and *au* as in English *loud.* With this knowledge you should be able to pronounce Latin words correctly according to the ancient norms. For instance, the Roman pronunciation of *Caesar* was very close to the modern German pronunciation of the word *Kaiser* 'emperor', perhaps not surprising since the latter is a Latin borrowing in German. The main rule is to pronounce each letter exactly as it stands and to use the same sound for a given letter in all contexts, as one would do for example with the English letters *m* or *p.*

There are relatively few complications. We have already met one in the word *lingua*. The group *gu* is pronounced [gw], so that *lingua* has two syllables. Similarly, the group *qu* is pronounced [kw], as in the word *aqua* 'water'.

This just leaves the question of the stress. In Latin words the stress is always on the second or third syllable from the end. The second last or penultimate is the most common, as in the word *latína*, but several words are stressed on the third from the end or antepenultimate syllable, like *fémina*. (You can find the rules for determining the position of the stress in the section on grammar at the end of the book.) Quite often it is possible to guess which syllable is stressed, as the general rule is that the stress in modern loanwords is still on the same syllable. In this book we sometimes use an accent on the words with antepenultimate stress, particularly if the stress of a loanword is different from the Latin one. In the word list at the back, which contains all the words used in this book, there is an accent on all forms longer than two syllables, and if you are uncertain about how to stress a word, you can check it there. In an ordinary Latin text there are no accents, but we use them here to help the reader.

The earliest period of Rome

The long history of Latin started about 2,700 years ago. It is not always so clear how and where a language comes into existence, but in the case of Latin at least there is no doubt about the place. In the beginning the language was spoken only in the city of Rome and its environs. According to the tradition of the Romans themselves the city was founded in the year 753 BCE (to use our modern system of dating) and modern archaeologists and historians believe that this is quite close to the truth. A small settlement seems to have grown up in the eighth century BCE which included just that spot which was to become the centre of Rome throughout antiquity, the *Forum Romanum* 'the Roman square'. One end of the square slopes slightly up towards the Palatine hill, where you can still see part of the *Via sacra* 'the Sacred Way', which was used for processions. Beside the road the remains of ancient huts have been found.

We do not know much about the people who lived in this small town but as far as we can tell they spoke an archaic form of Latin. During the first centuries it was probably just a spoken language, but fairly early on it must have begun to be written down. There is an inscription on a stone in the Forum Romanum which has been dated to the sixth century BCE. It has been damaged and is not completely decipherable, but the letters are Latin and it is clear that the language is Latin. Written Latin therefore is at least two and a half thousand years old.

During the first centuries the Romans were just an insignificant small group of a few thousand people among many other such groups to be found in Italy at that time. They lived in the region called *Latium*, which still bears virtually the same name. In Italian it is called *Lazio*, just like the famous modern Roman football team. To the north were the Etruscans, who lived in the area which is now called Tuscany and who were more numerous and more powerful than the Romans.

Obviously we do not know for certain what life was like in Rome in those early years, but the Romans possessed a rich store of traditions. According to legend, Rome was founded by a man called Romulus who in so doing killed his twin brother, Remus. When children, the two brothers had been left to die but had been nursed by a she-wolf and later rescued. A she-wolf is therefore one of the city's most important symbols, and a very old bronze statue of her still exists. When Romulus founded the city, he became *rex* or king. The same root is found in *regina* 'queen' and can also be seen in English words like *regent* 'someone who rules instead of the king or queen' and *regal* 'having to do with a king or queen'. Romulus was followed by another six kings, but the seventh and last king was overthrown and a different system of government was introduced. This is supposed to have happened in 509 BCE, a dating which is in all probability historically correct.

In the Romans' way of seeing things, kings were not something to be desired. To be ruled by a king was for them more or less like living in slavery, and they looked down on other states that had that kind of government. Their own state was from 509 BCE a republic, a *res publica*, which literally means 'public thing' or 'public affair'. In a *res publica* the highest authority lay not with a king but in principle with the *pópulus* or people. The idea of such a state has recurred time and again in history in many different forms. Both the leaders of the French Revolution and the founders of the United States took the Roman republic as an important model. The American Abraham Lincoln formulated the idea optimistically: 'government of the people, by the people, and for the people, shall not perish from the earth.' Both the idea and the key word come from the Romans. The English word *people* derives from Latin *populus*, via the French word *peuple*.

In reality, what the Romans had could hardly be called a democracy. There were two men together who held the highest office in the Roman republic, and they did so only for a year at a time. Their title was *consul*, a word which is now used for an office in one branch of the diplomatic service. Consuls were elected by the people at a public meeting known as the assembly of the people. They had considerable power during their term of office, but as it was short and the two equal consuls had to agree, no one person was able to dominate politics for very long. What in fact governed Rome after the era of the monarchy was an assembly called the *senatus*. The Roman Senate consisted of a few hundred men (anything from 300 to 1,000 at various points in its history) who had been elected to public offices by the assembly of the people. The Senate comprised exclusively people who had held public office; for example all former consuls were senators. Although they only held their office for a year, once they became senators they held that position for life. All really important decisions were made by the Senate.

Many countries today have a political assembly called the senate; the best known of course is the American Senate. The fact that the American institution bears that name is clear proof of how much

Roman ideals meant when the American constitution was written. The Latin word *senatus* is built on the same root as the word *senex* 'old man', so that the original meaning was something like 'the council of elders'. As members of the Senate kept their seat for life, the term was quite appropriate.

During this first period of its history Rome depended a great deal on its neighbours to the north, the Etruscans, and several of the kings were Etruscan. The transition from kingdom to republic also had to do with liberation from the Etruscans, and from that time on Rome began seriously to expand her dominion.

How Latin became Latin

Why did the first Romans speak a language of their own? How was it related to other languages?

To those of us who live in Europe in the twenty-first century it may seem strange that a small place with a few thousand inhabitants should have its own language. Languages like English, German, French, and Italian are spoken by many millions of people and are used over large areas. But it is not like that everywhere in the world. In Africa there are at least ten times as many languages as in Europe, although there are about the same numbers of people in the two continents. From a historical and geographical perspective you find that in the long run there is a strong correlation between the number of languages and the number of states or independent political entities. A very long time ago, when there were no large states but at most small tribes or clans, there were no large languages either. The reason is that the way people speak changes constantly. A group of people who live without much contact with other groups will gradually develop their own language, different from all others, although they may once have spoken the same language as people in adjoining areas.

The language of the small city of Rome similarly developed on the spot, so to speak. But it was not completely different from the languages nearby. Quite a few other languages had features in common with Latin. The most important of these were Oscan and Umbrian. Umbrian was spoken in that region of Italy which is still called Umbria, to the north and east of Latium. Oscan was used in large parts of southern Italy. Both were written languages, and a considerable number of inscriptions, which can for the most part be deciphered, have survived. These show that Oscan, Umbrian, and Latin are quite similar in terms of grammar and vocabulary, but not so close that they were mutually comprehensible. The differences must have been about as great as between, say, Swedish and German, or Italian and Spanish, and perhaps even as great as between English and German or between French and Italian. Oscan, Umbrian, and Latin, together with a few other minor languages, make up what linguists call the Italic languages, and it is generally assumed that the reason for the similarities lies in the fact that there once existed a common Italic language, though it is by no means certain that this was the case.

What is certain is that the Italic languages made up a group within a much larger group of languages, all of which must in some way have had a shared historical origin since they have a number of words and grammatical phenomena in common. This larger group is called Indo-European and includes most modern European languages, together with many of the languages of India, Pakistan, Iran, and Afghanistan. Within Indo-European, English belongs to the subgroup of so-called Germanic languages, which also includes German, Dutch, and the Scandinavian languages. This in turn means that English and Latin are related within the same large language family, just as English and Persian or English and Hindi are. It is generally thought that the likenesses among all these languages are due to the existence of a very early common Indo-European language, which, at least in part, many scholars have tried to reconstruct.

However, there are very few words in English and Latin which are similar because they come directly from the same

Indo-European source. One example is Latin *mus* 'mouse' and English *mouse*, which has related forms also in Sanskrit, Avestan, Armenian, and Greek. The consonants of this word are the same but the vowels are different as a result of sound changes. (Interestingly, the modern pronunciation in many Scottish dialects is nearer to that of Latin because they did not undergo the same vowel changes as the dialects south of the border.) Another set which are related are *mother, father, brother* beside their Latin equivalents *mater, pater, frater*, although here the changes have affected consonants and vowels, and made the similarity less apparent. Much closer to the Latin forms, of course, are the English adjectives *maternal, paternal,* and *fraternal*, but that is because the English words are borrowings direct from Latin rather than the result of shared inheritance from the ancient Indo-European ancestor language.

In fact, it is surprising that such words are even partially similar after more than 5,000 years of separate independent development. Latin and English share only a handful of words as a result of their common ancestry, and often they no longer have any sounds which are the same. For instance, the Latin pronoun *ego* and English *I* come from the same source, but it takes specialist knowledge to reveal the connection. The trick is to look for systematic patterns of sound correspondence. One such is that an English *f* often corresponds to a Latin *p*, as in English *father* beside Latin *pater*, or English *fish* beside Latin *piscis*. That one is fairly straightforward, but there are more surprising ones that can still be shown to be valid. For example, Latin *qu* sometimes corresponds to English *f*, sometimes to *v*, so that English *five* can be proved to be connected with Latin *quinque*. If there has been a meaning change as well, the connection may be even harder to see. English *quick* and Latin *vivo* 'live' can be linked by applying the above rule of correspondence to both consonants in the word, though the original meaning 'live' is only found in English in such fixed expressions as *the quick and the dead* or *quicksilver*. It is striking how in this way comparative linguistic research can reveal ancient links that go back to before the beginning of recorded history.

From small town to great power

The small state of Rome with its own small language had several neighbours. Half a millennium before Christ there were many small states in the Italian peninsula. North of the Romans lived the Etruscans, whom we have already mentioned, not in one state but in a number of separate city states. The Etruscans spoke their own language, which did not belong to the Indo-European family and which is not related to any other language which has been preserved. They used their own alphabet, and many inscriptions in Etruscan have survived. For several hundred years the Romans were very dependent on the Etruscans, both politically and economically, and they took over a great deal from them, including their alphabet. The letters in the Roman alphabet represent a slight modification of the symbols used by the Etruscans, who had in their turn borrowed the idea of writing with letters from the Greeks. As a result of the great influence of Latin, all the languages of western Europe have inherited the Roman alphabet, in some cases with additions such as the English and German use of *w*, the French *ç* (called *c cedilla*), Swedish and German *ä* and *ö*, Danish *ø* and so on. Two letters that are now widely used in European alphabets, *v* and *j*, have a different history, which we will come to later.

Besides the letters, the Romans acquired quite a lot else from the Etruscans, including some words which have gone on to be adopted by other languages such as *caerimónia* 'ceremony' and *fenestra* 'window' (whence French *fenêtre* and German *Fenster*). The meanings of these words tell us something about what the Romans learnt from their neighbours in the north. They imported many religious practices and ceremonies and the firm belief that the will of the gods could be read in the flight of birds or the entrails of animals that had been sacrificed. The Romans also got the idea of theatre from the Etruscans; the modern word *person* comes from the Etruscan loanword in Latin *persona*, which originally meant a theatrical mask— hence a role in a play and so finally 'person'. They also learnt how to build houses instead of windowless huts.

In other respects the Romans could not boast of any cultural achievements in our sense of the word for several centuries. They were first and foremost farmers. But the Romans would not agree that there was a lack of culture. In Latin farming is called *agricultura*, a word which is made up of *ager* 'field' and *cultura*, which originally meant the growing of crops but which gradually acquired the sense of spiritual growth or culture. The Latin word *cultura* is formed from the verb *cólere* 'grow' just as the English word *growth* is derived from *grow*.

Their other principal activity was military service, *milítia*. The Romans were excellent soldiers, and during the fifth and fourth centuries and the first half of the third century BC they fought war after war with their neighbouring states. Things did not always go well, but bit by bit the Romans conquered the whole of the Italian peninsula. Slowly but surely they also spread the Latin language over the territory they had conquered. One of the ways they did this was by giving out parcels of the land they had won to soldiers who had completed their military service. The soldiers naturally spoke Latin, and they and their families brought with them the language of the victors to the homelands of the vanquished, where they continued their main activity, farming. In this way islands of Latin emerged in all the other language areas. At the same time Latin was the language of the people who held power, so most people quickly learnt a bit of Latin, and after a few generations Latin had completely taken over.

A soldier, *miles* in Latin, could soon become a *colónus* or grower. A group of such *coloni* formed a *colónia*, a number of Romans living together in a conquered country. The English word *colony* clearly comes from this word.

Not everyone was a simple farmer even in early Rome; there were also rich and powerful people such as those who sat in the Senate, held military command or became consuls. Very early on there was a political distinction between the leaders, who were *patres* 'fathers', a common term for senators, and who were therefore called *patrícii* 'patricians', and those who belonged to the ordinary people or *plebs,* and who were therefore called *plebéii* 'plebeians'. In Rome these terms became outdated after a couple of hundred years, but they have survived to this day as ways of referring to people's social status.

By about 270 BCE their many wars and colonizations had made the Romans masters of the whole of the Italian peninsula, and they began to look with interest at the countries across the sea. On the north coast of Africa, in present-day Tunisia, there was a very successful city called Carthage. The Carthaginians were merchants and seafarers, and they controlled much of the trade and the coast in the western Mediterranean, including for example most of Sicily, an island which the Romans also had their eyes on.

The Romans fought three great wars against the Carthaginians, whom they called *poeni* 'Punic (people)'. You can read in the history books about these three Punic wars, which lasted altogether for more than a hundred years. In the end the Romans were victorious and destroyed the city of Carthage, but for a long time the outcome was uncertain. The most spectacular moment during these campaigns was when the Carthaginian general Hannibal entered Italy from what is now France by crossing the Alps with an army which included elephants, the tanks of the ancient world.

For ever after the Romans were inordinately proud of having defeated Hannibal and the Carthaginians, and it was this victory which made them a superpower in the Mediterranean. Yet when it came to writing, education and ideas, science, art, and music the early Romans did not produce much compared to many other peoples. In particular they lagged far behind their neighbours to the east, the Greeks.

How bad were the Romans?

The earliest Romans, those who conquered Italy and defeated Carthage, became some centuries later the models and ideals for their descendants. Classical Roman writers talk at length about the moral excellence of their forefathers, and since their time the theme has recurred again and again. Even today one still hears mention of 'Roman virtues', 'pithy Roman sayings', and so on.

The picture which posterity has created of the ancient Romans obviously contains elements of truth and myth, and is roughly as follows. In the first place they were simple men who cultivated their own land, but went to Rome to take part in government when required and who went to fight whenever it was necessary to put the neighbouring tribes in their place. The prime example was Cincinnatus, who was ploughing his small plot of land when he was informed that he had been appointed *dictator*, which meant that he could rule unchallenged but for no more than six months. The reason was a war: he had to rescue a Roman army which had been penned in by the enemy. Reluctantly, he left home, won the war, renounced his dictatorship after two weeks, and went back to farm his land again.

Part of this idea of the simple life was that the ancient Romans despised money and luxury, and did not take bribes. On the other hand they liked power. The story goes that the consul Dentatus received a delegation from the Samnites while he was sitting in his tent stirring his porridge, *puls*, in a clay pot. He refused their gold plate and other presents and said that he preferred to use a bowl made of clay himself while ruling over people who owned gold dinner services.

They were also extremely courageous and oblivious to physical pain. A Roman called Mucius tried to kill the Etruscan king Porsenna, but he failed and was captured by the Etruscans. He explained with pride. *Romanus sum* 'I am a Roman', and demonstrated to the king what kind of people the Romans were by putting his right hand into the fire and keeping it there until it had turned to charcoal. The king was duly impressed and relinquished the battle against such doughty warriors.

Finally, they were always just and law-abiding. It is true that they were waging war almost all the time, but their wars were always righteous, and had been prompted by some insult or injustice that the Romans felt they had suffered. For the sake of justice all human considerations had to be put to one side. The consul Torquatus had his own son under his command, and the son acted very bravely in killing one of the enemy. Unfortunately, in so doing he contravened his father's order not to engage in acts of war, and so Torquatus promptly had his son executed for disobedience.

Nowadays this picture of the Romans may seem less than appealing to many people. But it did remain attractive for many centuries and you do not have to go very far back in time to find societies which exploited it to their advantage. In the 1920s and 1930s the Fascists in Italy developed an ideology that was partly based on this imaginary picture, and their ideological brothers, the Nazis, also adopted some of these ideas.

But these are no more than fantasies, maybe with some foundation in reality. All the above examples and hundreds more of the same kind were written down by Roman or Greek writers who lived about the time of the birth of Christ, several hundred years after the heroic period that lasted up until the defeat of Carthage. It was in their interest to emphasize certain characteristics of the ancient Romans because they wanted to sway their contemporaries. Arguably, the conservative rulers of a later period used the ancient Romans for their own purposes.

Whatever the truth of the matter, this image is connected with a number of significant concepts in the Latin language. The most important of all is probably *virtus*, a word which has been borrowed into many languages including English *virtue*. It is built on the word *vir* which means 'man' and which is also to be seen in words like *virile* and *virility*. In origin therefore *virtus* meant 'manliness'. But it has nothing at all to do with sexuality, and means rather something like 'good qualities', namely those that a man was supposed to have. These include above all else courage, but also all-round ability, care for the family, a sense of business, reverence for the gods, respect for the law and the authorities, and more in the same vein. *Virtus* was seen as the best quality that a Roman could have.

Another keyword is *fortis* 'strong' and *fortitúdo* 'strength', a quality which was regarded as essential in a Roman. But he also had to cling to *ius* 'right, justice', so as to be just, *iustus*. The ideal was *vir fortis et iustus* 'a strong and just man', and also a *pater famíliae*, a family father. Those people who were not male heads of families, and hence considered strong and just, were marginalized. Early Roman society was exceptionally patriarchal. The housewife, *mater familiae*, did indeed play a role that was important in itself but only within the four walls of the home. If on the other hand you were a boy (*puer*) or a girl (*puella*) or a slave (*servus* 'male slave' or *serva* 'female slave') you were completely dependent on the *pater familiae* and his authority (*auctóritas*). A child was childlike (*puerilis*) and a slave was expected to be servile (*servilis*).

The fact that Rome was a society where people had slaves may be offensive to us, but the same was the case in all societies in antiquity, both in Europe and in the Middle East. Slavery lived on in Europe well into the Middle Ages, but was abolished quite a long time ago. Elsewhere Europeans used slaves on an industrial scale until the latter part of the nineteenth century.

A voice from early Rome

Our knowledge of ancient history mainly comes from written sources. Obviously the best and most reliable information comes from the writings of people who lived at the time. In the case of Rome, there is not a lot of this kind of material from the earliest times. The Romans certainly had an alphabet and made some use of it from at least 500 BCE, but very little has been preserved that is older than about 200 BCE, principally a number of inscriptions on gravestones and the like. What we know about the earliest period has been passed on by writers who lived much later, around the birth of Christ. The reason why so little has survived is probably because there was not very much to begin with anyway. In the earliest years of their history the Romans do not seem to have been a people much given to writing, and the first individuals who could be called writers do not appear until the third century BCE. The fragments that remain of their writing reveal that they were fairly clumsy. There was no written norm, and no instruction in the Latin language in schools.

So we do not really know much about how the oldest Romans thought and felt. There is, however, a book written by an individual who is always cited as an example of what the ancient Romans were like, Marcus Porcius Cato, often called Cato the Elder. He played an important part in the war against Carthage, and one of the things he is famous for is that he is said to have ended many of his speeches in the Senate with the words: *Praetérea cénseo Cartháginem esse delendam* 'Moreover it is my opinion that Carthage should be destroyed'. Cato died in 149 BCE, and the book which he has left behind, called *De Agricultura* 'On Agriculture', is one of the very oldest which exists in Latin. Most of it is devoted to very detailed instructions, sometimes highly technical, about how to build an olive press or how to bake a honey cake. Quite a few passages also tell us a lot about Cato himself and his attitude to life.

In the preface he says that farming is the most honourable occupation, and that the ancient Romans considered it a mark of the highest praise when they called someone *Bonum agrícolam bonúmque colonum* 'a good farmer and a good husbandman' (the addition of -*que* at the end of a word means the same as 'and' before the word). But when Cato starts to describe his own farm, it turns out that he is definitely not the person who does the sowing and ploughing or even the person who superintends these activities. He describes a farm which is managed by an overseer who is in charge of a considerable number of slaves. The role of the Roman, 'the good farmer', is to turn up every now and then, give instructions, call the overseer to account, and pocket the profits. This last is the most important for Cato. He is mean, not to say miserly, and farming is to him just a way of making money. The people who do the work, that is to say the slaves, are simply part of the production line. They get food and clothes so that they can work. If they can't do that they are surplus to requirements. At one point he reels off a list of things that should be sold: . . . *plostrum vetus, ferramenta vétera, servum senem, servum morbosum, et si quid áliud supérsit'* . . . an old wagon, old tools, an old slave, a sickly slave, and anything else that is not needed.'

So on closer inspection it turns out that all his talk about the honest farmer is deceptive. Cato was a rich man who invested in farming for whom the wellbeing of his employees was a matter of no concern. It would be wrong to say that all the ancient Romans were like Cato; we know very little about the rest. It is also the case that Cato lived at a time when the old ideals were being undermined by new circumstances. But it has to be said that the picture of powerful Romans which emerges from reading his book is far from attractive.

However, the culture of Rome fortunately does not consist solely of the myth of the severe but just patriarch. The door was soon to open on another era.

The meeting with Greece

For many hundreds of years the Romans lived on the fringe of the dominant culture of the age. The Greeks had made unique progress while Rome was still just a small town. They had created an unrivalled literature, had laid the foundations of western philosophy and science, and had made great strides in art and architecture. In addition, they were skilful engineers and successful warriors. In all this they did not start from scratch but were often able to build on what had been achieved much earlier in Egypt and in the great civilizations of Mesopotamia. But the Greeks went further than their predecessors in almost every field, and in turn passed on their advances to others.

During the great cultural flowering in the fifth and fourth centuries BCE, the region that roughly corresponds to modern Greece was divided into many small states. Towards the end of the fourth century the state of Macedonia subjugated all the small states and its king, Alexander, embarked on an extraordinary series of conquests, with the result that he became the ruler of all the countries that surrounded the eastern Mediterranean from Greece to Libya and of the territory that constitutes modern-day Iraq and Iran and right over to Pakistan and India. That empire soon fell apart, but it was the Greeks who ruled over the different states, which therefore kept Greek as the official language.

So to the east of the growing Roman empire there was a huge area which was in every respect more developed. The Greek-speaking world also extended to southern Italy and Sicily, where the Greeks had already had colonies since the eighth century BCE. When the Romans took over those areas they immediately came into contact with Greeks, Greek culture, and the Greek language. This was to lead to great changes for the Romans and their language. Before then, there had been a considerable distance between them and this people with their well-developed educational system and their great literature. The Romans may have had the alphabet for a long time, but they had almost entirely used it only to write down contracts and laws and for inscriptions on gravestones. Now, along with a lot else, they had the chance to learn that written language can also be used to create works of art and simply for the pure pleasure of reading.

The Greek influence developed gradually over a period of several hundred years. During that time the Romans also came to wield greater and greater political power in the eastern Mediterranean. By the birth of Christ they had subjugated both Greece itself and all the other areas which had had Greek as their official language ever since the time of Alexander. In consequence the Romans were deeply influenced by the Greek way of life, Greek science, Greek art, and not least Greek literature. In time, all Romans with any claim to education could read and speak Greek. The Greek and Roman civilizations can almost be said to have merged into one common culture. But it was a long process, and one that was never totally completed.

Literature was probably the field where Greek ideals meant most. The Romans in fact took over the whole idea of writing literature from the Greeks, and the first works were straightforward translations of

Greek originals. But gradually the Romans evolved their own topics and themes, and soon they were competing with their models and indeed trying to surpass them. Latin literature slowly freed itself from Greek influence, and in due course it was Latin literature that served as the model for the whole of Europe for the next two thousand years.

Theatre for the people

The oldest literature in Latin which has been preserved are a number of plays by a man called Plautus, written about 200 BCE and staged in Rome. The models for these pieces were contemporary Greek plays that Plautus translated, at the same time adapting them to the Roman context. They were about the life of what we would call the affluent middle classes. The characters were merchants and landowners and their wives, children, and slaves, and the plots revolved around themes like young lovers who are finally united or lost sons or daughters who turn up unexpectedly. The setting was always a port, with ships arriving from many different places. Rome was developing into just such a cosmopolitan community, and the plays quickly caught on there.

This kind of play has subsequently turned out to be very long-lived. Shakespeare took several themes and plots from Plautus—for example *The Comedy of Errors* is an adaptation of the plot of *Menaechmi*—and in our own times the same basic idea lies at the heart of long-running soap operas like *Dallas*. But Plautus was funnier. He does not worry a lot about plot, concentrating instead on quick-witted slaves and comical misunderstandings, and making fun of boastful generals and bossy fathers.

Slaves often play important roles in these plays and sometimes behaved in ways that they would have been forbidden to do in Rome. In one play, Plautus explains in the prologue that in the course of the play two slaves will marry, and he appreciates that the audience will be scandalized. Yet this, he says, is what they are allowed to do in other places, *in Graecia et Carthagini, et hic in nostra terra, in Apulia* 'in Greece and Carthage, and here in our own land, in Apulia'. In Apulia (modern Puglia), in the far south of Italy, which had only recently become part of the Roman empire, the customs were clearly those of Greece, whereas the Romans did not let slaves do anything which was legally binding, such as buying land, borrowing money, or getting married. Such acts might infringe the rights of the slave owner.

In this way Plautus' plays taught the Romans something about what went on in the wider world. He did not like the old Roman virtues although—or perhaps exactly because—he was a near contemporary of Cato. He calls the old Romans *pultíphagi* 'porridge-eaters' because they had not yet learnt to bake bread. The baker's oven was one of the many advances in civilization the Romans took over from the neighbours to the east and the south.

The plays are about family intrigues. A key word is of course *amor* 'love', and *amare* 'to love', but just as important is something else, the family's fortune or money. The general word for 'money' is *pecúnia* (derived from *pecus* 'livestock', since the bartering of animals preceded the use of money), but the Romans also had coins of silver (*argentum*) and gold (*aurum*). Hence in French the word for money is *argent*, from the Latin word for silver while the word gold is the source of *öre*, the name of the smallest unit of currency in Sweden, Denmark, and Norway (worth approximately a tenth of a penny). The value of money has, as we all know too well, changed with time.

The fortune itself often went by the name *res*, a word we have already met in the combination *res pública*. The basic meaning of *res* is 'thing'; one's fortune is all the things one owns. In one of Plautus' plays, a character is talking about how you have lots of friends when you are rich but none when you are poor, and he sums the situation up in the maxim *res amicos facit* 'the fortune makes the friends'. The Romans were very fond of such short, pithy sayings. Sometimes they sounded rather moralizing, but just as often they were, like this one, resigned or even cynical. Plautus is a master at delivering this kind of moral punch in the middle of all the comic confusion and practical jokes.

The age of revolutions

For several hundred years Rome was in principle ruled in the same way—by the officials and senators who had been chosen by the assembly of the people—but gradually the empire had become very large. And yet the people's assembly still consisted only of the free men from the city of Rome itself, and the senators came in fact mainly from a small number of very rich Roman families. All power and almost all the money was concentrated in a few people in a single city. This naturally led to widespread dissatisfaction amongst the poor in Rome and amongst everyone in the rest of the empire. In the long run such a state of affairs became untenable.

And yet it did not prove easy to change things. For a little over a century a serious power struggle went on in Rome. It started with a proposed land reform, which would have meant that the rich could no longer own huge tracts of land and work them with slaves. Instead they would have to give up land, which would then be divided into small lots and given to the poor and in particular to soldiers who had served their time. The man who advocated this reform was called Tiberius Gracchus. He was murdered in 133 BCE, and so was his brother Gaius Gracchus, who took up a similar idea ten years later. Their ideas, however, lived on and gave rise to a loose grouping of people, who called themselves *populares*, a word which derives from *populus* 'people' and means 'the people's party'. Their opponents were the rich senators and their followers, who styled themselves *optimates* 'the best'. In a way there was now a radical party and a conservative party.

The struggle between these groups went back and forth for many decades while the Romans were simultaneously making war on other states and extending their empire further and further. The army was obviously an important player in this power game, and the crucial balance of power was increasingly in the hands of successful generals, who allied themselves with one party or the other. Some of these names have become very well known, such as Marius, who was close to the *populares*, and Sulla, who belonged to the *optimates*. The political strife was intense, and on several occasions developed into a real civil war. It is easy to believe that the whole empire was on the point of falling apart. One Roman historian says of Rome just at the end of this period: *magnitúdine sua labórat* 'it is sinking under its own greatness'.

The best-known of the generals during the period of revolution is Gaius Julius Caesar. He belonged to an old Senate family himself and was very able both as a politician and a soldier. He was also a man imbued with an incredible amount of energy. In 58 BCE he became governor of the province of Gallia Cisalpina, which literally means 'Gaul on this side of the Alps', in other words northern Italy. From there, more or less on his own, he started a war against the Gauls who lived to the west and north; after eight years he had conquered all of what we now know as France, and in 55–54 BCE invaded Britain. Moreover, he had created a large army whose soldiers were loyal to him personally rather than to Rome. What is usually emphasized is how clever Caesar was. He was also completely ruthless. According to his own estimates, his armies killed 1.2 million Gauls and took 1 million prisoners, whom he sold as slaves and thereby enriched both himself and his soldiers. Today this kind of rampage would quite simply be labelled genocide.

After the Gallic war, Caesar found himself in conflict with the Senate. It was illegal for him to be in command of troops outside his own province, but he nonetheless marched south with his army so that when he came to the Rubicon, the river which constituted the border between Cisalpine Gaul and Italy, he was faced with a crucial decision. It is on this occasion that he uttered the famous words 'The die is cast'. What he actually said, according to the source we have, was *iacta álea est!* It is worth noting the order of words here.

Alea means 'die' (or 'dice' as we more usually say in modern English), and if we imitated the Latin word order in English it would be 'Cast die is!', which sounds very strange. It is not the most usual way to put it in Latin either, but it is much less uncommon than in English to rearrange the words like this within the sentence.

With this act Caesar started a major civil war, which in the end he won. As a result, for some years he was virtually the sole and auto-cratic ruler of Rome under the title *dictator*. In a short period, he managed to carry through a considerable number of reforms, of which several became a permanent part of the statute book. However, many people were opposed to his dictatorship, and on 15 March in the year 44 BCE he was assassinated, stabbed to death by a number of senatorial conspirators led by his friend Brutus. He is reputed to have uttered another famous remark as he died: *Et tu, Brute* 'Even you, Brutus'. This remark too deserves comment in a number of respects. The word *et*, which we have already encoun-tered, usually means 'and' but can also be used in the sense of 'too' or 'even'. *Brute* is of course his addressee's name, which has the form *Brutus* in the nominative. This form with the ending *-e* is called the vocative and is used when you speak to or call someone. In written texts we do not come across so many vocatives, but the Romans obviously used them constantly in their everyday lives when they said hello to each other or called their children.

After the death of Caesar, civil war broke out again and it was a full fifteen more years before the long and confused period of revolu-tions was over, and Rome finally acquired a functioning long-term leadership again. From the description of politics and war during this long period it sounds as if Rome was assailed by an endless sequence of misfortune and misery, but actually this was not the case. One reason for the trouble was that throughout this period the economy was in very good shape and many people wanted to have their share of the prosperity. Trade was very successful and a lot of people became incredibly rich. The level of education increased substan-tially across the board, and Roman society adopted many aspects of Greek culture as well as developing in its own way.

One thing which made particularly notable progress in this period was the written language. Even by this time only a very limited number of books in Latin existed. We do know that there were quite a few writers besides Cato and Plautus, whom we have already mentioned, and in particular we have many works by another writer of comedies, Terence. But, as far as we know, the works that have been lost are not terribly many and they were probably not of any great value. On the other hand, during the first century BCE there were a substantial number of extraordinarily good writers, and many of their works have been preserved. This is the beginning of the golden age of Roman literature, which continues on into the first century CE. The two centuries from about 100 BCE to 100 CE are often called Rome's classical period.

Writing, reading, listening, and speaking

What do we mean when we say that the Romans had a literature? We are obviously not thinking of printed books which are sold in book-shops, distributed by publishers and written by writers who for the most part have writing as their profession. In Rome things were rather different. The Romans lived in a society where the written language played a much smaller role than it does for us. In the towns many people were able to read and write, but among the population as a whole the majority were probably illiterate. There was also considerably less to read than we have nowadays. These differences have a lot to do with differences in technology. The Romans obviously did not have computers, and neither did they have printing presses or photo-copiers. Each text had to be written out by hand, and if a text was to be distributed in several copies, it meant that the original had to be copied again and again until the required number of copies had been made. That went for everything from posters to poetry. The only small texts which it was actually possible to mass produce were coin inscriptions, which could be stamped in great numbers. The inscriptions (and even pictures) on coins were therefore much used as propaganda by those in power.

Apart from coins there was no cheap way of producing texts. One way, albeit an expensive one, which was quite widely used was to carve inscriptions on stones or copper tablets. Inscriptions were very durable, and could be located in conspicuous places so that all the inhabitants of a town would be able to read them. This technique was suitable not only for tombstones and mausoleums but also for promulgating laws, regulations, and the like. We still have tens of thousands of inscriptions from all over the Roman empire.

If anyone had a more ephemeral message, they might well paint or scrawl it on a wall. Most of that has disappeared, of course, but the town of Pompeii, which was buried under ashes from an eruption of Vesuvius in 79 CE, gives us some idea of what this kind of writing looked like. Many of the walls have all sorts of messages scribbled all over them: advertisements for fruit shops, calls to vote for a particular election candidate, declarations of love, and any number of insults and obscenities. Here and there, too, there are poems, often ones composed by well-known poets.

However, inscriptions and walls were not suitable for bookkeeping or private letters or fiction. For that kind of thing there were two main options. One was wax tablets, strictly speaking pieces of wood which had been coated with a layer of wax. It was then easy to write letters in the wax with a pointed stick called a *stilus* (from which our word *style* comes and which literally means 'a way of writing'). Once the message was no longer needed, the wax could be smoothed out and a new text inscribed. This method was eminently suitable for notes, short letters, and the like which did not have to be saved. Indeed, people often bundled together several tablets to make a sort of notebook.

The material for larger texts which people wanted to save was papyrus. This looks and feels more or less like paper, but it is quite thick and stiff. It is made from the plant papyrus which, like reeds, grows along river banks and in marshes, primarily in the Nile delta. The Egyptians invented the technique of writing on papyrus, and it had spread throughout the Mediterranean area by about 2000 BCE. On papyrus you write with pen and ink so the writing is permanent. Unfortunately the material itself does not last forever. After a few hundred years papyrus rots away in a normal climate, which means that we do not have the original texts that were written in antiquity. What we have are copies, and how they came into existence I will explain later. However, under special circumstances papyrus can be preserved for a very long time, especially if it happens to end up in a completely dry place. The papyri which have survived from antiquity have usually been found in deserts, and in caves around the Dead Sea. The texts are mainly in Greek, Hebrew, and Aramaic, but there are some in Latin too.

Papyrus could be used as loose leaves for letters and that sort of thing. Long texts were written on strips of papyrus eight inches to a foot wide and up to ten yards long fixed to a wooden stick at each end. Usually the papyrus strip was rolled around one of the sticks. As you read, you unrolled the text, which was written across the roll, from one stick and rolled it up onto the other one. The text was written on one side of the roll only, which ordinarily had space for the equivalent of thirty or forty modern book pages. The Romans used to call such a roll *liber*, which is usually translated as 'book'. These books were much more difficult to handle than the kind we are used to and also much shorter. There might be enough space for a collection of poems or a play on a *liber*, but anyone who wrote something longer than that would have to break it down into short parts, each of which could fit on a roll. Ancient works were therefore not divided into chapters but into 'books', commonly of about twenty to forty pages in length.

The ancient book rolls were a good deal less practical than a modern book: you could not just turn to any individual page when you wanted to, and the process of unrolling and rolling them up again meant that they wore out quite fast. They were also expensive to produce, so probably only very few people had access to any books at all. Nonetheless, anyone with the money and the interest could build up a big collection, and in Rome public libraries were gradually established. Still, reading did not play anything like the same role for the Romans as it does for us today. For practical reasons, most people, even if they had learnt how to, probably read very little. And yet the Romans were intensely interested in their language and in the art of using it well. It was simply that their access to their language was in the traditional way, through their ears. Using your eyes to take in what someone had to say must have seemed to them a much more circuitous route to language than it does to us.

A written text was always seen as a way of recording the spoken word, and so whenever someone read something they always read it aloud. Of course people could always read to themselves, but rich people had educated slaves who read aloud to their master and often to his family and friends. What is more, writers often read aloud from their own works. This was an entirely normal way of introducing new works to the public, especially poetry, and such occasions gradually became important social events in Rome.

Writing good poetry and reciting it was actually a way of achieving success and fame in Rome. But there was another kind of verbal art which was much more important in Roman society, and that was oratory. This was not something people did for fun or to show off; it was rather an absolutely necessary skill for those who sought glory in public life, and the fact that this was so reflects important differences between their society and ours.

Speeches, politics, and trials

When modern politicians want to canvass public opinion, they write articles in the newspapers or get themselves interviewed on TV or radio. If there is a lot to be said, a report or a White Paper is published. They could also make a long speech in Parliament, but then there is a great danger that nobody will listen to it. In Rome, on the other hand, there were no newspapers in our sense of the word and no TV or radio or electronic media, and there was no system for circulating reports. The only way to reach a lot of people at once was to use one's own voice in front of an assembly of the people. Ambitious Romans had frequent opportunities to do just that, and the higher up the scale they were, the more important it was to be able to perform well in that context. Their careers depended on their ability to speak convincingly in public.

The most important speeches were obviously those made by politicians and those in power when big issues were decided, especially in the Senate. There were no fixed divisions between parties, so a single individual could sometimes bring about a shift in opinion. But it was not easy, as the senators were experienced men who had heard many fine words on other occasions. To succeed you had to be very good.

It was also important to be able to speak in court. In the modern world that is something lawyers do, but in Rome things worked very differently. Rome was truly a city ruled by law, not least in the sense that the citizens of Rome brought lawsuits against each other about everything under the sun. Landowners and the wealthy sued each other over business deals, loans, the boundaries of their land, or the collapse of a roof, while public officeholders could be prosecuted for abuse of power and corruption. Then, of course, there was always murder, robbery, and riot.

A person who was summoned to court normally engaged someone he trusted to defend him, and it was seen as a civic duty to defend one's friends in court. A training in the law was not compulsory for someone who took on the role of defender, although it might well be a very useful asset. But you did have to be able to speak well in public if you were going to help a friend out of a difficult situation. Trials were always open to the public; there were often several judges, who themselves did not always have any legal training, so it was more important to present a generally persuasive argument than to have mastered the legal subtleties of the case.

A Roman, then, had to be a good public speaker, and if he was, the road to success lay open to him. The best example, and the most able of all the Roman orators, was Marcus Tullius Cicero.

Cicero and rhetoric

Cicero was born in 106 and died in 43 BCE, and he lived during the turbulent era of the revolutions. He was born into what we would call the upper middle class, those who in Rome were called *équites* 'knights'. He received an exceptionally thorough education, the purpose of which was to train him to appear in court, to speak well in all situations, and, if need be, to take part in war. He studied first in Rome and later in Athens, where he had the chance to plumb the considerable depths of a Greek education.

When he was about twenty-five he began to appear for the defence in controversial trials and soon made a name for himself. He was elected to high office and thereby entered the Senate. He became a *homo novus* 'a new man', that is to say someone who became a senator even though no one in his family had ever been before. In the year 63 BCE he also became consul and hence head of state. It was truly exceptional for a *homo novus* to get that far.

In the remaining twenty years of his life Cicero played the power game at the highest level, with varying degrees of success. After the assassination of Caesar he was briefly the leading political figure in Rome, but he lost a battle for power with the general Antonius—known to cinema and theatregoers as the Antony of *Antony and Cleopatra*—and was in turn himself assassinated.

Cicero made many important speeches during his career, to the Senate and to the people as a whole. He published most of them in his own lifetime and some fifty still survive. These speeches were much admired. Cicero was an extremely skilful orator: he had a good voice, expressed himself very well, argued convincingly, and was above all a master at making his audience think and feel what he wanted them to. He was also amazingly successful. As counsel for the defence, he managed to get some of the dodgiest characters acquitted, and in the Senate he several times succeeded in winning the argument when there was no real political basis for his position, relying only on his ability to persuade.

Here is a small example. It is the beginning of his speech against Catiline, a senator who was secretly planning a *coup d'état* in the year in which Cicero was consul. Cicero found out what was brewing and called a meeting of the Senate, where he made a frontal attack on his fellow senator. The speech begins as follows:

Quo usque tandem abutére, Catilina, patiéntia nostra? Quam diu etiam furor iste tuus nos elúdet? Quam ad finem sese effrenata iactabit audácia? Nihílne te nocturnum praesídium Palati, nihil urbis vigíliae, nihil timor pópuli, nihil concursus bonorum ómnium, nihil hic munitíssimus habendi senatus locus, nihil horum ora vultusque moverunt?

How far will you, Catiline, abuse our patience? How long will this mad rage of yours mock us? Is there no limit to your boastful ambition and unbridled audacity? Does the nightly setting of guards on the Palatine hill mean nothing to you, nothing too the watches posted in the city, nothing the people's anxiety, nothing the coming together of all the loyal citizens, nothing the fact that the Senate is meeting in this heavily fortified place, nothing the looks and faces of these men gathered here?

Linguistically this is rather a difficult text, which you cannot read in Latin until you have had quite a lot of experience with the language. Here we will just look at a few of the things which show how the speaker went about his oratorical task. It is easy to see that Cicero's tactic was to show Catiline up as a dangerous man from whom everyone should keep their distance. The aim was not to debate whether Catiline was or was not a rebel against the state, but to make everyone feel that he was. The tactic was so successful that he did not think it was even worth trying to speak in his own defence in front of the Senate, and so he simply left Rome. Cicero succeeded in what is always an orator's chief aim: to make his audience think what he wanted them to think.

To that end, he exploited many of the orator's tricks of the trade. Some of these are easy to recognize. For example, he starts out with three provocative questions one after the other. They were not meant to be answered, for there is no reasonable answer that could be given; in reality, they are statements. Today we call such questions rhetorical. In the following sentence, Cicero repeats the word *nihil* 'nothing/not at all' six times to hammer home the fact that Catiline is ruthless and callous. These are just two examples of devices which could be used to make a speech effective.

Many others wanted to be able to perform like this, and Cicero's speeches were used as models which were carefully studied in Roman schools. But although these speeches are in fact incredibly well constructed, not many people read them today, for the simple reason that they are designed for specific occasions and you often have to know a good deal about Roman politics and law to understand them at all. They are rich and varied in their choice of vocabulary, but to the modern reader this can make them seem wordy and even boring; the effect must have been completely different when they were delivered.

Cicero was not just a master of public speaking himself; he was also a great theorist. He wrote several important books about what he called *ars oratória* 'the art of public speaking'. *Ars* obviously means 'art', and *oratoria* 'oratorical, having to do with public speaking' is an adjective which has been formed from the noun *orator* 'speaker'. This word in turn comes from the verb *orare* 'to make a speech, to orate'. The same discipline was also known by the Greek name *ars rhetorica* 'the art of rhetoric', from the Greek word for a public speaker, which was *rhetor*.

Rhetoric was one of the many disciplines that the Greeks invented. It was linked, in their view, on the one hand with poetics, the theory of poetry or of creative writing in general, and on the other with politics, the theory of the state. Rhetoric was about how to persuade people by means of the spoken word and by Cicero's time the Greeks had already written textbooks and theses on this subject and had been teaching it for several hundred years. Cicero learnt everything the Greeks had to teach in his youth and thereafter honed his skills through a lifetime of practice, while in his spare time he wrote books in Latin on rhetoric. A hundred years after his death, another Roman, Quintilian, wrote the most detailed and best-known handbook on the subject, the *Institutio Oratoria* 'Training in Oratory'.

In most other subjects, what was taught in the ancient world has long been superseded. The physics of antiquity, for example, is of interest only to historians of science, and the same goes for for most other fields of study. But rhetoric is different. Those whose concern is the arts of public speaking and persuasion often take Quintilian and Cicero as a foundation. The reason probably lies in the fact that this subject was so important to the Romans that their best talents consumed much of their energy and imagination on it, and hence their views still hold good today. The most successful modern hand-books of rhetoric owe much of their contents to the teachings of the ancient writers on the subject.

You can get some idea of what it is all about by looking at the basic terms. If you were planning a speech, you had to concentrate on five things: the first was *invéntio* or 'invention', in other words find-ing the line of reasoning and the arguments which were to be used in the speech. The next phase was *disposítio* or 'arrangement' of the different parts, which was followed by *elocútio* or 'expression', that is to say putting the argument into the right words. This particular sub-area of rhetoric is the origin of the modern discipline of stylistics. After this comes *memória* or 'memory': when the speaker had worked out and written down a speech he had to learn the whole thing by heart, and rhetorical teaching included a number of inter-esting techniques for training the memory which are still useful today. Finally, there was *pronuntiátio* or the 'delivery' of the speech, including modulation of the voice, gestures, and so forth.

In a sense, then, making a speech was the most important literary activity in ancient Rome. But there were other ways of using the language which were of great importance, and to which other prominent Romans eagerly devoted their energies.

The language of history

In this book I have written quite a bit about the history of the Romans from the earliest times and down through the centuries. That we know anything about this is due to the fact that the Romans themselves were very interested in writing their history. The idea was another one which came originally from the Greeks, who had started to record their own history several hundred years before the Romans, and many of the sources we still have for the history of Rome were actually in Greek. But once the Romans got started, they produced a number of excellent works. Several of the Roman historians are still well worth reading today if you are interested in the subject.

The first to get a mention is usually Sallust (in Latin Sallustius), who was one of the officers closest to Caesar, and who also became a senator and governor of the province of Numidia (roughly, modern Algeria). He probably plundered his province, since he became rich enough to buy himself a house with a huge garden in the best part of Rome. When he was about forty, he retired there and devoted himself to writing.

What has survived are just two short books, of which one is about that same Catiline whom Cicero had attacked. It is very readable, and was used in schools for many hundreds of years. Sallust writes very well, in an abrupt style, and he spices his narrative with neatly phrased reflections about the way people are, and the way they should be, as for example *Régibus boni quam mali suspectiores sunt* 'To a king good people are more to be suspected than evil ones' (word for word in Latin: 'To kings, good than bad more suspected are'). He set a fashion among Roman historians to look for moral lessons in the events of history.

One of the things that distinguishes Roman historians from modern ones is the fact that they often had their main characters perform and make speeches. This was actually historically accurate in the sense that the Romans did make speeches to the Senate and to the troops before a pitched battle, or to the people at times of crisis. Of course, the historian could not know exactly what had been said, but it was part of his task to try to render the important speeches as he imagined they might have been delivered. This is the same technique as is employed by the scriptwriters for historical documentaries on television. History books could often be used as tools in the training of future orators.

Caesar, Sallust's commander and protector, was himself a very skilled writer, and the works of his that survive are also historical, in a way. He wrote his own account of the war he waged in Gaul, which is seven books long (but remember that a Roman book or *liber* is much shorter than a modern one), and another one, three books in length, about the subsequent civil war which he precipitated. Both these works are deliberately couched in a seemingly neutral and objective style, as if they were simply reports home to Rome about the events that had taken place. A characteristic feature of his style is that Caesar never writes about himself as 'I' but always writes 'Caesar' as if he was discussing someone else. However, when you look more carefully at what Caesar says, you soon find that it is to a large extent propaganda which aims to explain and defend his actions. For the most part he marched his army around and fought pitched battles, which makes the narrative rather monotonous, as millions of schoolchildren have discovered, since his account of the Gallic war has quite undeservedly taken up a great deal of time in the traditional Latin syllabus. For many, its opening sentence has been the first authentic text in Latin which they have encountered:

Gallia est omnis divisa in partes tres, quarum unam íncolunt Belgae, áliam Aquitani, tértiam qui ipsorum lingua Celtae nostra Galli appellantur.

The whole of Gaul is divided into three parts, of which the Belgians inhabit one, the Aquitanians another and the third is inhabited by those who in their own language are called Celts and in ours Gauls.

In this sentence Caesar gives us a brief introduction to the inhabitants of the new country. In the north-east were the Belgae and in the south the Aquitani, while in the large area between the two, that is to say most of modern France, lived the Gauls. Many of the words in the text are easy to recognize. *Divisa* means and is clearly related to 'divided', *partes tres* means 'three parts' ('one part' would be *una pars*). The three words *unam, aliam, tertiam* obviously correspond to 'one', 'another, i.e. second', and 'third'. The word for language is *lingua* and *lingua nostra* means 'our language'. *Appellantur* 'they are called' reminds us of the French verb *appeler* 'to call'.

Many others came after Sallust and Caesar. One of the best-known is Livy, who lived around the time of the birth of Christ and devoted his whole life to writing a complete history of Rome from 753 BCE, the year of the city's foundation, until 9 BCE. This work is called *Ab urbe cóndita* 'From the foundation of the city'. It contains 142 books, corresponding to about 6,000 printed pages, and about a quarter of it has been preserved. There were probably not many complete copies in any case, even in antiquity, for, as we have said, the expense involved in producing each individual copy was enormous.

The parts that have survived are from the early period. It was Livy who passed on most of the tall stories about brave and just Roman warriors. He saw it as the duty of the historian to provide posterity with an example. He was not therefore so interested in examining and criticizing his sources, although he did not consciously lie or make things up. He sought to give the Romans a splendid and glorious version of their own history, and one that was also readable. In this he succeeded; he is a very adept storyteller, and very good at giving lively descriptions of situations and events. It is most fun to read the very first part, where the sources were few and fanciful, and where Livy was able to embellish the stories using his own imagination. The bit about the Roman war against the Carthaginians used to be required reading for schoolchildren, and here we find such pearls as the description of Hannibal's march across the Alps. Unfortunately, there are also a great many descriptions of pitched battles and stratagems, which are hardly of interest to anyone except military historians.

Imperium romanum: *Augustus and the Roman empire*

After Caesar had been assassinated, it transpired that in his will he had adopted the nineteen-year-old grandson of one of his sisters. In our source it says: *Gaium Octávium in famíliam noménque adoptavit* 'He adopted Gaius Octavius into the family and the name'. From that day forth the young man was called Gaius Julius Caesar, with the additional name Octavianus (in English Octavian). At first the established politicians tried to ignore him, but in so doing they made a big mistake. Within a couple of years, he was camped outside Rome with his own army and had forced the Senate into appointing him as consul at the tender age of twenty-one. There followed some fifteen years of intrigue and civil war, in which the main protagonists were Octavian and Antony, who had been Caesar's closest ally. When Antony and Cleopatra, the Queen of Egypt, were finally defeated and died, Octavian, who was then thirty-five, became the unchallenged leader of the empire. He had shown himself to be ruthless and cruel, and it seemed likely that he would preside over a reign of terror, but things turned out differently.

Octavian did not want to be dictator or consul for life, and he explained to the Senate that he was restoring power into their hands. However, he retained for himself a number of powers which in practice were crucial. It is fair to say that he gave Rome a new constitution according to which one man had most of the power, but the Senate and consuls and other officers of state were still there as before and had a great deal of say in government. One way in which the Senate thanked him was to give him the name *Augustus* which means 'venerable' or 'majestic'. That is the name by which he has become known to posterity, and he bore it from 27 BCE until his death at the age of seventy-six in 14 CE.

Augustus was the first of a new kind of ruler. He was succeeded by his stepson Tiberius, and after him there came a long line all the way down to the last ruler of the western empire, who was deposed in the year 476 CE, half a millennium after Augustus had introduced his new form of government. In English these rulers are called emperors, but in German the word is *Kaiser*, a word which derives from the name Caesar, and which entered the Germanic language family at an early stage and is also found in modern Germanic languages like Swedish, Danish, Dutch, and Icelandic. This of course is not incorrect, since *Caesar* was part of the full title of all the emperors; but their official designation was *Augustus,* the honorary name which they all bore. Their title also included the word *imperator,* which is the source of the English word 'emperor' and which in turn came to us via the French *empereur.*

The word *imperator* literally means 'commander' and belongs with the verb *imperare* 'to command' and with the abstract noun *imperium* 'command, power, authority'. Whoever had been given the power to command by the Senate, usually for a year or for the duration of a particular military undertaking, had *imperium* and was called *imperator.* What Augustus introduced was the principle that he always had the highest power, *summum imperium,* and therefore was always *imperator.* Of course, that also meant that he was always able to get his own way, by force if necessary, throughout the whole territory in which his authority ran. Hence this territory was also called *imperium,* from which comes our modern word *empire.* The Roman empire was then the *imperium romanum.*

Augustus ruled for a long time and by and large he ruled well; civil strife came to an end, the economy was strong, and the quality of the administration in the provinces was improved. This was the beginning of a very long period of stability. It was more than two centuries before the empire was beset once more by a lengthy crisis; but even that passed, and imperial rule continued until the dissolution of the empire in the fifth century AD, when various Germanic tribes invaded the western part and divided it up amongst themselves.

Name and family

The Roman way of naming people was very different from ours. Roman men from distinguished families always had three names, as in Marcus Porcius Cato or Gaius Julius Caesar or Marcus Tullius Cicero. Just like us, there was a first name, called the *praenómen*

39

'forename', though with the difference that there were very few first names, no more than about twenty in all. It was possible to abbreviate most of them to one or two letters without misunderstanding. Marcus was shortened to M, Quintus to Q, and so on. The name Gaius is, strangely enough, abbreviated with the letter C, because this letter was once, when the alphabet was in its infancy, used both for the 'k' sound and for the 'g' sound. For the most part these first names did not have meanings as far as we know, but some of them are easy to interpret: Quintus means 'the fifth', Sextus 'the sixth' and Decimus 'the tenth'. Families with many children evidently resorted to the numerals as a way of keeping tally!

The middle name, which ended in –*ius*, was called the *nomen* 'name' or sometimes *nomen gentis* 'family name'. This represented the wider family or lineage to which one belonged and might be borne by a large number of people. Compare the Scottish use of clan names such as Campbell, McDonald, and Stewart. Finally, there came the *cognómen* or surname, which indicated one's immediate family, a much smaller group of people.

Roman men who did not belong to one of the leading families but who were nonetheless free citizens for the most part only had two names, a *praenomen* and a *nomen*, and no distinction was made between lineage and family. At the very bottom, of course, were the slaves, who only had one name. It was never a Roman first name, but was often a descriptive label such as Syrus 'the Syrian'.

Women in Rome mostly had one name too, even if they belonged to a distinguished family. That name was often quite simply the name of the father's lineage in the feminine. The daughter of Marcus Tullius Cicero was called Tullia. There were also other patterns. The daughter of Marcus Vipsanius Agrippa was called Vipsania Agrippina, and her three daughters were called Agrippina, Livilla, and Drusilla. The first got her mother's name and the next two were called after their famous great grandmother, Livia Drusilla, who had been married to Augustus.

Names then clearly showed a person's position in society: the more names you had the higher up the social ladder you were. To have three was very good, but important people could have even more, as they were given different honorary names which recorded real or invented exploits. Most men, though, had to make do with two, and women and slaves had to put up with one. Sometimes people were given an extra name because of a change in status. We mentioned earlier that the young Gaius Octavius was adopted by Caesar in his will, something which to us rings very strange, but adoption was quite a common practice among Rome's leading families. It was done partly to ensure suitable heirs for large fortunes and partly to strengthen ties between families. The person who was adopted would then get his new father's *nomen* and *cognomen*. The young Gaius Octavius therefore became overnight Gaius Julius Caesar, taking the names of his dead adoptive father, but he added to these Octavianus, which shows that he previously belonged to the Octavius family. Finally, the Senate gave him the honorary name Augustus, and his complete name became Gaius Julius Caesar Octavianus Augustus.

Slaves who were given their freedom also acquired new names. As free men they were allowed to have both a first name and a family name, and for the latter they usually took the name of their former owner. The very rich dictator Lucius Cornelius Sulla set a great number of his slaves free, with the consequence that there were suddenly thousands of people with the name Cornelius in Rome.

Which name people actually used in their everyday lives clearly varied. Famous people were generally referred to by their last name or *cognomen*. Marcus Tullius Cicero is known as Cicero, and Gaius Julius Caesar was usually called Caesar. But there are exceptions. The successor and stepson of Augustus was named Tiberius Claudius Nero but was always known as Tiberius, which is one of the few Roman first names. Later one of his nephews became emperor. His name was Tiberius Claudius Drusus, but he was always called Claudius. In principle one could be known by any one of the three names.

Years and months

The Romans had a way of reckoning time which continues to be of interest, as we mainly still use their system and have kept their names of the months. The oldest Roman calendar was already introduced at the time of the monarchy, and the inspiration probably came from the Etruscans. In the beginning it seems there were only ten months, the ones we call March to December, with January and February being added later. How that might have come about is rather unclear, but it is absolutely certain that the original Roman year started on the first of March, as can be deduced from the names of four of the months, which in Latin are called *mensis September, mensis October, mensis November, mensis December. Mensis* means 'month', and the other parts of the names clearly derive from the numerals *septem* 'seven', *octo* 'eight', *novem* 'nine', and *decem* 'ten'. Hence in the beginning March must have been the first month.

The names of the months that do not come from numerals most often have to do with Roman religion. Somewhat surprisingly, the names of the months are adjectives which are attached to the noun *mensis. Mensis Martius* means something like 'Martian Month'. *Martius* is an adjective formed from Mars, the name of the god of war. In the same way *mensis Maius* is the month of the goddess Maia, and *mensis Ianuarius* is connected with the god Janus. This is the god who is depicted with two faces, one on the front and one on the back of his head. He had to do with beginnings and endings, and we can conclude that the month name *Ianuarius* was coined with the idea of marking the start of the new year.

Two of the months were given names by the Senate. The one which had originally been called *Quintilis* (from *quintus* 'fifth') was renamed *Iulius* to pay tribute to Julius Caesar, and the next one, originally *Sextilis* (from *sextus* 'sixth') was called *Augustus* in memory of the first emperor. These demonstrations of servility have had a depressingly long-lasting effect.

There is, though, one good reason to remember Caesar in connection with the calendar. It was he who saw to it that the calendar year had the length that it still has today. As we know, the earth orbits the sun in approximately 365 and a quarter days. Astronomers in antiquity had known this fact ever since the days of the Babylonians. But in Rome until 47 BCE the twelve months of a normal year consisted of only 354 days, and to avoid a serious lack of fit with the actual seasons an extra month was inserted now and again. This was an impractical and confusing system, so Caesar turned to astronomical expertise from Egypt to establish the new calendar, called the Julian calendar, with the number of days in each month which we still have and with a leap day every fourth year. We still use this calendar today, though with a slight modification of the leap day system which was introduced in the sixteenth century by Pope Gregory XIII and adopted in Britain in 1752.

The length of the year and the names of the month are things we have inherited from the Romans. They were, however, less successful in other aspects of the calendar, and in particular in dealing with the problem of how to identify an individual year.

As we have said, in the beginning March was the first month, and it remained this way until 153 BCE, when it was decided that the consuls should take office on the first of January each year. In this way, the beginning of the year was also changed. The consuls' first day in office was crucial, as the Romans named their years after the two people who were consuls at the time, and these names were used for all dating. For example, it says in the biography of the emperor Augustus: *natus est Augustus M. Tullio Cicerone C. Antonio consúlibus* 'Augustus was born during the consulship of Marcus Tullius Cicero and Gaius Antonius', which is the Roman way of saying he was born in 63 BCE. This is obviously a very impractical system, since if you wanted to know when something happened, you had either to know by heart the whole chronological order of consulships or else go and check them in the official record. Nevertheless, the Romans stubbornly stuck to this system throughout antiquity, although some writers tried to replace it with a more manageable system, according to which events were dated from the foundation of the city of Rome, which was supposed to have taken place in 753 BCE. Our modern system of dating by reference to the birth of Christ was invented in the sixth century CE and did not become common until many centuries after that.

The Romans also had a very strange way of naming the days of the month. They numbered them starting from three fixed days in each month, which had their own names: *Kalendae*, the first of the month, *Nonae* the fifth, and *Idus*, the thirteenth, except in March, May, July, and October, when the Nonae was the seventh and the Idus the fifteenth. From these days other dates were reckoned by counting backwards. For example, they had to say *ante diem quartum Nonas Februarias* 'on the fourth day before the Nones of February' when they meant the second of February, or *ante diem décimum Kalendas Martias* 'on the tenth day before the Kalends of March' for 20 February. Fortunately, that system disappeared for good in the Middle Ages and was replaced with the system we still use, with the simple numbering of the days from the first to the last day of the month.

A last residue of the Roman dating system is to be found in the term for a leap year in French and Italian, *année bissextile* and *anno bisestile* respectively. This is so-called because the Romans dealt with the problem of the extra day in a leap year by doubling one day, namely the sixth day before the Kalends of March (i.e. 24 February), and described this day as *bisextus* or *bisextilis*, which means 'double sixth'.

Latin becomes the language of Europe

Under Augustus the Roman empire grew to the size which it then kept for about four hundred years. It included all the land to the west of the Rhine and south of the Danube, and all the countries along the eastern and southern coasts of the Mediterranean. For this reason the Mediterranean was sometimes called *mare nostrum* 'our sea', and the Romans were in complete control of all its coasts. The two official languages in the empire were Latin and, in the east, Greek, as we have already mentioned. Yet at the time of Augustus most of the population certainly spoke other languages than these. In the eastern part Latin never gained a firm foothold, but in the west most people gradually adopted Latin as their language.

We have already mentioned that Italy was multilingual. What is now France had recently been conquered and there the majority spoke a Celtic language. In Spain and Portugal too there were many speakers of Celtic languages, but there were also Ligurians and the Vascones, the ancestors of today's Basques, with their own languages. In north Africa, in modern Morocco and Algeria, the majority of the population probably spoke Berber, and languages belonging to that group are still used by large numbers of people in those countries. In the middle of what is now Tunisia lay Carthage, which had been founded by Phoenicians from modern Syria, and hence many people there spoke the Phoenician language (related to ancient Hebrew), which the city's founders had brought with them.

All these areas came under Roman rule. Italy obviously had a special status, but all the other regions became provinces, which meant that they were ruled by a governor appointed by Rome. The governor naturally had a staff of Romans and in addition there were always one or more garrisons, but apart from these, in a new province there were not necessarily many people who knew Latin. This state of affairs gradually altered in the peaceful conditions which obtained during several centuries of empire, as more and more people learnt Latin, giving up their native language in its favour. The soldiers and the attendant military organization constituted an important factor. The army used Latin for all its business, which meant among other things that the young men in the provinces who became Roman soldiers had to learn that language. Colonies of veterans were also set up in the provinces, from which sometimes sprang quite large towns whose language was of course Latin.

Probably, though, an even more important factor was the fact that in times of peace the local economies of most provinces improved. Commerce and trade increased, existing towns expanded, and new ones emerged. Business people found a ready use for their knowledge of spoken Latin and often too needed to be able to read and write it. In the towns it probably did not take long for the main language to be Latin. In many places schools were started, and the language of schools was Latin and sometimes Greek, but never any of the other local languages.

We cannot trace this development in detail, but it was not long before there were people from Spain, France, and North Africa who were writing in Latin and for whom Latin seemed to be their native language. One of the earliest was an expert in oratory called Seneca, who was active already at the time of Augustus. After a few hundred years the people in the towns throughout the southern part of western Europe and in north Africa probably spoke Latin. How it was in the villages, where most people lived, is not so easy to say, as our sources are generally written by town-dwellers. However, there is some evidence that languages other than Latin were still surviving in several country districts at the time of the break-up of the Roman empire in the fifth century CE, so the shift to Latin must have taken a very long time.

That this shift was nonetheless deep and permanent in its effect in large parts of this territory is confirmed by the fact that the languages spoken today in Italy, France, Spain, and Portugal descend directly from Latin. The same is true in parts of other countries such as Belgium and Switzerland. In addition, Latin gained a strong hold in a country a long way to the east, namely modern Romania. This roughly corresponds to the Roman province of Dacia, which was conquered very late, not until just after 100 CE. Moreover the Romans gave it up again after about 150 years, so that it is very strange that the language there, Romanian, should derive from Latin. There are several theories about how this happened, one being that people from the provinces to the south, which might once have been Latin speaking, moved north into this region, but no one knows for sure.

Anyway, Latin was preserved as the spoken language in large tracts of western Europe and in an area near the Black Sea. How Latin later gave birth to other languages is a question we will return to later, but in some important provinces Latin disappeared. Nowhere is this more true than in north Africa. For many hundreds of years the population there had spoken Latin, at least in the towns. In the fifth century a Germanic tribe, the Vandals, conquered the greater part of the area, and after them it was for a while under the rule of the eastern emperor in Constantinople. But Latin survived, at least to some extent. What caused it to disappear entirely was the Arab conquest in the seventh century.

In another western province Latin was clearly never sufficiently established. England and Wales (but not Scotland) were conquered by the Romans after the time of Augustus during the first century CE. It remained as the Roman province of Britannia for about three hundred years, but it seems that the Roman way of life was never completely accepted, and the inhabitants kept their Celtic languages until the Germanic invasion in the fifth century.

Despite these exceptions, a consequence of long Roman rule was that people in large parts of Europe went from speaking many different languages to a single language, Latin. It clearly meant a great deal for the unity of the Empire that almost everyone in the western part spoke the same language, and this has also been crucial for the development of language in Europe right up to the modern day.

Poetry and poets

The great blossoming of Latin literature came in the period between 100 BCE and 100 CE, in what is normally called the classical era, and just at the time when the Roman empire was expanding most rapidly and was experiencing its greatest success.

But what, one may ask, was it that the Romans wrote? The answer is that they studied the masterpieces of Greek literature very carefully and then produced similar works themselves. At first, they made several translations or adaptations of Greek works, but little by little they grew more ambitious and started to write their own original compositions, though in many respects still keeping within the guidelines established by the Greeks. Put like this it sounds quite boring, but in fact Latin literature achieved considerable success. The Romans did indeed follow the example of the Greeks; these provided exceptionally good models, and then they tried to create similar things in Latin but preferably even better. They called this process *aemulátio*, which means the attempt to emulate or outstrip someone or something, and quite often the Latin works did indeed match or even excel their models.

The literature which the Greeks and Romans wrote is quite unlike what is found in the bookshops today. Most of the books written these days are novels, that is to say long narratives in prose. There are some Roman novels, but they never became very popular either in antiquity or later. The heyday of the novel did not come until the eighteenth century, and then it appeared in modern languages such as French or English. In ancient times, by contrast, most creative literature was in verse. Plain prose was reserved for speeches, history, and various kinds of non-fiction, which I will deal with later. Almost everything that could be called narrative or storytelling or entertainment came in the form of poetry, where the texts are required to follow strict rhythmical patterns; a number of examples are given below. The authors are also very attentive to how they choose their words and other forms of expression; Latin poems are often very carefully crafted and linguistically refined. One reason why the authors took so much trouble in this respect is probably that literature was essentially an aural medium. A modern reader sits in silence, quickly scanning page after page, but in antiquity people read aloud.

The earliest form of imaginative literature in Rome of which anything survives are plays, which we have already discussed. After the early comedies of Plautus and Terence not a lot came of the art of drama in Rome, but other kinds of literature became more interesting. A number of poets wrote mainly about love, and the best of them have hardly been surpassed to this day. Catullus was one of the first. His love for a woman called Lesbia gave rise to a number of passionate poems. Here is one:

> Dicebas quondam solum te nosse Catullum,
> Lesbia, nec prae me velle tenere Iovem.
> Dilexi tum te non tantum ut vulgus amicam
> sed pater ut gnatos diligit et generos.
> Nunc te cognovi. Quare etsi impensius uror,
> multo mi tamen es vilior et levior.
> 'Qui potis est?' inquis. Quod amantem iniuria talis
> cogit amare magis sed bene velle minus.

> You said one day you only knew Catullus, Lesbia,
> And you'd refuse to embrace even Jove instead of me.
> I loved you then, not only as common men their girlfriend
> But as a father loves his sons and sons-in-law.
> I know you now. So though my passion's more intense,
> Yet for me you're much cheaper and lighter-weight.
> 'How can that be?' you ask. It's because such hurt compels
> A lover to love more but to like less.

This is one in a series of poems where we can follow the development of the relation between Catullus and Lesbia, from the joy and delirium at the beginning of their affair through the quarrelling and deceit we see here to a final phase of bitter memories and recriminations.

But the poet Catullus did not only write about this intense love of his. He was a bright, talented young man who for a few hectic years moved in Rome's inner circles. He was only thirty when he died and he had published just one collection of poems, which contains many other things apart from the Lesbia poems: humorous poems for his friends, some poems about gods and goddesses, and not least love poems to the boy Juventius. That a man might be in love with both women and men did not cause any great surprise in antiquity and there was no special term for people who were. It was not regarded as deviant behaviour.

One of Catullus' real specialities was libellous poems. When he was living in Rome in the 60s and 50s BCE, the economy was expanding and the politics turbulent. Parties, factions, and generals were engaged in a ruthless struggle for power and the tone of public conversation was, to put it mildly, outspoken. This suited Catullus down to the ground. He set about both those in power and other people he did not like with great gusto, and the poems are sometimes unashamedly rude. One short poem, which is relatively moderate in tone, is famous. The reason is that the person he was having a go at was already, in Catullus' time, one of the most famous people in Rome, the dictator-to-be Julius Caesar:

> *Nil nimium studeo, Caesar, tibi velle placere*
> *nec scire utrum sis albus an ater homo*

> I am none too keen to wish to please you, Caesar,
> nor to know whether you are a white man or a black.

After Catullus there were many poets who dedicated themselves to writing about love. The most famous is Ovid, who lived a couple of generations later during the reign of Augustus and at the time of the birth of Christ. His poems are both beautiful and knowing, but he writes in a more gentle manner than Catullus did. He does not attack anyone and does not seem to suffer any intense passions himself. Rather, he is good at relating all kinds of elegant love affairs, both his own and those of others. His most famous work is a sort of handbook for lovers in verse called *Ars amatoria* 'The Art of Loving', which deals with what gentlemen must do to meet ladies, and ladies gentlemen, in the right social circles in Rome. It also discusses what to do after they have met and has been considered scandalous because it gives some good advice about the best positions to adopt for sexual intercourse and related matters. Even so, it is a lot less explicit than today's handbooks let alone modern pornography.

Ovid was very industrious and wrote a great deal of other poetry. The work that has been most widely read is called *Metamorphoses*, or 'Transformations'. The word is a Greek loan, just as many centuries later it was in English and other European languages. The transformations in question are those that occur in the world of fairy tales and the gods, as for instance when the nymph Daphne changes into a laurel bush in order to escape the god Apollo. The stories are well told, and contain large chunks of ancient mythology, so it is not surprising that they have been used in the teaching of Latin in schools for many centuries. One of the most famous episodes concerns the sad story of Pyramus and Thisbe. They grew up next door to each other in ancient Babylon, but when they fell in love their parents tried to stop them seeing each other. They spoke to each other through a crack in the wall between their two houses, and agreed to escape and meet each other outside town. A fatal misunderstanding makes Pyramus think Thisbe has been eaten by a lion, and racked with guilt he takes his own life. When Thisbe, who is in fact unharmed, finds him she too commits suicide.

As in many of the stories, the transformation that then occurs seems somewhat contrived. Pyramus kills himself under a mulberry tree, and the berries turn black from his blood. That is why mulberries are white as long as they are unripe, but turn black when they ripen. The story of Pyramus and Thisbe has been taken up many times since Ovid. The best known is a passage of burlesque in Shakespeare's *A Midsummer Night's Dream*, where a group of tradesmen rehearse their amateur performance of this story which then becomes a parodic play within the play.

Love poetry was important and well liked, but it was not accorded the highest praise by Roman writers. This was reserved instead for epic poetry, and it was also under Augustus that a great epic, the most famous Latin poem of all, was written. To write a long, gripping tale the Greeks and the Romans usually adopted the hexameter. The first and greatest poet to do so was Homer, author of the *Iliad* and the *Odyssey*. After him, many others tried to compose similar long poems, both in Greek and in Latin, but for the most part they have been quite deservedly forgotten.

But one Roman, Virgil, succeeded. He first demonstrated his exceptional talent in a series of poems about pastoral life, the *Bucolica*, or *Eclogae*. These charming pieces introduce simple shepherds in a rural setting who mysteriously also sometimes talk and feel like poets or even prophets. The famous Fourth Eclogue foretells the birth of a child who is to save the world. Not surprisingly, Christians interpreted this as a prophesy of the coming of Christ, and it earned its author pride of place among pagan writers in the Middle Ages.

Later, Virgil ventured to rival Homer himself and write a long poem, an *epos*, which contained similar themes to both the *Iliad* and the *Odyssey*, but written in Latin and in accordance with Roman tastes. He succeeded brilliantly: the resulting work, the *Aeneid*, has even been considered by some critics to be the greatest poem in the whole history of literature. Here are the first few lines in the original Latin, in a literal prose rendering and in a famous English translation by John Dryden:

> *Arma virumque cano, Troiae qui primus ab oris*
> *Italiam, fato profugus, Laviniaque venit*
> *litora, multum ille et terris iactatus et alto*
> *vi superum saevae memorem Iunonis ob iram;*
> *multa quoque et bello passus, dum conderet urbem,*
> *inferretque deos Latio, genus unde Latinum,*
> *Albanique patres, atque altae moenia Romae.*

I sing of arms and of the man who, made fugitive by fate, first came from the coasts of Troy to Italy and the Lavinian shores; hard pressed both on land and at sea by the force of the gods above on account of the unforgetting wrath of fierce Juno, he suffered much in war until he founded the city and brought in the Gods to Latium, whence came the Latin people, the Alban fathers and the walls of glorious Rome.

> Arms, and the man I sing, who, forc'd by fate,
> And haughty Juno's unrelenting hate,
> Expell'd and exil'd, left the Trojan shore.
> Long labours, both by sea and land, he bore,
> And in the doubtful war, before he won

The Latian realm, and built the destin'd town;
His banish'd gods restor'd to rites divine,
And settled sure succession in his line,
From whence the race of Alban fathers come,
And the long glories of majestic Rome.

This kind of rhythm can be sustained indefinitely, and indeed the whole *Aeneid* runs to some 10,000 lines. The plot is already pretty clear from the lines we have quoted. The hero, Aeneas, was on the losing Trojan side in the war between the Greeks and the Trojans, which took place on the west coast of what is now Turkey. He escaped across the sea together with a number of companions, and after many adventures they landed on the coast of Latium, where they became the ancestors of the Romans. Aeneas himself is said to have been the ancestor of the Julian clan, of which among others the Emperor Augustus was a member.

The poem is a saga of heroes and heroines, gods and goddesses. Aeneas' mother is the goddess Venus, and the whole thing is obviously designed to provide the Romans, and in particular the emperor, with a famous and fitting ancestry. Aeneas fits the bill in every way. He is handsome and strong, pious and brave, serious and wise, indeed just a bit too perfect in some people's eyes. In any case, what makes this great poem worth reading for us is less the glorification of Rome and the Romans than the powerful emotions that are conveyed. Virgil's underlying tone is one of magnificent melancholy which can easily captivate readers. The poem is basically about *miseri mortales* 'wretched mortals'; in other words you and me. This atmosphere is nowhere more evident than in the famous episode when Aeneas, in his wanderings, arrives in Carthage, which is ruled by Queen Dido. Soon they are caught up in a passionate love affair and Dido thinks that Aeneas is going to marry her and become king of Carthage. But the messenger of the gods, Hermes, comes to him and tells him that this will not do. Aeneas' mission in life is to go to Italy and found Rome. Obediently, he orders his men back to the ships and sets sail again, while Dido in her despair burns herself on a pyre, cursing the deceitful coward.

The plot is every bit as convoluted as a TV soap opera. One difference, though, is that Virgil sympathizes with both sides, with Dido who is betrayed and with Aeneas who betrays her out of a sense of duty. In Virgil's world everyone has a heavy burden to carry. A close friend of Virgil's was another famous poet, Horace. He takes life a bit less seriously than Virgil but is perhaps just as important. Many of his poems too are in hexameters, but their tone is conversational, even chatty, rather than tragic and heroic. They are nimble, carefully argued texts, but for all that ones where the associations sometimes seem to move in unpredictable directions.

Horace is best known for his collections of relatively short poems called Odes. These are written in a variety of metres, normally with stanzas of four lines each. The poems are about various things, such as politics, friendship, and love, but a lot of them are also about how to live, wisdom in verse as it were. The beginning of one of the poems runs:

> Otium divos rogat in patenti
> prensus Aegaeo, simul atra nubes
> condidit lunam neque certa fulgent
> sidera nautis;
>
> otium bello furiosa Trace,
> otium Medi pharetra decori,
> Grosphe, non gemmis neque purpura
> venale nec auro.
>
> Non enim gazae neque consularis
> summovet lictor miseros tumultus
> mentis et curas laqueata circum
> tecta volantis.
>
> Vivitur parvo bene, cui paternum
> splendet in mensa tenui salinum
> nec levis somnos timor aut cupido
> sordidus aufert.
>
> Quid brevi fortes iaculamur aevo
> multa? Quid terras alio calentis
> sole mutamus? Patriae quis exsul
> se quoque fugit?

Literally translated this means:

[The sailor], caught in a storm on the open Aegean prays for peace when a dark cloud has hidden the moon and the fixed stars no longer shine for sailors. For ease [prays] Thrace furious in war, for ease [prays] the Mede with his decorated quiver, peace, Grosphus, which is not to be bought with jewels or purple or gold. Neither treasure nor the consul's *lictor* can dispel the miserable disturbances of the mind and the cares that fly around the panelled ceilings. He lives well on a little, that man whose father's salt-cellar shines on his modest table, and whose quiet sleep sordid greed and fear does not take away. Why do we strive so hard in our short lives for so many things? Why do we change our countries for ones warmed by a different sun? What exile from his own country ever escaped himself as well?

And here is what it sounds like in a verse translation by John Conington, a former Professor of Latin at the University of Oxford:

> For ease, in wide Aegean caught,
> The sailor prays, when clouds are hiding
> The moon, nor shines of starlight aught
> For seaman's guiding:
> For ease the Mede, with quiver gay:
> For ease rude Thrace, in battle cruel:
> Can purple buy it, Grosphus? Nay,
> Nor gold, nor jewel.
> No pomp, no lictor clears the way
> 'Mid rabble-routs of troublous feelings,
> Nor quells the cares that sport and play
> Round gilded ceilings.
> More happy he whose modest hoard
> His father's well-worn silver brightens;
> No fear, nor lust for sordid hoard,
> His light sleep frightens.
> Why bend our bows of little span?
> Why change our homes for regions under
> Another sun? What exiled man
> From self can sunder?

As often in ancient poetry there are allusions which need explaining. Thrace is the home of the Thracians, who together with the Medes were peoples that the Romans were at war with. Lictors were a kind of policemen who also served as bodyguards for the leading figures in the state; hence to have a crowd of lictors around one was to have reached the pinnacle of society. Grosphus is the person to whom the poem is addressed. Moderation and calm, and the ability to enjoy life as long as one has it, are the things Horace prefers to talk about. The message is low-key and unsensational, but it has appealed to many over the centuries. Amongst poets writing in English who imitated the structure and style of the Horatian ode we may mention Marvell, Gray, and Keats. Here is the beginning of a famous poem by Andrew Marvell entitled 'An Horatian Ode upon Cromwell's Return from Ireland':

> The forward youth that would appear
> Must now forsake his Muses dear,
> Nor in the shadows sing
> His numbers languishing.
> 'Tis time to leave the books in dust,
> And oil th' unused armour's rust,
> Removing from the wall
> The corslet of the hall.
> So restless Cromwell could not cease
> In the inglorious arts of peace,
> But thorough advent'rous war
> Urged his active star.

Virgil and Horace, like their younger contemporary Ovid, became writers who have been read in schools from their own time right up until today. Latin was the most important school subject for almost two thousand years, as I shall explain later. The reading of poetry was always part of the school curriculum (from Latin *currículum* 'a race' built on *cúrrere* 'to run'), and so these poems have become better known than any others in the whole history of Europe.

Of course, the Romans did not stop writing poetry after the time of Augustus, when the most famous poets lived. But none of their successors really reached the same level either in achievement or, above all, in fame. A good number of poems from later antiquity have survived and several of them are very readable, for example the satirical poems by Juvenal, but hardly anyone but specialists actually reads them nowadays.

Philosophy: Lucretius, Cicero, Seneca

The word philosophy is Greek and means something like 'love of wisdom'. For the Greeks it included most kinds of systematic search for what is true and right. As is well known, their achievements in the realm of philosophy were paramount, and still today much of what the best Greek philosophers such as Plato and Aristotle wrote has lost none of its significance and importance.

Roman philosophy was entirely based on this great Greek tradition, with its various attempts to explain the world and to establish the norms by which one should live one's life. The Romans did not introduce many new philosophical ideas but they did transfer the thoughts of the Greeks into Latin, making a few modifications along the way. Nonetheless, the Roman philosophers are very important for two reasons. First, they communicated the essence of Greek philosophy to everyone who could read Latin, which was to prove very valuable in the later history of European thought. Second, they created a terminology for philosophical reasoning which was then there to be used by the many significant original thinkers who subsequently wrote in Latin, from Augustine and the Church Fathers of late antiquity right down to Descartes and Spinoza in the seventeenth century.

In fact the first major philosophical work in Latin turned out to be influential even later than that. Its title is *De rerum natura* 'On the

Nature of Things', and it was written by Lucretius, who died in 55 BCE. This work also falls within the poetic tradition since it is a long didactic poem in hexameters, the same metre as Virgil used for the *Aeneid*. Lucretius was a passionate adherent of the Greek philosopher Epicurus. To the extent that people know anything at all about Epicurus today it is as an advocate of pleasure as the supreme good; pleasure-loving people are therefore sometimes known as Epicureans. But Lucretius took no notice of that side of his philosophy. To him, Epicurus was the man who had the courage to explain the whole world rationally with the aid of the theory of atomism and so sweep aside all superstitious fear of the gods and of unknown powers. Already near the beginning of the poem we find the line *Tantum religio potuit suadere malorum* 'Such evil has religion been able to cause!' (In the word order of Latin: 'so-much religion has-been-able to-cause of-evils'.)

This poem on the nature of things consists of six books, each of which is more than a thousand lines long. The first two books are about atoms, and how everything in the world is built up out of them, and how in the end everything breaks back down into atoms again. Books three and four are about the soul, the will and sensations, and stress materialist and rational explanations for what we experience and feel. Books five and six are about the universe and the external forces that act on human beings, such as bad weather and illness. Plagues are explained, for instance, as due to bad air and the transmission of infection, and in consequence they have nothing to do with punishments visited on us by the gods. The whole work concludes with a striking illustration of this line of argument, a grand and terrifying description of the plague in Athens.

Elsewhere in the poem Lucretius is not always good at finding really striking examples or parallels to illuminate his work. A lot of the text is inevitably dense scientific analysis, even if it is conducted in verse. Sometimes he encounters, and indeed complains of, the difficulty of transferring Greek scientific terminology into Latin. At one point he talks about *patrii sermonis egestas* 'the poverty of the language inherited from our forefathers'. From a strictly literary point of view, therefore, the text is rather uneven. Some parts, such as the introduction, are among the best things that have ever been written in Latin, and the great master of Latin poetry, Virgil, learnt a lot from reading Lucretius. Other parts, by contrast, are rather wooden. But then we must remember that the purpose behind this poem was not simply to create a work of art. Lucretius was a missionary for Epicurus in Latin, and his passion was to make human beings appreciate that the world was ruled by understandable natural forces. He was an apostle of science, materialism, and rationalism.

For a long time it seemed as if his message did not get through. In Rome he was never read very much, and in general the philosophy of Epicurus was pushed into the background by the Stoic ethic of duty and piety. Christianity took over most of the ideas of Stoicism, leaving Lucretius and his teachers to stand in the corner with the pagans for almost two thousand years. However, Epicurean thought was revived in the sixteenth and seventeenth centuries. The eighteenth century saw the Enlightenment and the new science, which abandoned the link with religion and reinforced the interest in the ideas of the Epicureans. In the nineteenth century, the fundamental ideas of Epicurus and Lucretius were incorporated into one of the most important systems of thought ever constructed in the western world: scientific materialism, whose name directly reveals the source of its inspiration. Karl Marx wrote a doctoral thesis on Epicurus and the attitudes of the two thinkers have much in common, as witness for instance their passionate belief that the lot of human beings can be improved if they are freed from the yoke of religion. Today Marx is just as unread as Lucretius ever was, but his ideas and those of likeminded people have influenced western thinking for more than a century so thoroughly that what once seemed controversial and new is now deemed trivial and obvious.

Marcus Tullius Cicero, who as we have seen was above all a great orator and politician, also wrote several philosophical works. He did not claim to come up with original ideas, but saw it as his task to present the thoughts of the Greeks in Latin in an appropriate literary form. To this end he wrote fictitious dialogues, in which Cicero himself and his friends were often protagonists. The topics are things like death and the possibility of life after death, duty, good and evil, friendship and old age. The emphasis is on giving guidance about life rather than on logical reasoning. Opinions are often set against each other without Cicero himself directly taking a stance. They were all written at an amazing rate, most of them within a year when Cicero happened not to have much else to do, and they can still be read with profit, particularly as a starting point for one's own personal reflections.

The writer Seneca lived about a century after Cicero, and was known in the first instance as a philosopher. Like Cicero, he achieved a very prominent position in Roman society. He was the tutor of Nero, who became emperor at a very young age, and Seneca and another man acted as the emperor's guardians. However, after some years he fell from grace and was forced to commit suicide. Seneca wrote many books advocating the philosophy of Stoicism, which he for the most part took over from his Greek predecessors. This view involved doing one's duty, using one's personal resources for the common good, despising wealth and worldly rewards, looking forward to eternal life, and revering the highest god.

These ideas are very close to those of Christianity, and indeed speculation did occur at quite an early stage that Seneca was really a Christian or had at least been in touch with Christians. There is even a forged correspondence between him and the apostle Paul. Timewise, it all fits quite well, since Seneca died in 65 CE and Paul in 67 at the latest. Seneca's philosophy was greatly valued for a long period of European history, which obviously has to do with the fact that it is so consonant with Christianity. Seneca himself, however, has had very few admirers, since he did not live by his own precepts. He held the view that one should despise riches, but nonetheless acquired a very large personal fortune. He thought that we should endure everything with fortitude, but turned out to be less than a hero in real life.

How to judge this kind of discrepancy between thought and deed is a matter for debate, but whatever one concludes on that score, it is of interest that two of the most prominent philosophers of antiquity, Cicero and Seneca, were closely involved in political activity and leadership. Both also wrote other literary works, and made early careers as orators. This says something about the position that philosophy and literature had in Roman society. On the one hand they had great prestige, and writers often played leading roles in the state; on the other hand, they were pastimes. To achieve real success in life, it was no help to be a philosopher or a poet or a historian. You had to be a public speaker.

The schools and Quintilian

Since success in Rome depended so much on the ability to speak in public, it was natural for parents to want their children to learn to speak well. That was essentially what schooling in Rome was about. There had been schools and teachers for children in ancient Greece, and the Romans took over the idea. Primarily, of course, it was the wealthy families in the towns who sent their children to school, although the very richest were able to afford private teachers in their homes. It is difficult to say exactly how many children received a school education, but in the towns quite a large percentage of the population were able to read, and there seem to have been schools in most towns.

In their first years at school children were taught to read and write and do arithmetic, very much as today. The language of instruction was of course Latin. Most pupils probably did not get any further than that. Those who went on had to learn a foreign language, Greek, and start to be trained in public speaking. That training consisted, in part, of the children making speeches on given subjects; such speeches were called *declamationes* 'declamations'. They also had to learn the theory of oratory, which we have already described, and which involved techniques for finding arguments, for memorizing and so on. We know quite a lot about how this was done from a large handbook in twelve books written by Quintilian called *Institutio oratória* 'Training in oratory', or more freely 'Manual of Public Speaking'. This deals with the education and training of a public speaker, and covers everything from infancy to adulthood. It provides an overall picture of education in Rome.

In particular, it shows how the goal of becoming a good public speaker was allowed to take priority over all other educational considerations. Quintilian is undoubtedly a very perceptive and clever man, who emphasizes the importance of having a broad perspective and a good variety of skills, but the goal throughout is very clear. The important thing is to turn the pupil into a successful orator. One consequence of this attitude was that the Latin language received a great deal of attention in school. A knowledge of language is the speaker's basic tool and a fundamental demand was that the pupils should speak correctly. Grammar and linguistic correctness therefore had pride of place right from the beginning. Later came exercises in style at different levels, from simple everyday language through elaborate descriptions to violent outbursts of emotion. A public speaker had to be aware of the resources of the language at every level and be able to make use of them in the best way possible. Given such schooling, it is hardly surprising that the best Roman writers have never been surpassed stylistically. To speak well and also, when necessary, to write well was quite simply the highest goal of education.

However, this in turn meant that schools did not pay attention to other kinds of knowledge. Pupils undoubtedly had to read a lot, preferably the writings of the best Latin and Greek authors, but the intention was not primarily to discover what they wrote about but to study and imitate their language and style. All kinds of literature were seen as material for rhetorical exercises. In this way pupils came to read a fair amount of history and philosophy, but there was little room for other disciplines. Mathematics stopped after elementary arithmetic, and anyone interested in subjects like physics, astronomy, biology, and so on had to follow their interest up outside school. Technology, economics, and medicine had no place in a Roman's education.

With such a school system, one might imagine that there would be a debate about teaching methods. This did take place to some extent, but rather than being about the content of the curriculum it mostly centred on the criticism that the training in oratory was far too theoretical and unrealistic. One contribution to this debate was by Seneca, who, as we have said, was also a very well-known public speaker. At one point he writes, *Non vitae sed scholae discimus* 'We learn not for life but for school', by which he meant that the class-room exercises did not train pupils to be better at anything except doing classroom exercises. That phrase was soon twisted around and is often quoted as an unchallengeable truth: *Non scholae sed vitae discimus* 'We learn not for school but for life'. Whether that is in general true is certainly worth discussing, but in any case it is not what Seneca had asserted.

The sciences

Although schools focused on linguistic exercises, there was a great need for knowledge about other matters in Roman society. There was no possibility of access to higher education because the Romans never had the first inkling of anything comparable to a modern university. Older people probably passed on their vocational skills through some kind of apprentice system, but we do not know much about it. However, manuals in a wide variety of subjects have come down to us. As we have already said, the basic industry was farming, and there are several handbooks on that subject, starting with the one by Cato the Elder which we have already mentioned and going right on into late antiquity. The most detailed was written by a landowner called Columella, who lived in the first century CE.

The Romans also undertook a whole range of building projects. Vitruvius, who lived at the time of the Emperor Augustus, wrote a large handbook on architecture, *De architectura,* the only one that has survived from antiquity. It was very influential, especially in the Renaissance and afterwards, when people wanted to return to ancient ideals of style both in architecture and other kinds of art.

A particular speciality for which the Romans were known was the construction of the means of carrying water over long distances, namely aqueducts. A successful civil servant, Frontinus, who was the manager of Rome's water supplies, wrote a book about the aqueducts of Rome, which has been preserved. The same man also published several works about another Roman speciality, warfare, and one of these too has survived.

An especially useful skill for farmers, builders, and even soldiers is the ability to survey the land. While the Greeks had developed geometry as a part of mathematics, the Romans had no time for geometrical theory as such; but they used selected aspects of it to create practically applicable procedures for surveying the land, and we possess a number of their pretty indigestible treatises on this subject.

In all these practical fields the Romans went some way beyond existing Greek models. In many other areas they were content just to translate Greek knowledge into Latin. A good example is medicine, where the Greeks had had a strong tradition ever since the great Hippocrates. In Rome several handbooks of medicine were composed, among others one by Celsus, but they were all based almost totally on Greek models. The same goes for the manuals of veterinary medicine, prescription books for pharmacists, and the like.

The person who probably did most to transfer the knowledge of the Greeks into Latin was a prominent officer named Pliny. He was an admiral in the Roman navy, which had its main base in the bay of Naples. When Vesuvius erupted in 79 CE, Pliny tried to help the victims of the disaster but was killed himself. We can read this dramatic story in a famous and very detailed letter written by his nephew, Pliny the Younger, who was also present at the eruption. Pliny the Elder, who must have had an incredible capacity for hard work, spent a large part of his time reading—or having read to him—specialist literature in Greek on most subjects, of which he then continuously dictated translations or summaries in Latin. He gradually collected this material into a large encyclopedia, which he called *Naturalis historia* 'Natural History'. In this title, the Greek word *historia* retains the general meaning 'inquiry' or 'science', whereas we mostly use it only to mean inquiries into the past. The title of the book you are reading is of course adapted from Pliny's famous work, in the hope that it will provide a suitable blend of useful information and entertaining anecdote, just as his volumes do.

In one form or another the *Naturalis historia* takes up most of what today is called '(natural) science' but which was long called 'natural history' after the title of Pliny's work. For a long time, even as late as the eighteenth century, Pliny was in fact the most important authority in areas such as botany, zoology, anatomy, mineralogy, and many more. But modern science has gradually overtaken him in area after area, and now his work is seen almost exclusively as one of the curiosities in the history of learning.

The same generally goes for the other Roman writers in different specialist areas. For a large part of the history of Europe these writings were the best to be had, but in the course of the last couple of centuries they have become very dated. Some of their material has become basic knowledge for beginners in different disciplines, and much has turned out to be wrong. What has by and large been preserved are the Latin names and terms which, with or without modification, live on in today's scientific language.

Everyday language

What did people say in Latin when they talked about the weather or complained about the taxes or were gossiping about their neighbour's wife? For a language that is spoken today it is easy to find out about such things simply by listening. Latin we can only read, not listen to, so it is hard to know what everyday speech was like. Quite a lot can be gleaned from the texts we have; but most writers do not adopt a colloquial style, preferring instead to write in a deliberately artistic way, using a wide range of vocabulary, often with long sentences and always with the utmost respect for the rules of grammar. People do not speak like that nowadays, and of course they did not do so in Rome either. Moreover, as we have seen, most writers came from the upper classes, and their way of speaking was probably very different from that of the majority of Romans. The elements of spoken language that can be found in Cicero or his peers are therefore not very representative.

It is possible to get some idea of how common people spoke from the comedies of Plautus, whom we mentioned earlier. Here is a short dialogue between two housewives, Cleostrata and Myrrhina, who meet in the street:

CLEOSTRATA: *Myrrhina, salve.*
MYRRHINA: *Salve, mecastor: sed quid tu's tristis, amábo?*
CLEOSTRATA: *Ita solent omnes quae sunt male nuptae: Domi et foris aegre quod sit, satis semper est. Nam ego ibam ad te.*
MYRRHINA: *Et pol ego istuc ad te. Sed quid est, quod tuo nunc ánimo aegre'st? Nam quod tibi'st aegre, idem mihi'st dividiae.*

CLEOSTRATA: Hello, Myrrhina.
MYRRHINA: Hello: but why are you so sad, my dear?
CLEOSTRATA: Everybody feels like that when they have made a bad marriage: indoors or out, there's always something to make you miserable. I was just on my way to see you.
MYRRHINA: Well fancy that! I was on my way to visit you. But what is it that has upset you so? Because whatever upsets you upsets me too.

This is almost ordinary spoken language, with short sentences, expressions which are typical of everyday speech and quite a lot of repetition of the same words. Strangely enough, it is more difficult to translate than many more solemn texts. The reason is that there are so many idioms. Let us consider a couple of examples. Myrrhina ends her first speech with the word *amabo*. Literally, this means 'I shall love'. But the implication here is something like 'I shall like you (if you answer my question)' and often it is simply an expression that is used when someone is asking a friendly question. It can be translated 'my dear' or even simply 'then'.

Later on she says *et pol ego istuc ad te*. *Et ego ad te* is easy: 'And I to you'. The word *istuc* means 'yours, where you are' and hardly needs to be translated. The little word *pol* is the problem. It is an abbreviated version of Pollux, which is the name of a god, or more accurately a demi-god. It is a small imprecation or a very mild swear word. It occurs a lot in spoken language and is almost impossible to translate satisfactorily. I have tried here with the expression 'fancy that'.

Spoken language is not always easy to understand for someone who has not grown up with it. For example, a newly arrived immigrant in Britain may frequently find it less difficult to understand a news broadcast than a conversation in a pub. In the same way, it is often easier for us to understand the arguments in Latin about politics or philosophy than to follow the language of the street. But the spoken language is often more fun when you do understand it, and it can tell us a lot about how people actually lived a couple of thousand years ago. Apart from the plays, a few other texts contain language drawn directly from the spoken Latin of ancient Rome.

When the ashes of Vesuvius buried Pompeii in 79 CE, they preserved many of the things in the town, including the walls. When the first archaeologists started to excavate the town a couple of hundred years ago, as we have said, they discovered that these walls were covered with writing. They had been used for all sorts of messages, such as advertisements and election posters. But a lot of it is quite like what you would find on the walls of any modern town, not least in the public lavatories. There are all kinds of messages, and a fair number of them are about sex. The authors want to do this or that, or accuse some named individual of doing it or not being able to do it. Latin has many useful words, including a wide selection of verbs for different kinds of vaginal, oral, and anal intercourse, and the wall inscriptions use them to the full! Whether these inscriptions really contain everyday language is a matter for debate. What is there is in all likelihood mostly what people did not have the courage to say rather than what they actually said. Even today they still have the power to raise eyebrows.

Another source of everyday language is a text which is usually known as the *Cena Trimalchionis* 'Trimalchio's Dinner Party'. It is an extract of about thirty pages from a long novel, one of the few in ancient Latin literature. Only short sections of this work, which was called *Satyrica* (often cited in the genitive plural, *Satyricon*), have survived. The manuscripts tell us that the author was called Petronius, and he is generally thought to be the same Petronius who was both a highly placed official and a leading partygoer among Rome's jetset. The emperor Nero is said to have engaged him as an *elegantiae arbiter* 'arbiter of good taste'. The story of this extract concerns a spectacular dinner party at the house of Trimalchio, one of Rome's nouveaux riches. Most of the guests are former slaves who have, like the host, found success and fortune, and the dialogues between them reveal how they spoke. This is what it sounds like when one of them, Echion, speaks about his son's education:

Emi ergo nunc puero aliquot libra rubricata, quia volo illum ad domusionem aliquid de iure gustare. Habet haec res panem. Nam litteris satis inquinatus est.

So I bought the boy some law books because I want him to taste a bit of law at home. That's something which can earn him some bread. His head has been stuffed enough with literature.

These people were very ambitious for their children, and hoped, just as many parents do today, that they would have a better life as a result of their studies. Petronius, who had a secure position in high society, looked down on that kind of aspiration. This speech contributes to the portrayal of an amusing social upstart, something which the choice of language reinforces. Compared to ordinary written language it is full of blunders, which are hard to represent in the translation. For example, Echion uses *libra* instead of *libros* as the plural of *liber* 'book', revealing his uncertainty over the inflection of very common and ordinary words. It would be as if someone were to say *childs* instead of *children* in English.

Some of these peculiarities are very exciting for linguists studying changes in the language. For instance, Echion says *aliquid de iure* 'a little law', literally 'something of law'. In ordinary written Latin this should have been *aliquid iuris*, where the form *iuris* is the genitive of the noun *ius* 'law'. But Echion uses the preposition *de* and a noun instead of the genitive of the noun, which is exactly what happens in the modern Romance languages. In French 'a little law' would be *un peu de droit*, literally 'a little of law'. This means it is possible to observe the beginning of a major change from nouns with case endings, as found in Latin, to prepositions with nouns, which are characteristic of the modern Romance languages. There are quite a few things of this kind, which point ahead to future changes, in the speeches which Petronius puts in the mouths of his emancipated but still uneducated slaves.

In other words, it appears as if certain changes were taking place in the spoken language, although they almost never occur in the more 'correct' written texts from the same period. This is very much as we would expect. All spoken languages vary and change with time, whereas the written languages which are taught in schools are considerably more conservative. Written language changed very little during the whole of antiquity, and as a result obviously became more and more unlike the spoken language.

The kind of Latin which is not quite like the official written language, and which we see exemplified in the inscriptions of Pompeii and the dialogues of Petronius, is often called 'Vulgar Latin'. This is an unfortunate term, although it has been in use for a long time. First, 'vulgar' has a derogatory meaning in English, as do the equivalent words in German and French: *vulgär, vulgaire*. They all come from the Latin word *vulgaris*, which means 'popular' or 'common', and is often also derogatory. This in turn is derived from the word *vulgus* 'common people'. Secondly, it is easy to get the idea that Vulgar Latin is an independent language, completely different from ordinary Latin, when it is in fact exactly that: the ordinary Latin that the people spoke. That it differs somewhat from the written language is no more strange than the fact that spoken English is different from written English in a number of ways. But no one calls spoken English 'Vulgar English'!

Laws and legal language

The emancipated slave Echion wanted his son to study law as a way of making a living. He did not have such great ambitions as to imagine his son becoming an orator and defending others, but he had to know something about the law. In this he was probably right. In the Roman world, laws were very important. Civil servants spent a lot of their time forming judgements and making sure that people lived by the law. Those who broke the law were often treated very harshly, but the law also protected people from violence and arbitrariness.

People were not equal before the law. On the contrary, the laws gave distinct and clear rules about who had power over whom, and about the extent of such power. Slave owners, for example, had absolute power, even including the right to kill their slaves. But there were still limits: the owner could be forced to sell a slave who had run away because of unjustified cruelty, so in some circumstances even slaves were protected by the law.

Rome was a very patriarchal society, and a father of a family, a *pater familiae*, was able to decide most things within his family, but there were restrictions. His wife, for example, remained in control of her own money, and her finances were legally separate from those of her husband.

These rules are examples of how people's rights and obligations were defined. There were obviously also many other rules about buying and selling, disputes and damages, and not least crime and punishment. All functioning societies must have rules of this kind, but the Romans invested more time than any society before them (and many since!) in formulating clear, consistent rules and in making them work. They also thought and wrote a lot about the principles underlying their laws and rules, and can be said to have invented the science of law or jurisprudence (from *iuris prudentia* 'wisdom of the law').

The fundamental principle itself is *ius* 'right' or 'law'. It is defined in the following way: *Ius est ars boni et aequi* 'Law is the art of the good and the right'. People who are not lawyers probably often have their doubts about that, yet Roman legislators did not just make rules for things that needed regulation; they also had thoughts and ideas about the foundations of justice and its administration. They established principles regarding the interpretation and application of laws, and they defined many fundamental concepts. Roman law, which was gradually developed by many famous jurists, completely surpassed all pre-existing systems. It is documented in what is called the *Corpus iuris*, a collection of laws and many other texts which were put together as late as the sixth century CE under the Emperor Justinian in Byzantium.

After the fall of the Roman empire in western Europe both legal science and the administration of justice waned, but from the eleventh century properly founded legal education resumed in Bologna, in what is usually considered Europe's first university. This education was totally based on Roman law, and for many centuries thereafter Roman law was the foundation of the legal system in most European countries. Even as late as the nineteenth century, Roman law survived almost intact in the legal systems of many countries in south and west Europe, from Portugal to Germany. It is still important for students of law in the western world to know the basics of Roman law, which is an independent subject in most Faculties of Law.

One reason for this is that the Romans created a complete system of terms and concepts which were well thought out and readily applicable. They have formed the basis for jurisprudence for some two thousand years, and they still turn up in modern debates. An example is *ius naturale* 'natural law'. In one of the texts in the *Corpus iuris*, it is defined as follows: *Ius naturale est quod natura omnia animalia docuit* 'Natural law is what nature has taught all living creatures'. Whether or not there is a concept of natural law is still a fundamental question in sociology. Under all circumstances *ius civile* exists and in English this is usually called 'civil law'. It is the law which applied to all citizens, *cives*, in a given country.

These concepts are not always easy to translate. The Latin *culpa* is roughly equivalent to English 'guilt' or 'fault' but in contrast the Latin term *stipulátio* is much more restricted in meaning than the English loanword *stipulation*. A *stipulatio* is an oral contract which is established through a formal exchange of question and answer. The *stipulator* says, for instance, 'Do you agree that you will give me 50 pounds?' and the *promissor* or respondent states, 'I agree.' In legal English reference to this Roman form of contract may be made by means of the term *stipulation*, but in our everyday language most of our uses of the word *stipulation* would not count as instances of *stipulatio*.

Roman legal decisions were often short and in need of detailed interpretation. Here is one small example. The highest judge, the praetor, promulgated the following decision:

Nautae, caupones, stabularii quod cuiusque salvum fore receperint nisi restituent, in eos iudicium dabo.

As far as sailors, hotelkeepers and innkeepers are concerned, if they do not give back intact whatever has been given into their keeping, I will allow them to be tried.

This two-line decision is to be found in what is called the *Digesta*, a part of the *Corpus iuris*. Its purpose is to protect travellers, who often had their possessions with them on board ship or in an inn. It is followed by approximately three pages of comment, in which a great deal is explained. It is pointed out that by 'sailors and innkeepers' is meant in fact the captain of a ship and the owner of an inn. The point is that it is the boss who has the responsibility, not his subordinates. Moreover, the things left in keeping do not have to be owned by the people who left them there, providing for things that were in the process of changing ownership, and so on and so forth. It is clear that this decision was applied in many different cases, and that the lawyers carefully made a note of all the complications that ensued, and wrote a new comment every time. In this way they gradually created a mode of writing and thinking which has survived to this day and which is still made full use of. Most of us are probably no more fond of consulting a lawyer than of going to the dentist, but a society must have laws and the state must have the power to ensure that the laws work and are respected. For this purpose the Romans had an army and a good number of very competent lawyers. It turns out that the lawyers created something rather more stable and long-lasting than the generals and the soldiers managed to do.

Tacitus, the emperors, and Britain

Sallust and Livy, whom we have already mentioned, were well-known historians, but the most famous of them all may be Tacitus, who lived about 100 CE. He wrote the history of the period of the emperors from the death of Augustus in 14 CE until the death of Domitian in 96 CE, so he was dealing with events that had taken place very recently. Only part of this work has been preserved.

Tacitus explained that he was writing *sine ira et studio* 'without anger or favour'. This expression is still quoted today as a description of how historians are supposed to work. Tacitus certainly cannot himself be accused of *studium*, which in this context means giving undue preference to someone, since he very rarely speaks well of anyone at all. He particularly disliked the emperors. Personally he was a highly placed and successful man who belonged to a distinguished senatorial family. He had had bitter personal experience of oppression under Domitian, and he often talks about freedom, although what he means is primarily freedom for the Senate to make decisions without interference from the emperor, as had been the case in Rome in the olden days. Most Roman writers were conservative but it is probably fair to call Tacitus a reactionary. He it was who created posterity's images of some of the best-known emperors, including Tiberius, Claudius, and Nero. His portraits are very cleverly worked; the historical events are mentioned too, of course, but the personalities of the main protagonists are described almost as if they were characters in a novel.

At the beginning of his description of the reign of Tiberius, he tells how Agrippina, who was married to one of Tiberius' nephews, acted with great courage and initiative during a military crisis on the Rhine. He goes on to say: *Id Tiberii animum altius penetravit* 'That made a lasting impression on Tiberius' (literally: 'That penetrated deeply into the mind of Tiberius'), because, he could not bear, Tacitus explains, that a woman should show such initiative and acquire so much influence. Tiberius took no action on that occasion, but the reader begins to get a sense of how he is going to get the better of Agrippina later on. Through such comments and hints, Tacitus builds up a picture of Tiberius as a sly, unforgetting, and vengeful person. The first Roman emperors were hardly paragons of virtue, but it has to be said that those who got Tacitus as their historian had singularly bad luck. He knew how to make them appear demonic. That, of course, is one of the things that makes him such compulsive reading, but perhaps posterity has had a tendency to see that era a bit too much through his eyes. Real blackguards are much more interesting than ordinary, weak, moderately competent individuals.

But Tacitus was not just concerned with the emperors and their personalities. His history tells us a great deal about what happened in the wider empire and even in neighbouring countries. He was particularly interested in events along the Rhine, which made up the eastern border of the Empire, and in the people who lived on the other side of the border. He wrote a separate little book called *Germania*, in which he describes the peoples who lived in what is now Germany and beyond.

The Germans were important to the Romans because they represented a continual military threat. Indeed, it was various Germanic tribes who invaded the empire in the fifth century and finally brought about its downfall. However, the danger they posed was probably not the only reason Tacitus wanted to write about them. He was also interested in their kind of social organization and their habits and customs. He saw them as a primitive people, more free and honest than the civilized Romans, but also more naïve and impulsive. The way he describes them is a bit like the things European explorers used to write about the peoples they encountered in distant places a century or so ago. But Tacitus had not travelled to Germania himself, and probably got his information instead from Roman traders who had been there. He knew about many Germanic groups, among them the Angli, who at this time lived inconspicuously in northernmost Germany. Tacitus also took a special interest in Britain, and made an important contribution to the history of the island. He wrote a biography of his father-in-law, Gnaeus Iulius Agricola, entitled simply *Agricola*. This man was a prominent military commander and politician, whose main achievement was his seven years as governor of the province of Britannia from 78 to 84 CE. The southern and eastern part of the island had come under Roman rule some thirty-five years earlier, but there was still much resistance against the occupiers. Agricola fought successful campaigns in Wales and in the north, where he advanced as far as the Firth of Forth and the Clyde.

Agricola records the details of these campaigns, and also contains a great deal of information about the Britons. They were Celts, closely related in language and culture to the inhabitants of Gaul. In the eyes of Tacitus, they were ardent lovers of freedom, but incapable of resisting the Romans in the long run because of their inability to act together. He says *Nec aliud ... pro nobis utilius quam quod in commune non consulunt* 'There is nothing more useful for us than that they do not consult together'. Still, they made valiant attempts to regain their liberty. One of their heroines was Queen Boudicca (the name is sometimes written Boadicea), who was elected by other chiefs as the head of a rebellion: *Neque enim sexum in imperiis discernunt* 'For they do not discriminate between the sexes when it comes to command'. However, her army was swiftly defeated, and she had to commit suicide. Later, the Britons fought (and lost) a large pitched battle against Agricola and his troops in the north, and Tacitus composed an imaginary account of a speech to the army by one of the British commanders. He is made to describe the indignities of the Romans in graphic detail, and summarizes their deeds in a famous phrase:

Ubi solitúdinem fáciunt, pacem appellant

When they produce a desert, they call it peace.

The author is in fact quite ambiguous in his attitude to the Roman conquest as such. On the one hand, he admires the feats of his father-in-law, not only when he wins the battles but also when he works hard to change the hostile attitude of the Britons, enticing them to use Roman baths and give their children a Roman education. On the other hand, he thinks that this is just a very efficient way to deprive them of their former freedom:

Apud imperítos humanitas vocabatur, cum pars servitutis esset

Among the ignorant it was called civilization, when it was really part of the slavery.

Clearly, the Romanization of Britain was in some aspects similar to the Westernization of many countries of Africa. But Tacitus was really much more concerned with the conquerors than with the conquered. He thought that his own people had lost their freedom, and were exporting their moral decay to others.

Christianity: from dangerous sect to state religion

In his *Annals* Tacitus gives a detailed account of the great fire in Rome in the year 64 CE, during the reign of Nero. After the fire, there were many rumours that it had been the work of an arsonist, perhaps even of the emperor himself. To divert these rumours, Nero blamed a group who were already unpopular and whom people called *Christiani*, because, as Tacitus explains:

Auctor nóminis eius Christus Tiberio imperitante per procuratórem Pontium Pilatum supplício adfectus erat.

Christ, from whom that name [i.e. 'Christian'] originated, had been sentenced to death by the procurator Pontius Pilate during the reign of Tiberius.

This is one of our very earliest references to Christ and the Christians. Apparently there were already Christians living in Rome thirty years after the death of Jesus. Tacitus has no sympathy for their teaching, which he calls *exitiábilis superstítio* 'a pernicious superstition'. The Christians were captured and executed in a variety of cruel ways, as Tacitus documents: for example, they were used as living torches.

They were driven underground but still did not disappear. Less than fifty years later Pliny the Younger, governor of Bithynia, in modern Turkey, wrote to the emperor Trajan and asked what he was supposed to do when people were accused of being Christian. It seems there were many such cases, and Pliny's inclination was that it was better to give them the chance to repent than to put them to death at once. The emperor agreed, but thought that it was better not to look into things too closely, and simply punish those who were reported and convicted.

Christianity continued to spread and the punitive actions of the state remained quite sporadic, but it was some time before the Christians started to write in Latin. The religion had originated in the eastern part of the empire, where Greek was the official language. The authors of the New Testament also wrote in Greek, and that became the language of the Church in the East. The first important Christian writer in Latin was called Tertullian. Around the end of the second century CE he wrote a number of works, one of which was a defence of the Christians called *Apologéticum*, addressed directly to the rulers who sat in judgement over them. Several of his other books were about tricky theological questions like absolution and the Trinity. Their most striking characteristic is their spiteful and uncompromising attitude to everyone who thought differently from

Tertullian himself, which unfortunately set the tone for theological disputes down the ages.

In the third century CE Christianity was still just one of many new kinds of religion and sect which were flourishing within the Roman empire. There are very few Christian texts from this period. However, the Emperor Constantine, who reigned at the beginning of the fourth century, gave preferential treatment to the Christians and was himself christened shortly before his death. His successors were, with a few exceptions, Christians, and by the end of the century Christianity had become the official religion of the state.

During the fourth and fifth centuries most, and indeed the most important, writers in Latin were Christian. The new religion attracted the most talented people, as well as those who could sense which way the wind was blowing. And there were plenty of gaps that needed filling. The many new Christians in the western part of the Roman empire were for the most part unable to read Greek, and so it became necessary to create a Christian literature in Latin. The most urgent thing, obviously, was to make the Bible accessible. Parts of the New Testament and of the Old Testament had been translated into Latin early on, but the quality varied widely. A complete and reliable translation of the whole Bible did not appear until the beginning of the fifth century, a monumental work that was due to the learned and hard-working Jerome. He made an entirely new translation of the Old Testament from the Hebrew and revised the existing translation from the Greek of the New Testament. Not without pride did he call himself *homo trilínguis* 'a trilingual man'.

Interestingly enough, Jerome had the same kinds of problems with his readers as almost all later translators of the Bible have had. They complained because he made changes to what they were used to hearing in church. This was most evident in the case of the Book of Psalms, which had long been used in a very bad translation from Hebrew into Latin via Greek. The Psalms were frequently recited in church services, and the opposition to Jerome's new-fangled ideas was so great that the old translation was in part allowed to go on being used. However, Jerome's translation was gradually accepted by everyone, and later came to be known as the *Versio vulgáta*, literally 'the common version' but usually now called in English the Vulgate. This is the Bible that has been used ever since antiquity in the Roman Catholic Church, and which is used even today in those places where Latin is maintained as the language of worship.

The text of the Bible was not of course the only thing the Christians needed. Hymns and texts for other parts of the religious service were also important. Much of what was written at that time has been preserved in the order of service over the centuries. One example is the beginning of one of the best-known hymns:

> *Te deum luudámus*
> *te dóminum confitémur,*
> *te aetérnum patrem omnis terra venerátur.*

which is translated in the Book of Common Prayer as

> We praise thee, O God:
> We acknowledge thee to be the Lord.
> All the earth doth worship thee: the Father everlasting.

In this text there are words which are actually common in Latin but which acquire new meanings in Christian texts. The word *dóminus* means 'master' or 'lord'. It is usually used in reference to the master of a slave, but in Christian contexts it always mean the Lord with a capital 'L', in other words God. The word *confitéri* means 'confess' and is in origin a term used in court, but among the Christians it acquires the meaning 'to confess one's faith in', and the related noun *conféssio* 'confession' in turn comes to mean 'a confession of one's faith'. English borrowed the vocabulary of Christianity from Latin a thousand years or so ago, so to us these meanings seem entirely natural and even obvious, but for the Romans of late antiquity things must have been very different. The Latin language did not have any terms for the core Christian concepts, so they had to be created either by giving old words new meanings, as in the example we have just seen, or else simply by borrowing words from Greek.

In many instances the changes were quite radical. We have already talked about the important place that the art of public speaking had in Roman life, and the normal verb for 'to make a speech' was *oráre*. The speech itself was called *orátio*. But in Christian Latin the verb *orare* meant 'to pray (to God)' and *oratio* meant 'prayer'. Another common Latin word is *gratia*, which means 'thanks' or 'favour'. In Christian Latin, on the other hand, it had a precise theological meaning, namely 'grace', most commonly in the phrase *Dei gratia* 'the grace of God'.

Among the many loanwords from Greek we may mention *baptizare* 'to baptise' and *ecclésia* 'church'. In a sense such words were less confusing, as they had only their Christian meanings. At the same time, their pronunciation and spelling made it clear that they were foreign. The word *baptizare*, for instance, contains the letter *z*, which does not occur in indigenous Latin words and which represents a Greek sound usually pronounced [ts] in Latin.

As we have seen, the Christians created a large new vocabulary for themselves. In the beginning it probably sounded strange and perhaps even funny to many people, but as Christianity in time came to take over the whole empire, all these Christian words and meanings were incorporated into Latin. This is the normal course of events when a new phenomenon enters society: it brings its own vocabulary with it. Christianity led to enormous changes in people's everyday lives and their way of thinking, and hence many new words and expressions were needed. The people who brought this about were of course not just translators and hymn-writers but a whole host of missionaries and preachers, priests and bishops. Many of them were also writers. They wrote sermons, hymns, long, dense commentaries on the Bible, controversial pamphlets against the pagans, and not least theological treatises, frequently with the aim of attacking heretics.

It was not easy to know at the time who actually was a heretic, or *haeréticus*. It depended on who was successful in having their view of original sin or the Trinity finally accepted as the true teaching of the Church. The winners were rewarded not least by having their attacks on their opponents preserved even down to modern times, whereas the books of the losers have in general disappeared. Someone who won on every occasion was Augustine, the greatest of the Catholic Church Fathers. He started life as a teacher of rhetoric, but converted to Christianity at about the age of thirty. He became a priest, and later bishop, in the small town of Hippo near Carthage in present-day Tunisia, where he spent fully forty years until his death in the year 430, just at the moment when the Vandals conquered and occupied the province.

Augustine is one of the most productive writers in world literature. He devoted much of his energy to the analysis of theological questions in a series of long treatises, in an unending fight against Donatists, Pelagians, Priscillians, and others who on some point disagreed with him and (later) with the whole Church. He also wrote an enormous number of sermons, hymns, and other occasional pieces. However, more than anything else he is famous for two works. The first, *Confessiones* 'Confessions', is always to be found in surveys of the history of world literature, as it is the first personal autobiography which is not just concerned with what happened but which also tries to describe the writer's personal development. It covers Augustine's life from his birth until his conversion. The other work is called *De civitate Dei* 'The City of God'. The immediate cause for him to write this was the assault on and plundering of Rome by the Visigoths in 410 CE. This was an unparallelled event, in that it showed that the capital of this great empire could be taken by its enemies just like any other city. Some saw it as a punishment visited on the Romans because they had abandoned the old gods and converted to Christianity, and Augustine's work started life as a refutation of this idea. But it grew in the writing into an ambitious philosophical study of the relation between the Earthly City and the Kingdom of God.

Augustine summarizes the whole of Christian teaching, combining it with a wide variety of ideas derived from non-Christian philosophy. In this way he and his predecessors created a whole system of thought, a Christian philosophy. For someone who is not a Christian many of his ideas are strange or even repugnant. This is especially true of the idea of original sin, the idea that man is born evil and has to be redeemed by the Saviour. But for almost one and half millennia his thought constituted one of the foundations for all discussions of the human predicament. He was one of the last ancient philosophers but at the same time one of the foremost intellectual figures of the era that was to come.

Part II
Latin and Europe

Europe after Rome

No one knows why the Roman empire collapsed in the west. Within a few decades at the beginning of the fifth century, the territory where Latin was spoken went from being a single empire under a single emperor to being a number of separate states, most of them governed by Germanic kings. The empire had evidently grown weaker, since otherwise it would not have been so easy for the various Germanic groups to help themselves to chunk after chunk, but historians are still debating the reasons for this weakness. Current research points particularly to the fact that the population seems to have diminished drastically in the period before the Germans arrived, but once again no one knows why this should have been the case.

The new states were not that different from those that already existed or which came into existence beyond the borders of the Roman empire, to the east and the north. As time passed, the differences in society and culture between the former empire and what had traditionally been regarded as the homelands of the barbarians became smaller and smaller. There were two principal reasons for these changes. First, much of what had characterized Roman society disappeared. The large and efficiently run army was disbanded, as was the system of civil servants and tax collectors which underpinned it. People shook off their taxes, but that meant they no longer received military protection. Trade and communication were in turn reduced, and people moved out of the towns, some of which ended up as nothing but heaps of ruins. Most people now lived in the countryside or in small towns and had little contact with the surrounding world. In this way conditions became almost the same as they had been in the areas that had never belonged to the empire.

Second, all western and northern Europe gradually acquired the same religion. Christianity became stronger at about the same rate as the Roman empire grew weaker. By the sixth century the greater part of the former empire was populated by Christians, and from the seventh century vigorous missionary activity began to be undertaken in the north and east. By the eleventh century, Christianity had triumphed in modern-day Ireland, Great Britain, Belgium, the Netherlands, Germany, Austria, Switzerland, Poland, the Czech Republic, Slovakia, Hungary, Slovenia, and Croatia, and was well advanced in Scandinavia.

Rome was the centre of the Church in this whole area, and in principle the Pope had sovereignty over all the bishops. The areas to the east and south, such as modern Ukraine, Romania and Greece, had also become Christian but in these areas the missionaries emanated from the Eastern Church, which had Constantinople as its centre. The Roman Church had Latin as its language, and it insisted on that in all contexts and in all countries. Missionaries obviously had to be able to speak the local language, but the service itself had to be conducted in Latin and all priests therefore needed to be able to speak Latin, at least to some degree. The Bible and all other religious works were also in Latin.

Since there were very few people outside the Church who could read and write, the consequence was that Latin became completely dominant as the written language throughout Europe. In every country there were also a number of people in high administrative positions who spoke Latin, and that ability was useful, among other things, in international contacts. Strangely enough, Latin became the most important written language and the international spoken language in virtually the whole of Europe, and over a much larger area than the western part of the Roman empire, where the language had been spoken in antiquity. Latin retained that pre-eminence for the best part of a millennium, and this explains why it has had such an enormous influence on almost all branches of European culture.

In what follows I will first discuss how it was that Latin disappeared as a native language while at the same time acquiring its unique role as the common language of communication for individuals from many language groups. I will then look in some detail at that language, how it varied from region to region, and how it differed from ancient Latin. I will introduce quite a few examples of how Latin was used, and is still being used, in many fields, and of how thoroughly it has infiltrated the modern European languages, including English. I won't say anything about the death of Latin, as the language is still very much alive.

From Latin to the Romance languages

During the fifth century CE all the Latin speakers in the Roman empire saw great changes. Germanic tribes poured across the border and, not content with ravaging and plundering, stayed and seized power permanently in region after region of the old empire. Within a few decades both the authority of the emperor and his means of enforcing it had disappeared, and in the year 476 the last emperor in the western part of the Empire, Romulus Augustulus, was deposed and had no successor. Suddenly, all the rulers were German and not Roman.

This was certainly a revolutionary moment but the invasions meant less for the language situation than one might have imagined. The Franks, Vandals, Burgundians, Goths, Lombards, and all the other Germanic groups naturally came with their own languages, which all belonged to the Germanic family—which includes modern languages like English, German, Dutch, and the Scandinavian languages. One of the languages of the invaders, Visigothic, is well known from a translation of the Bible, the so-called Gothic or Silver Bible, which has survived. Unfortunately, we do not know much about the other Germanic languages in the Roman empire as no texts or inscriptions have been preserved. What they had in common, however, was that all of them, including Visigothic, soon disappeared. There were probably not very many Germanic speakers, and although they certainly assumed power and ownership of the land, they were surrounded by people who spoke Latin, and after

87

a few generations they started speaking the same language as the people they ruled over.

The great exception, of course, was the invasion of England. The Angles, the Saxons, and other groups, notably the Jutes from Jutland (part of modern Denmark), not only conquered the earlier inhabitants, but their own Germanic language soon became the language of the majority. Latin did not survive as a spoken language. It is uncertain how many spoke it even in Roman times, for it seems that most people were still using the original Celtic language, called British, when the Germanic ships arrived. But a few hundred years later, the British language was found only in the western part of the island, where it stayed on, eventually being transformed into Welsh and Cornish. (Celtic, in the form of Gaelic, was in due course reintroduced to Scotland from Ireland.) The language of the Angles and Saxons came to dominate the island, and in due course also a large part of the rest of the world.

Within the rest of the empire, society did not at first change greatly as a result of the Germanic invasions. The new rulers often left the local administration in place, and in many respects life in the towns went on much as before. There were, for instance, still schools of the Roman kind well into the sixth century in a number of places, and still writers who were able to write Latin according to the old models. Gradually, however, the situation got worse and worse throughout western Europe. It became increasingly uncommon for people to use the written language, and the school system had collapsed completely by the seventh century in the greater part of Europe. Only in some towns in Italy was it possible to continue to go to school. The art of reading and writing did not disappear totally, however, due to the fact that the Church set up its own education system, a topic to which we will return later.

Nonetheless, the ability to read and write became very rare in Europe, especially during the seventh and eighth centuries, when many regions had neither a school system nor a functioning public administration. There was also a very low level of mobility among the population; almost everyone spent the whole of their lives on their farms or in their towns or villages. In such conditions, linguistic change is to be expected. All languages change with time, but how slowly or quickly they change depends to a large extent on the society and culture in which they are embedded. Some situations promote rapid change, others slow it up.

Roughly speaking, we can say that linguistic change depends on the interaction between two conflicting and incompatible tendencies. On the one hand we want to use language as an effective means of communication; on the other we want to sound as much as possible like the people closest to us and we prefer to speak a little differently from strangers. The first tendency may create large languages, with millions of people who speak in the same way and are able to understand each other without difficulty. The second tends to form small dialect areas, where the inhabitants of each town can immediately hear the difference between their own dialect and that of the neighbouring town, and where people may not even understand those who live a few miles away. Hence large, strong states are linked to large languages. During the Roman empire it was extremely useful to be able to speak with people in the same language in every town, and that was exactly what many travellers did. The shared written language also obviously reinforced the tendency towards a common norm across the whole of the Empire. In the new situation that obtained after the collapse of the Empire, the motivation for a common language disappeared. Almost no one travelled, and contacts between any given place and its surrounding regions were reduced to a minimum. The written language had very little influence, since almost no one learnt to read or write.

As a result, there was no longer anything to hinder the development of local dialects. It seems that the spoken language changed very fast between the sixth and the eleventh centuries throughout the area where people used to speak Latin. Moreover, the changes went in partly different directions in different regions, so that each region or sometimes even each town had its own form of speech. Little by little the changes accumulated to such an extent that people who lived a great distance apart were no longer able to understand each other straightaway.

It is not possible to say much in detail about how all this took place, as the sources we have from the period immediately following the fall of the Roman empire are very meagre. Those who wrote at all wrote in Latin, and in the few schools that did function people as far as possible learnt the same written language as Cicero and Virgil had used in the century before Jesus was born, more than half a millennium earlier. No one wrote their spoken language down, and so we do not know very much about how it must have sounded. Nonetheless, we can draw some conclusions from the mistakes less well-educated writers made when they tried to express themselves in Classical Latin. Such mistakes occur already in antiquity and allow us to build up a rough picture of the development.

As we might expect, spoken Latin was already changing in antiquity, while the written language that the schools taught remained the same, so that by the fifth century the differences between writing and speaking had become quite considerable. The situation can be compared to English, which is still mainly spelled the way it was pronounced in the seventeenth century. Similarly, for those who lived in late antiquity the way Latin was written down was rather archaic beside their own pronunciation.

An example is the fact that the sound [m] at the end of words ceased to be pronounced quite early on. Since a good many Latin words end in -*m*, this small change had a big effect. Another change is that the pronunciation of vowels shifted quite markedly, so that for instance *u* was pronounced as [o] and *i* as [e] in some contexts. The combined effect of these changes meant that, for example, where people wrote *imperium romanum* they actually said [imperio romano]. And this pronunciation corresponds exactly to how this expression is pronounced and spelled in modern Italian and Spanish: *imperio romano*. Already in late antiquity Latin had moved a few steps in the direction that was to lead to the modern Romance languages.

Nonetheless, at this time there was still quite clearly only one language. There are many Latin texts from the fifth and sixth centuries from different parts of Europe, but it is not possible to discover any dialectal changes at all, although many have looked for them. The misspellings that reveal the actual pronunciation are the same wherever the texts are from. The few Latin texts that have survived from the seventh and eighth centuries mainly indicate that their authors barely had enough education to get the words onto the page. Some are so full of strange features that we can only half understand them. In the ninth century Charlemagne implemented a major educational reform. After this there is a considerable resurgence in the writing of Latin throughout the territory that had once been the Roman empire, only now the written language reveals nothing at all about the everyday pronunciation as writers once again adhere faithfully to the ancient norms which they have learnt in school.

But what language did people actually speak in the ninth and tenth centuries? Was it still Latin or was it already the new languages French, Spanish, Italian, and so on? This is not an easy question to answer. We do not have much evidence as to how the spoken language sounded, but that is not in fact the biggest problem. The big question is how to determine which language people are speaking. In principle there are two ways. Either you discover some facts about how they speak and compare them with other known languages, or else you ask the speakers themselves what their language is. In most instances the result is the same either way. If you listen to the way people speak in, say, Norfolk it sounds like English, and people in Norfolk, if asked, will maintain that they speak English.

Things are much more difficult when it comes to the people who lived in France in the ninth century. We know enough about how their language sounded to say that it did not sound particularly like Latin. Indeed, it was not so different from the language that people started calling *français* a couple of centuries later. From that point of view it seems reasonable to say that they spoke French. On the other hand, there is absolutely no evidence that the people who lived in France at that time used this name for their language. On the contrary, in some Latin texts from the ninth century there are expressions like *rustica romana lingua* 'the rustic Roman language' or just *lingua romana* 'the Roman language', referring to the spoken language. In normal Latin usage *lingua romana* and *lingua latina* mean exactly the same thing, the Latin language. On this evidence, then, it seems as if the French of that period thought they spoke Latin, though perhaps a somewhat rustic variety.

As far as Latin is concerned, it is not very important what people thought they were speaking. What is quite clear is that those who wrote did so in Latin. The situation remained like that in all the countries where people had spoken Latin until new written languages were created. This happens for the first time in northern France, where a number of writers in the eleventh century started writing a language which was based on the spoken language of that time. This was radically different from Latin, and after many changes it has developed into modern written French. In Italy and Spain similar things happened, but not until a couple of hundred years later, in the thirteenth century. Gradually all the Romance areas acquired their own written languages.

These new written languages obviously competed with Latin. Until they were created everything was written in Latin, and so they took over the function of Latin. But this happened only slowly and gradually. In the beginning it was mainly writers of imaginative literature who wrote in the new languages. Little by little people started using them in private letters and simple documents such as receipts and IOUs. Institutions like the courts and government offices instead clung on to Latin for hundreds of years. Even more conservative was the Church, which kept Latin as its major language for longer than any other institution. Higher education and all kinds of science were also areas where Latin remained in use for a long time.

In sum, both the written Romance languages and Latin were used in parallel for a very long time, from the eleventh right down to the twentieth centuries. It was close to a thousand years before the new ways of writing definitively ousted the old ways within the former Roman empire.

Missionaries, Latin, and foreign languages

In the year 432 a monk by the name of Patricius left the monastery of Lérins in France to preach Christianity in Ireland. He succeeded beyond all expectation, and is still remembered as St Patrick, the patron saint of Ireland. He was the first in a long line of Christian missionaries who dedicated their lives to spreading the word of God to places where people did not speak Latin. Ireland had never belonged to the Roman empire and the population spoke Irish, a Celtic language. Patrick mastered the language and obviously used it in his mission, but it seems that the men of the Church used Latin for reading and writing. The Irish language certainly started being written with Roman letters soon after Patrick's mission had begun, but the texts that have survived from the oldest times do not betray any Christian content.

In Ireland the monastic system proved very successful, and in consequence many of the Christians lived as monks. The monasteries evidently became very effective schools, as proficiency in Latin was maintained there at a very high level during the following centuries, when the ability to read and write became increasingly rare in most of the rest of Europe. The Irish obviously had to learn Latin as a completely foreign language, and they probably learnt to speak, read, and write all at once in the monastic schools. For them it was classical Latin from beginning to end. By contrast, on the Continent people thought that they were speaking Latin, but their spoken language was so different from the written language that they had great difficulty learning to write in the classical way even when they did manage to acquire some kind of schooling.

For several hundred years the Irish monks preserved proficiency in classical Latin better than anyone else, a fact which was to prove to be of great significance. They also became eager missionaries themselves. At first they turned their attention to England, where there had been Christians in the Roman period, but the Christian religion had disappeared almost entirely after the invasions of the Angles and the Saxons in the fifth century. However, about the year 600 the Irish started missionary work in the north-west, almost at the same time as a bishop sent out by the Pope from Rome started preaching in Canterbury in the south-east.

All England became Christian within a hundred years, and so Latin came back to the island again as an important foreign language. Monastic life and monastic schools flourished, and by the eighth century no one was better at Latin than the best of the English. The most important Latin writer of that century was Bede, who had the honorary name of *venerábilis* 'the venerable'. Bede was a monk in a monastery close to what is now Newcastle-upon-Tyne, and dedicated himself with great energy to a life of writing. Most of what he produced was in the form of Bible commentary and other kinds of religious literature, but he is best known for his detailed history of England. His main goal is to describe how England was Christianized, but he also writes at length about the history of the island more generally, starting with Caesar's landing in 59 BCE and coming right down to the year 731, when he himself stopped writing.

Bede wrote excellent Latin, for the most part in complete accordance with classical rules, although the language was obviously not his native tongue. He was an enthusiastic historian, whose writings hold the reader's interest because of their many anecdotes about all kinds of people, often but not always with a moral to them. He made a lasting contribution to western history by consistently dating events from the birth of Christ. England at the time of Bede was a multilingual society. At the beginning of his history he establishes that there are five languages, *Anglorum vidélicet, Brettonum, Scottorum, Pictorum et Latinorum* 'namely those of the Angles, the Britons, the Scots, the Picts and the Romans'. The language of the Angles was of course an early form of English, that of the Britons was what we call Welsh, the Scottish language was what we now call Gaelic, while the language of the Picts has entirely disappeared, and no one even knows which family of languages it belonged to. Latin is also mentioned, but Bede says that it is a language which everyone had in common through the study of the Scriptures. This is another way of saying that it was no one's native language, and that the Christians used it as a learned language, which is the role that Latin had gradually acquired throughout western Europe.

Missionaries travelled from England to spread Christianity to the East. The most famous of these is a man from Wessex named Winfrith, but who called himself Bonifatius in Latin, a name which has in turn been anglicized as Boniface. He was a contemporary of Bede who, at the request of the Pope, preached among the Germans in many different areas from Frisia on the coast of the North Sea all the way down to Bavaria in the South. All these activities are documented in his extensive correspondence which has been preserved. He was finally murdered by pagans in Frisia, and as a martyr was of course made a saint. The mission in the east was connected to the fact that the empire of the Franks spread wider and wider in the eighth century, so that by the beginning of the ninth it included modern France, Belgium, the Netherlands, Switzerland, Northern Italy, Germany, Austria, and a great deal more. The man who accomplished this enormous expansion was Charlemagne, who also made a major contribution to the developments which resulted in Latin becoming the most important language in Europe for many centuries thereafter. This he did in two ways. First, he engaged in a war of conquest in the east which he combined with what one might benevolently call missionary zeal. This mostly meant that his soldiers killed anyone who was not prepared to accept Christianity. The survivors ended up belonging to a Church which possessed great resources, and which could also rely on the state's intervention if it asked for it. This Church conducted all its business in Latin. In this way, Latin gained its position as the language of religion and administration in large swathes of central Europe.

Second, Charlemagne was an enthusiastic advocate of education. He focused a great deal of effort on raising the level of attainment and reforming the schools. In this he was helped by an Englishman named Alcuin, who did much to ensure that the future priests—for these were the people who went to school—learnt correct Latin according to classical rules. Alcuin was also a central figure among a whole circle of learned men who were anxious to revive the knowledge of antiquity and its literature. With some justice this movement is usually referred to as the Carolingian renaissance. The authors who belonged to this group obviously wrote in Latin, and frequently made great efforts to write according to ancient models. A well-known example is a biography of Charlemagne himself written by a man called Einhard. This is set out according to exactly the same schema as the great biographies of the Roman emperors which Suetonius had composed in the second century CE. Einhard tells us all sorts of things about the emperor Charlemagne, one thing being that he was *eminenti statúra* 'of extraordinary height'. That is true. His preserved remains show that he was about six foot six inches tall. He was also *in cibo et potu témperans* 'moderate in the consumption of food and drink'. The emperor knew Latin very well, and could speak it as fluently as his mother tongue, but curiously he never really learnt to write. He was not taught to do it as a child, and his attempts to do so as an adult were not very successful.

As a result of Charlemagne's efforts, by the beginning of the ninth century almost the whole of western and central Europe had acquired a unified Church with priests who were relatively well educated in Latin. Hardly anyone else had any education at all. This was the beginning of a period which lasted for something like half a millennium in which Latin was completely dominant as the written language in Europe, and furthermore was used as a spoken language among the educated. The Carolingian empire soon fell apart again, and Europe underwent many political changes in the centuries that followed, but Latin continued to expand into new areas for several hundred years. To illustrate the role that the language assumed, let us have a look at what happened in Britain.

Latin in Britain

In the eighth century, England was the area where education and scholarship in Latin were most advanced. We have already discussed

Bede and his history of the Christian Church in the island, and the missionary work of Boniface. An even more renowned Latinist was Alcuin from York, who as we have seen also emigrated to the Continent and became closely associated with Charlemagne. Alcuin was a famous teacher, and his role was something like a minister of education for the new empire.

While Alcuin was very energetically furthering Latin studies on the Continent, serious trouble started in his home island. Alcuin died in 804, and a few years before that, in 793, the Vikings had made their first, terrifying raid against the monastery of Lindisfarne in Northumberland. In the ninth and the tenth centuries there were many more attacks and indeed large-scale invasions by Scandinavian warriors. The monasteries and the churches were favourite targets. This meant, among other things, that most of the places where Latin was taught and written ceased to exist. The great tradition of learning disappeared almost without trace. A century later, it seems that few people knew Latin at all. Alfred the Great, who ruled from 871 to 899, wrote that there were very few people south of the Humber who could translate a Latin letter into English, and not many north of the river either.

But Alfred himself did much to improve the situation. In the first place, he took important steps toward the unification of all England under one ruler, thereby ending a long period of political disorder. Secondly, he believed in education and did whatever he could to advance knowledge in his kingdom. It is true that he chose to propagate English as a written language rather than Latin, but his main achievement was to translate important works from Latin, especially handbooks for the use of the clergy. The reason he did so was not that he did not want the men of the Church to read Latin; it was just that he realized that they could not do it. At the same time, of course, the English language entered a new domain in written form.

Almost a hundred years later, towards the end of the tenth century, the English Church was reached by a reform movement that had its roots in Cluny, in France; the main protagonist in Britain was Dunstan, archbishop of Canterbury and later declared a saint.

Religious reform also meant more study, and so more Latin. The language reclaimed much of the territory it had lost in the centuries of disorder.

After 1066, the linguistic situation of Britain changed drastically. Before that year, English was used in writing as well as orally, and its sole competitor was Latin. Afterwards, English was relegated to the role of spoken language of the underprivileged. The ruling class spoke French. In writing, Latin became the completely dominant language, although French was also used. English in practice ceased to be a written language for a couple of hundred years.

The two centuries after the Norman Conquest were a period of rapid economic and cultural development in Britain (as well as in much of western Europe), and Latin became the written language in almost all areas of society. The famous texts from this period are composed in the language. As early as 1085, William the Conqueror ordered a general census of people and land. This was recorded in the very important Domesday Book, which contains invaluable detailed information about the economic and social situation in early medieval England.

Another well-known document is the *Magna Charta*, the Great Charter, promulgated by King John in 1215 under pressure from those opposed to his autocratic rule. The precise significance of the document has been much discussed. However that may be, the king made important concessions to the citizens, as can be seen from this phrase at the beginning:

Concessimus etiam ómnibus líberis homínibus regni nostri, pro nobis et herédibus nostris in perpétuum, omnes libertates subscriptas.

We have also granted to all free men of our kingdom, on behalf of us and our heirs forever, all the liberties written below.

Naturally, Latin returned to its previous status as the only language of the Church. In general, the level of education rose rapidly, and in the twelfth century several good Latin authors emerged.

One of them was the prolific and very learned John of Salisbury. After a good basic training in England he went to Paris, and then to

Chartres, to study under the most famous teachers of the time, among them the philosopher Peter Abelard. When he finally returned to England in 1138, in his late thirties, he became secretary to the archbishop of Canterbury, Theobald, and then to his successor, Thomas Becket. He was sent on many diplomatic missions by the archbishop and by the king, Henry II, especially to Rome but also elsewhere. Eventually, he became an archbishop himself, in Chartres. In spite of all these activities, he found time to write several important works, among them the *Policraticus*, which deals with the moral principles underlying good government, and the *Metalogicus*, which tackles some basic philosophical questions.

John was a leading European intellectual, an Englishman who had been trained in France. As far as language is concerned, he wrote only in Latin, and probably spoke that language in many contexts: in church services, of course, but also in learned discussions and in his diplomatic activities. While he was unusually brilliant, he was by no means the only one of his kind. For example, Thomas Becket himself, the archbishop who was murdered in 1170, conducted his correspondence in very elegant Latin. There were several more ecclesiastical authors, as well as historians, philosophers, and others. Britain at this time could compete with France as the leading nation in education and learning.

In the thirteenth century, Latin was still completely dominant. This was the time when large institutions for higher education became established in Europe. The University of Oxford was one of the first, and one of the most important. Naturally the language of the university was Latin, both in speech and in writing, and it remained so for a long time. It must have seemed that Latin would be the language of the educated forever. But in the following century, things began to change. English as a written language came back with a vengeance in the late fourteenth and the fifteenth centuries. It was used by authors of fiction, such as Chaucer, but it was also introduced in official administration, in business, and in other fields. At the same time, French disappeared completely both as a spoken language and as an official written language in Britain, though, as we shall see, it had left an indelible mark on the English language which survived it.

Over the following centuries, the use of Latin declined gradually, and in many areas very slowly. English made its way into the educational system, but Latin remained indispensable for higher studies until about a hundred years ago, and was a required entrance qualification for the study of certain arts subjects at Oxford and Cambridge until the late twentieth century. Within the Church, Latin was used universally until the Reformation, and for many purposes much longer. In diplomacy, Latin was obligatory until the seventeenth century, and in the learned world, most people wrote in Latin up to that time too. For example, Newton used the language for his most famous work on physics, the *Principia Mathematica*.

The early immigrants brought knowledge of Latin into North America. The language naturally was important in education in the colonies, just as in Britain. It was no coincidence that the constitution of the United States was heavily influenced by the ideas of the Roman republic. The eighteenth-century politicians were well acquainted both with the Roman state and with its language. One obvious trace of that acquaintance is to be seen in the many towns and states with Latin-based names, for example Cincinnati, Urbana, and Virginia.

Latin has a very long and varied history in Britain. First, it was the language of the occupying Romans in antiquity, and was probably spoken by many people. It then disappeared for a few hundred years, to be reintroduced as the language of the Church around 600. It flowered for a couple of centuries, was almost obliterated again, but was firmly established once more and became a language for all educated people from the twelfth century and for several hundred years thereafter. Only in the last century was it finally superseded by English in all domains of use.

Latin in schools

As we have seen, in Roman schools the main aim was to teach the pupils to speak well so that they could become lawyers and politicians.

When the Church took over it had other priorities, and the monastic schools were, in consequence, very different from the schools of the Roman empire. One of the people responsible for forging the new education system was Cassiodorus. He lived in Italy in the sixth century, and was for most of his life a high-ranking civil servant. At that time Italy was ruled by the Ostrogoths, and Cassiodorus, who belonged to a distinguished Roman family from southern Italy, made a career for himself at the court of the Ostrogothic king. Among other things he was in charge of the chancellery, and wrote a large number of official letters in an ostentatious and difficult Latin. When he was about sixty, he left the royal court and retired to a monastery which he had founded on his ancestral estate. There he dedicated himself to a Christian life and to writing Christian works, of which he composed a large number over a period of several decades. He was over ninety when he died.

One of these works is a handbook designed to help student monks, which gives a very clear indication of the direction education was to take for several centuries thereafter. The handbook has two parts, the first of which is entirely devoted to how to study the Bible and the writings of the Church Fathers. The schools followed suit. The main purpose was to provide a Christian education, and at the heart of that was the need to be able to read the Bible in Latin. A common method employed throughout most of the Middle Ages was to let the pupils begin their acquaintance with the Bible by reading the first lines of the first psalm in the Book of Psalms, which goes as follows.

Beatus vir, qui non abiit in consilio impiorum et in via peccatorum non stetit et in cáthedra derisorum non sedit.

Here is the very literal translation from the authorised 'King James' version of the English Bible (1611):

Blessed is the man that walketh not in the counsel of the ungodly nor standeth in the way of sinners nor sitteth in the seat of the scornful.

If the translation reads strangely, it is at least in part due to the fact the Latin is in turn a translation from Hebrew and the translators have tried to represent the Hebrew original as literally as possible, which does not easily chime with the normal rhythms and patterns of Latin. Here is a more modern version from the New Living Translation:

Oh, the joys of those who do not follow the advice of the wicked, or stand around with sinners, or join in with scoffers.

This helps to make sense of the passage, but obviously was not of much use to medieval children! They had to learn Latin at the same time as they were learning all the psalms. Once they had learnt the first verse, they had to learn the second and then the third and so on until the last verse of the last psalm, number 150.

As a language teaching method this is hardly brilliant, but it was quite practical for a future monk to be required to learn all the psalms by heart in Latin. In a very rigidly ordered existence, they were part of the ritual at the frequent prayer sessions that the monks had to take part in. In a week they managed to get through all the psalms and a good deal more besides. The next week they went through the whole lot again. The week after that . . .

The whole point of this education, then, was to learn to pray in the right way in the right language. When the ancient schools disappeared, the idea of educating someone for a career in society disappeared too. Thereafter, for the pupils in the monastic and cathedral schools the purpose of a Latin education was primarily prayer and the service of God. The language of course had other important functions, but its religious use was and remained the fundamental one, because education was in the hands of the monasteries and churches, which is where it stayed for more than a thousand years. Throughout Europe, the church authorities were in charge of education until the French Revolution and in some places much longer than that. Cassiodorus stands at the beginning of a tradition which determined the role of education almost up until our own times. But his handbook had a second part. This describes non-religious education, which was divided into the seven 'liberal arts', *artes liberáles*, which are: *grammática, rhetórica, dialéctica, arithmética, música, geometría, astronomía*, or grammar, rhetoric, dialectics (also known as logic), arithmetic, music, geometry, and astronomy. It was not enough just to read the Bible; even the pious had to learn a good deal more besides.

This was not Cassiodorus' own idea, but rather the end result of lengthy debates amongst leading Christians in late antiquity. Men like Augustine and Jerome, who had received a long and thorough traditional kind of education, asked themselves whether it was right to go on reading and enjoying the pagan philosophers and poets. They did represent culture, but at the same time they might tempt people away from the path of righteous learning into sin or doubt or even downright apostasy. Eventually they reached a compromise: Christians should be allowed to read non-Christian works, but only so as to find better ways of reinforcing their faith. It was not a good idea to give up reading the ancient writers, since they were the best, but one should not let oneself be led astray by their arguments. The aim was to absorb their knowledge and their elegant written style, and to use them in a different way, to wrest the weapons from the hands of the pagans, as the saying has it.

The result of these reflections was that the pupils should also have a quantity of classical education served up to them in harmless, bite-sized chunks. The seven liberal arts provided the appropriate institutional framework which lasted throughout the Middle Ages. Of these seven, the first three provided the foundation and were of the greatest practical value. They were called the *trivium*, literally 'three ways', and they were the only ones that were taught, together with religion, in elementary school. In Sweden that led to the lowest level of schooling being called 'trivial school', just as in English some schools came to be called Grammar Schools because they taught (Latin) grammar, while in English the adjective *trivial* has come to mean 'minor, unimportant' because it originally referred to things taught at the beginning of the school curriculum. The first art, then, was grammar, obviously meaning Latin grammar. Theoretical concepts like gender (*genus*) or tense (*tempus*) were learnt from a grammar book. The one which was used in teaching beginners was almost always a small compendium written in the fourth century by a man called Donatus, whose name, with time, became almost synonymous with grammar itself. The terms in Donatus are not difficult for someone who has been taught the grammar of a European language. He starts with the names of the parts of the sentence or *partes orationis*. These are: *nómen, pronómen, verbum, advérbium, particípium, coniúnctio, praeposítio, interiéctio*. The corresponding English terms are: noun, pronoun, verb, adverb, participle, conjunction, preposition, and interjection. As is clear, we have taken our terms for the parts of speech over lock, stock, and barrel from Donatus.

There is a small difference in that under *nomen* he included both what we call nouns and what we call adjectives. This last term comes from later grammars, which distinguish the *nomen substantivum*, literally 'substantive name' and the source of the rather more specialized English term *substantive*, and the *nomen adiectivum*, literally 'adjacent name', so called because one of its most common uses is to stand beside a noun. Thus grammar in Cassiodorus' school was not that different from what was, until relatively recently, taught in our schools too. Rhetoric, by contrast, was a condensed version of what Cicero and Quintilian had taught, and does not directly correspond to anything in the modern syllabus. Even so, it had a much smaller role when compared to the importance of this subject in antiquity, and it was not used to train people in making speeches in Latin, since that was not important in the Middle Ages. Rhetorical devices were, however, useful in writing and sometimes in preparing sermons. Dialectics or logic dealt with fundamental philosophical concepts and the ability to draw formally correct conclusions from a set of premisses. It was a subject which at first had had hardly any place in Roman schooling, but interest in it increased in late antiquity. Christians felt they had to have some knowledge of philosophy in order to defend their faith against well-educated pagans.

Apart from the foundational language subjects grammar and rhetoric, philosophy was the only one of the seven liberal arts to be taught in Cassiodorus' school. The remaining arts, the so-called *quadrívium* or 'four ways', were, according to the ancient way of looking at things, four further sub-branches of philosophy. More precisely, mathematics (*mathemática*) was one of the principal fields of philosophy, and was in turn divided into arithmetic, geometry, astronomy, and music. That the first two belong under the heading of mathematics would probably not cause much disagreement, and astronomy definitely contains a considerable amount of maths, although we now believe that observation is also important. The place of music is more surprising. The reason it was classified as a sub-part of mathematics is because of harmonics. Already Plato had known that there are certain mathematical relations between, for instance, the length of a string and the pitch of the note it produces: a string which is twice as long will produce a note which is half as high. For this reason, mathematics, a branch of philosophy, was in antiquity regarded as the very foundation of music.

But not many pupils got as far as the *quadrívium*, and those who did probably derived only a limited amount of pleasure from their studies. What you could read about these subjects in Cassiodorus and even in the bigger handbooks which later became available was very meagre. It consisted of condensed and partly misunderstood digests of ideas which originally came from a variety of Greek authorities. In subjects other than religion, knowledge in the Middle Ages became quite restricted, even for people who had had all the schooling that was on offer. Apart from the knowledge of Latin, which covered grammar and some of the basic principles of composition, most of the rest was a training in logic.

This was not probably not such a bad thing. It was certainly the case that those who had attended the monastic schools were often able to make use of their abilities elsewhere than in monasteries or the Church. And this is hardly surprising. Since there were no other schools, it was obviously necessary to recruit people for any job that required the ability to write Latin from among those who had been to the Church schools. And people who were able to write were always in demand, mainly by princes and kings who needed help with administration and correspondence, of which there was a considerable amount even in hard times like the eighth century, when large parts of Europe were reverting to a local subsistence economy.

As time passed schools gradually improved, and education not only lasted longer but became more substantial. Even so the foundation was always Latin, since it was impossible to move on to other subjects without this basic linguistic tool. It goes without saying that Latin was also the language in which the classes were conducted and any textbooks written.

Around the twelfth century there was a period of real prosperity in western Europe both economically and culturally speaking. It was a time when there was enough money and know-how to build such magnificent places of worship as Notre-Dame in Paris or the cathedral at Chartres. The cathedral schools in these towns also developed into true intellectual centres, where there was advanced education and where teachers and students were able to question the established truths. The relation between religion and the philosophical ideas of antiquity provoked particularly intense debate in the best schools. Out of these schools developed the first universities, such as Paris and Oxford, and before long more had been founded in many other places.

Although the universities were much more advanced than the schools, they kept the language of the schools. Latin was the only language in the universities of Europe from their beginning and for many centuries thereafter. Not even the Reformation in the sixteenth century brought about any great change in this respect. Priests certainly had to conduct their services in the local language in Protestant countries, but they still had to learn to read, write, and speak Latin, since that was the language of the universities in which they received their training. It was not until the eighteenth century that universities started to use national languages, and in some places Latin was still the language of instruction into the twentieth century.

In schools things were not quite the same. Latin was generally the only school language until the fourteenth century, but by that time the Church schools started to face competition as the need arose for people who were able to read and write in the national language of the country in question. Little by little, therefore, these languages entered the Church schools as well, and Latin shifted from being the sole language of instruction to being the most important foreign language. It retained that status for as long as Latin was necessary in higher education, which meant in most cases down to the nineteenth century. Since then Latin has had a much less eminent place in the schools of Europe, even though several million students study it every year. Nowadays the students who choose it are those who want to acquire a better understanding of the history and culture of Europe in all but the last centuries. Of course, the interest is greatest in countries like Italy and France, whose national languages derive from Latin, and where written Latin has been in continuous use since the time of the Romans. In Britain the language has had a significant role for a rather shorter period, roughly from the seventh to the eighteenth centuries. On the other hand, Latin is perhaps the principal language through which people can have access to the earliest history of these islands, so to the extent that people want to be in touch with their roots, it is of great importance here too.

Speaking and spelling

People for whom Latin was not a native language obviously had to learn to pronounce the words at the same time as they learnt to spell and write. But how could they know how they were supposed to sound? As Latin was no longer anyone's native language, there was no one to imitate. In fact this was already a problem in late antiquity. By the fourth century pronunciation had changed a fair amount by comparison with the years around the birth of Christ. All languages change with time, and Latin was no exception. The teachers in the schools noticed that the spelling in the classical texts did not really square with the way both they and their students pronounced the words, and hence there were already debates about the rules of pronunciation among Donatus and his contemporaries.

When the Emperor Constantine established Constantinople as the second capital of the empire, the problem grew yet larger. In the new eastern capital there was an urgent need to recruit people to carry out the imperial administration, which was conducted in Latin, but the people in that part of the empire spoke not Latin but Greek or some other tongue as their native language, and needed a very thorough training in Latin. This is the reason why Priscian compiled his grammar, the weightiest of all the ancient grammars and one which devotes quite a lot of space to the pronunciation of the language. The situation became even more difficult once Latin became a foreign language in the monastic schools which had hardly any contact with the former Roman world, as happened for instance in Ireland, and later in Germany and Scandinavia. In some places the pronunciation must have been quite peculiar.

Fortunately, it is not difficult to work out from the spelling how to pronounce most Latin words. The alphabet had been invented precisely for this language, and most of the sounds of Latin are also found in all or almost all European languages. There is, for instance, never any doubt about how to pronounce the letters in words like *bona* 'good', *mitte* 'send!', *lectus* 'bed'. Some of the sounds, however, caused problems. In several cases this is due to the fact that the pronunciation of Latin had already changed in ancient times. A well-known example is the letter *c*, which in Latin in the classical period always represented a *k*-sound. Cicero would certainly have pronounced his name [kikero] and the word *concepta* 'ideas' was pronounced [konkepta]. However, in late antiquity the pronunciation changed when the sound came before the vowels *e* and *i*. What exactly the resulting sound was varied from region to region, as can still be seen in the different Romance languages. In Italian they use what phoneticians call a palato-alveolar affricate, the same sound as at the beginning of English *chilly*. In French on the other hand the corresponding sound is [s] in *Cicéron* and *concepts*. The Germanic languages have adopted a good many Latin words, and there too the pronunciation reflects this change. English has taken over the [s] from French in words like *Cicero* and

concepts. German, by contrast, has the pronunciation which originally occurred in Old French, namely [ts] as in *Cicero* [tsitsero] and
Konzept [kontsept].

How did people who knew Latin pronounce these words five
hundred or a thousand years ago? We cannot know for sure, as there
are no recordings or even detailed descriptions, but everything
points to their already being pronounced in the different ways we
have described in the different countries at that time. One good
reason to believe this is the way loanwords are pronounced. There is
no better explanation than to assume that they carried with them
into the new language the pronunciation they had in Latin, the language they had been borrowed from. There were probably fixed
norms for the pronunciation in all parts of Europe, but nonetheless a
degree of local variation was permitted from region to region.

It was not just the Germanic languages which borrowed from
Latin. Even the Romance languages did so frequently, although they
had originated in Latin. A case in point is precisely the word *concept*
in French. It is a typical learned word which probably did not exist at
all in early spoken French, and it is not to be found in any of the written texts which have come down to us from the first 350 years of the
language's attestation. In fact it shows up for the first time in 1401.
In English the corresponding word occurs in the sixteenth century. It
is the same with thousands of words in the languages of Europe, as
we shall see below.

Apart from loanwords, there is at least one more good reason to
believe that the pronunciation of Latin was partly different in different places, namely our knowledge of the way Latin was traditionally
pronounced in different European countries in the nineteenth and
early twentieth centuries. This is well documented and indeed, here
and there, there probably still are individuals who stick to this style
of pronunciation, which really varied considerably from country to
country. Nowadays the differences are smaller. In the course of the
twentieth century there was a kind of reform movement, with the
result that people now use more or less the same pronunciation
wherever they are. This is a pronunciation which reflects the way

the language sounded in the classical period and which was briefly described at the beginning of this book.

Traditional pronunciation, by contrast, like loanwords, provides us with a chance to learn a good deal about how the language sounded over the centuries. There is no reason to go into detail; it suffices to be aware that the language sounded different in different places and that it also changed gradually in some of these places. We will, however, spend a little time on the history of the pronunciation of Latin in England.

It is in the area of vowels that the traditional English pronunciation of Latin has most diverged from classical norms. One cause was the different stress and rhythm rules of English. These have meant that, from the earliest Old English times onwards, English speakers lengthen stressed vowels when they are not followed by two consonants, pronouncing a long vowel in words like *focus* and *pater* where Latin had a short one. Conversely, a long vowel tends to be shortened before two consonants even if it had been long in Latin. For example, in English pronunciation *actum* 'waged' and *factum* 'done' rhyme (as do the words *act* and *fact*), even though in Latin the first has a long *a* and the second a short one.

More striking are the changes in the quality of the long vowels, as a result of the so-called Great Vowel Shift, which took place in English in the fifteenth and sixteenth centuries. This caused the vowels in words like *game, seem, rose,* and *wine* to cease to be pronounced as long [a], [e], [o], and [i] respectively, and to have instead their modern values. The pronunciation of Latin vowels followed suit. One place where this pronunciation can still occasionally be heard is in some of the Latin phrases that pepper legal and philosophical talk. If a case is adjourned indefinitely, the lawyers may say *sine die* (literally 'without a day') and pronounce this expression something like 'sign-ee die-ee'. We also usually say *habeas corpus* with the first word sounding something like 'hay-bee-ass', and we have a diphthong in the first syllable of *modus* and the last syllable of *operandi* in the expression *modus operandi*, well known to all lovers of detective fiction. The logical terms *a priori* and *a fortiori* are usually pronounced with the first word like the name of the letter A and the last vowel like the word *I*. There is also a residue of this pronunciation in astrological names like *Gemini, Leo,* and *Pisces.* To this source too may be traced the difference between the British and American pronunciation of the prefixes *semi-* and *anti-*. This tendency is, however, on its way out, and some Latin expressions that have entered everyday language now have something nearer a classical pronunciation. The word *qua* in the phrase *sine qua non* for instance is now usually pronounced [kwa] where once it was pronounced [kwei].

Among the consonants some habits came in via the teaching of Latin in French, such as the pronunciation of both the initial *i* in words like *Iulius* and *Ianuarius* and the *g* of *genius* and *gens* with the sound (technically called an affricate) that we still have in *January* and *gentle*. Also from French is the 'soft' pronunciation of *c* as [s] in words like *censeo* and *cella*.

As long as English had a trilled *r*-sound (of the kind that still survives in Scottish and some regional accents) there was no problem over producing something close to the Latin *r* before a consonant (as in *cornu* 'horn') or at the end of a word, as in *pater*. However, after the loss of this sound in southern, and hence standard, English pronunciation many English speakers had difficulty in distinguishing pairs such as *parcis* 'you spare' and *pacis* 'of peace', or in producing the correct stressed vowels in words like *cerno* 'I see' and *virtus* 'virtue'. Similarly, since English *l* has a 'dark' quality at the end of the word (e.g. in words like *feel, fall*) and before consonants (as in *felt* and *film*), the traditional pronunciation of words like *alter* 'other' and *mel* 'honey' errs in the same direction. There have been various attempts at reform over the years. In the university of Cambridge in the sixteenth century there was a strong lobby in favour of the return to classical pronunciation habits advocated by the great Dutch classical scholar Erasmus in his dialogue *De recta Latini Graecique sermonis pronuntiatione* 'On the correct pronunciation of Latin and Greek' (1528). This was opposed, however, on various grounds, not the least being that it would make the pronunciation of Latin different in Oxford and Cambridge! The idea of reform reappeared some four centuries later. A group of scholars and teachers in the 1870s proposed a new reformed pronunciation for classical Latin and this had gained fairly widespread acceptance by the beginning of the twentieth century. This reformed pronunciation, as one commentator wryly noted, did not actually involve using any non-English sounds or even English sounds in non-English positions, but at least it ensured reasonable approximations to most of the classical consonants and vowels.

Those who teach Latin today follow more closely the precepts that are normal in modern language teaching and insist right from the outset on something much nearer to the classical qualities and quantities of the vowels, the correct assignment of stress, the 'hard' pronunciation of *k* and *g* in all positions in the word, and an accurate rendering of the letters *r* and *l* before consonants and at the end of the word. It is probably true to say that modern attempts to pronounce the language are more faithful to ancient norms than at any time since the fall of the Roman empire.

Just as the English pronunciation deviated from the classical standard, so there were of course corresponding local tendencies in other countries all over Europe, so when people came together there must have been something of a muddle of different pronunciations. Indeed, we learn as much from Erasmus' dialogue in which he mocks the pronunciation of Latin by the different ambassadors at the court of the Emperor Maximilian.

It is in general difficult or impossible to know exactly how Latin was pronounced in a given country at any given time, and most people would probably not think it was a matter of much interest anyway. One group of people in Britain and elsewhere, however, for whom the question is of some importance are those who sing in choirs. Several of the pieces in the repertoire are religious works whose words are in Latin. What pronunciation should be used? Anxious choirmasters and mistresses have sought the advice of specialists on matters such as: what did Bach's Latin sound like? Should one style of pronunciation be used in a mass by Mozart and another in a mass by Verdi? To avoid complete confusion, it is usually suggested that choirs and others who are required to read or sing aloud a Latin text written after the period of antiquity should stick to a single pronunciation. The one generally recommended is that in use in Italy. This a practical and sensible choice, both because it is quite close to the classical pronunciation and because the Italian pronunciation of Latin has always had the greatest prestige. Italy is the country in which Rome lies, and Rome was the first capital of the empire and later became the centre of the Church. Pronouncing Latin in the Italian way is not difficult. Here is a list of the most important differences between the Italian and the classical pronunciations:

- the letter groups *ae* and *oe* are both pronounced [e];
- the vowel letter *y* (which in Latin only occurs in Greek loans) is pronounced [i];
- the letter *h* is not pronounced at all;
- the combinations *ci* and *cci* and *ce* and *cce* are pronounced as the first sounds in *chilly* and *check* respectively.
- the combination *ti* before a vowel is pronounced [tsi], as in *natio* [natsio].

Increasingly, however, the modern interest in performances on authentic period instruments has led a number of choirs to experiment instead with pronunciations that correspond more closely to the precise way Latin was pronounced at the time and place when the piece was composed. However, if you have no specialist reason to need to know exactly how Latin sounded at different periods, you can always use the classical pronunciation which I explained at the beginning of the book.

There remains the question of how Latin was spelled in the Middle Ages. The main rule was of course at all periods to follow the classical spelling, but certain departures from classical practice were nonetheless very common. For instance, the combination *ae* was generally pronounced [e], and it became common practice to spell it that way too. Most people in the Middle Ages did not write *saecula* 'centuries' and *praemium* 'prize' but *secula* and *premium*. Often, as with the latter example, the loanwords in the modern languages are spelled this way too. Another common departure from classical usage was to write *ci* instead of *ti* before a vowel—for example *consequencia* instead of *consequentia* 'consequence'—and once again this is not unconnected with the way such words were normally pronounced in the Middle Ages. These spellings and pronunciations led to a large number of words in modern English and French which have retained the *c* in the spelling as *consequence, difference, absence* and literally hundreds of others where the original Latin had *tia*: *consequentia, differentia, absentia*. *Praesentia* 'presence' is an example where both the the older *ae* and *ti* spellings have been replaced by the medieval spelling pronunciation. Still, these are minor differences, and anyone who can read classical Latin can easily read texts in medieval spelling (although there are sometimes quite a few other peculiarities that I have not mentioned).

The last example we will look at in connection with spelling is a difference between our modern practice and the spelling in use both in antiquity and during the Middle Ages. The reason for this difference is a small spelling reform for Latin which was made as late as the sixteenth century. It concerned the letters *j* and *v*. The classical system had no way of distinguishing [i] and [j] in spite of the fact that both sounds existed in the language. They were both written *i*. The words *iustitia* 'justice' and *intellectus* 'intellect' were spelled with the same letter at the beginning, even though the pronunciation is [j] in the first word and [i] in the second. Another example is the name *Gaius Iulius Caesar*, in which the *i* in *Gaius* and the first *i* in *Iulius* are both pronounced [j].

Similarly, it was not possible to distinguish between [u] and [v] (which by the way in early Latin was pronounced as a back semivowel, i.e. like *w* in English). Both sounds were spelled with the same letter; the [v] in *uilla* 'villa' is represented by same letter as the [u] in *urna* 'urn'. However, the shapes of the letters varied. In ancient Roman inscriptions the letters usually look exactly like our modern capital *I* and *V*. During the Middle Ages different styles of handwriting developed, which gradually gave rise to our small letters, in which the two letters usually looked like modern *i* (most often, however, without the dot) and *u*. In some styles, though, you also find the variants *j* and *v*, but these were not used according to modern rules. In the sixteenth century a French scholar had the brainwave of using *u* and *i* for the vowel sounds and *v* and *j* for the consonants. This was a very good idea which was adopted in the spelling of several modern languages, including for example German and the Nordic languages. In this way, the two new letters *j* and *v* were added to the alphabet, and they were inserted into the alphabetical order immediately after the two corresponding vowels. In English, these letters were also introduced, but there are more consonants to worry about. The rare letter *y* (originally a letter for a vowel in the Greek alphabet) is used for one sound, and *j* for the other, as in *yet* and *jet*. This distinction did not exist in Latin. The consonant that is denoted *i* or *j* was pronounced like the first sound in *yet*.

When it comes to Latin, which the reform was really intended for, this new spelling has never been completely accepted. The usual modern spelling of Latin is a compromise in which the distinction between *u* and *v* has been adopted but not the one between *i* and *j*. It is this practice which we follow in this book, and so we make a difference between *villa* and *urna* but not between *iustitia* and *intellectus*. There are, however, many editions and dictionaries where *j* is used and the spelling is consequently *justitia* and *Julius* for example. Moreover, there are also many experts who do not like these reforms at all, and hence still write *uilla* beside *iustitia* and *Iulius*. On this point, then, there is still disagreement about how to spell Latin. The controversy will soon be half a millennium old and may in due course be resolved. Either way, Latin should survive a lot longer yet.

Books and scribes

In antiquity people wrote on papyrus, a material which in normal conditions only lasts a couple of hundred years. As a result, hardly any texts other than inscriptions have survived from the classical era around the birth of Christ. Most of what was written at that time was obviously lost when the papyrus rotted. That we nonetheless still have a considerable amount of ancient literature is due to the fact that the books were often copied before they decayed, and so the text was preserved for a bit longer. Fortunately, a new material, parchment, came into use in late antiquity. This is made of the skin of animals, and the sheets are stiff, often yellowish in colour, and very strong and durable. They could not be rolled up, so instead the large sheets were folded to make pages of a convenient size, which were then put into bundles and stitched together down one side. The sewn-up spine was in turn fastened to a hard cover. In this way the book was invented, and in essence books are still made the same way today.

Books made of parchment caught on in about the fourth century AD. Papyrus was still used for several centuries, but it gradually disappeared completely. It is true that the manufacture of parchment is by comparison a time-consuming process, but the skin of domestic animals could be found everywhere whereas papyrus had to be imported from Egypt. As trade across the Mediterranean decreased and eventually dried up almost completely, no papyrus came to western Europe any more. This change in technology was very much to Latin's advantage. When someone copied a Latin text from a roll of papyrus onto parchment, that text was able to survive for several thousand years. The ancient texts that we still have are the ones that were copied onto parchment. To make a copy was a considerable investment of time and money, so it is not surprising that much was not copied and disappeared forever. At least, though, we have the books that the Romans themselves regarded as the best and the most important, since they were obviously the ones that were copied first.

Unfortunately, we do not have many parchment manuscripts that were made in late antiquity. There are a few from the fifth century, including a couple which contain Virgil's *Aeneid*, but most have disappeared with time. What we have instead are later copies of those copies. Quite a number of works by the classical writers are preserved in copies dating from the ninth century as a result of the prompting of Charlemagne and those around him. In other cases the oldest surviving manuscript is as late as the fifteenth century, when the classical enthusiasts of the Renaissance made systematic searches for old manuscripts and had them copied.

The fact that someone makes a parchment manuscript is no guarantee that it is going to survive for ever. It can become worn if it is frequently handled, and can be damaged by damp or floods. Fire has deprived us of many manuscripts. Sometimes their owners have used them for book covers or some other everyday purpose. Sometimes, too, people have erased all the writing on the pages with a scraper or a suitable chemical and have then written a new text on top, creating what is called a palimpsest. In this case it is occasionally possible to restore what was originally there, and a number of ancient texts have been rediscovered in this way. Of course, the oldest manuscripts have seldom been preserved, but we still have many Latin manuscripts anyway. No one to my knowledge has tried to count them, but there are probably several hundred thousand still in existence. Today most of them are in libraries or archives. The greatest collections, such as those in the library of the Vatican, the British Library or the Bibliothèque Nationale in Paris, number their manuscripts in tens of thousands.

The vast majority were produced by church scribes, mostly in the monasteries. The transition to parchment took place at about the same time as Christianity established itself in the Roman empire, and it seems that it was mainly the Christians who used the new technques right from the start. Hence, it is no accident that a large percentage of the surviving manuscripts are copies of books that were important for the Church: the texts of the services and prayers, the gospels and the Psalter, collections of hymns, and so forth. Obviously too there were many complete bibles, commentaries on the books of the Bible, writings of the Church Fathers and other Christian literature which we will come back to later.

But all the other Latin that we have from the earliest period right down to the invention of printing, except for the inscriptions, is in manuscript, whether it is Christian or not, and one may well ask why the monks bothered at all to copy anything that did not relate to Christianity in some way. The answer is that this was a conscious choice from the beginning of the monastic system in late antiquity. As we have already seen, Cassiodorus and others who founded monasteries considered it essential that Christians should take over and pass on part of the ancient cultural tradition, and especially its written literature. Copying manuscripts was also seen as a very fitting occupation for monks and nuns. Good monasteries always had a *scriptorium* or writing room, where some members of the community were kept busy copying manuscripts which the monastery already possessed or which had been borrowed from somewhere else.

The number of manuscripts possessed or produced obviously varied a great deal from monastery to monastery, but all in all this was a sizeable industry as there were hundreds of monasteries. The choice of texts was probably often fortuitous, to some degree at least, since the monasteries had copies made of whatever happened to be available or accessible. At any rate, the upshot is that a pretty good assortment of pre-Christian texts has been preserved for us today. We have already discussed several of them in the first part of this book. But there are still many gaps. A case in point is Livy's great history of Rome, of which only 35 out of the original 142 books have been preserved. By contrast, Christian writers were much more extensively copied. For instance, the Church Fathers Augustine and Jerome were incredibly prolific, and almost every line has survived.

Throughout the medieval period people continued to write in Latin both on Christian and less Christian topics, so that the number of books that could be copied increased constantly from century to century. Obviously, a good deal of this production disappeared without trace but much did not, and the vast majority of Latin texts that we have today were written after antiquity. The monks and nuns who did the copying were instrumental in transmitting to us almost everything that we know about from the time before printing. For a long time they wrote only on parchment, but from the fourteenth century onwards it became common to use paper. This was a very old technique first invented in China soon after the birth of Christ. Paper was used in the Muslim world from the eighth century, but only in the thirteenth century did it start to be produced in Europe, more precisely in Spain. At about the same time the Church also started to lose its long monopoly on education and on everything that had to do with writing. As paper is cheaper than parchment, it became financially possible for people to make their own copies of texts or to write new ones themselves. There are many such manuscripts from the fourteenth and fifteenth centuries and even later. It was not simply the art of printing which displaced the monasteries from their central role in book production. By the time the printing presses came into their own at the end of the fifteenth century, the monasteries had already lost their pre-eminent position in this market.

Nevertheless, for almost a millennium responsibility for communicating the culture of antiquity rested almost exclusively with the scriptoria in the monasteries. The manuscripts they produced were not always easy to read. Usually the problem is not the handwriting, although the styles obviously varied a lot both from scribe to scribe and from period to period and place to place. Experts can draw important conclusions about the date and place of origin of a manuscript by studying the handwriting. This discipline is called palaeography, and it is an important aid to everyone who works seriously with Latin texts.

Most handwriting styles, even when they are idiosyncratic, are very clear and consistent, so once one has learnt to recognize the letter shapes, it is not difficult to work out the letters which make up a given text. Unfortunately, the problems do not stop there. A huge stumbling block, especially for beginners, are the abbreviations. As parchment was very expensive, it was important to make the best possible use of the available space. In addition, the scribes were not keen on writing more letters than they had to, so they had a number of ways of abbreviating words. One of the most common was to draw a line over a letter, which usually meant the same as an *m* after that letter, so for instance *uerbū* instead of *uerbum*. By itself that is not so hard. Unfortunately, though, the line might also mean other things, such as the omission of a syllable containing an *r*, so you could also write *ūbū* for *uerbum*, which makes things a bit harder for the inexperienced reader. And that is only the start; there were many dozens of abbreviations and hundreds of ways of using them.

Another problem is punctuation. In many manuscripts there are hardly any punctuation marks at all, and even when they are there, they are not the same as we use today and the principles that dictate their use are often completely different from our own. One has to work out for oneself where there should be a full stop or a comma in the text. Capital letters do not help, as our modern practice of starting a new sentence with a capital letter did not come in until quite late. In most manuscripts there is a capital letter at the beginning of the text, and maybe then just one at the beginning of each new section. Of course, things are different with different manuscripts. The ones that are easiest to read are the de luxe ones, perhaps commissioned by the archbishop or that were to be presented to a king or some other potentate. They are written in a large, elegant, and spacious hand with few abbreviations, and there are decorated initial letters and sometimes illustrations as well. This is the kind of manuscript often shown in pictures or in exhibition cases in museums. However, the vast majority are everyday manuscripts written in a close hand with many abbreviations and no decorations at all.

The greatest problems with manuscripts are encountered once you get beyond the external things like handwriting, punctuation, and abbreviations. It is only then that you discover that perhaps in places you cannot understand what it says, that the Latin is quite simply incomprehensible. At that point you begin to suspect that there is some kind of mistake, and that what it says in the manuscript is not what the author wrote. But what can you do about it? If there are other manuscripts containing the same text, and if you have the time to travel all over Europe or can obtain microfilm copies, you can check your version against these other ones and see what makes best sense. But even supposing you find something more intelligible in another manuscript, can you then be certain that that is what the author wrote? If two manuscripts differ in respect to a given point, at least one of them must be wrong, but how can we know which one contains the correct text, or whether indeed they are both wrong?

The answer to these questions is neither short nor simple, and leads to another branch of scholarship which is called textual criticism. This is an important part of a Latinist's everyday life. Manuscripts are full of mistakes, especially if they contain very old texts, as they have generally been copied many times and with each copy mistakes inevitably occur, however careful the scribe is. (If you do not believe me, copy a couple of hundred pages by hand and then check word for word what you have written!) Furthermore, mistakes in one copy will often be compounded in the next copy, when the scribe tries to correct what is clearly wrong but makes the wrong guess at what was in the original.

To sort out this kind of thing you have to study all the existing manuscript versions of a text in order to try and establish the relations between them and to assess which ones are the most reliable. Then you have to study all the puzzling passages in the text and decide which copy to follow at each point. If they all contain something which is difficult or impossible to interpret, you may have to make an educated guess at what the original manuscript said. Even describing this trying and lengthy procedure is enough to make most people yawn! But some are fascinated precisely by the difficulties, which require not only considerable patience and knowledge but also a special kind of cleverness, a bit like a very advanced sort of crossword. Really good textual critics are rare birds—or *rarae aves*, as they said in Latin—and their names are legendary within the small circle of people who understand what this kind of work involves.

A good many textual critics have worked on the ancient writers during the last five hundred years, so the texts of Horace and Cicero which are printed today have been purged of obvious scribal errors. Even so, uncertainties remain, and editions intended for specialists have lots of small notes at the bottom of the page. These constitute what is called the critical apparatus, which contains information about the variants in the manuscripts and about what is not in the manuscripts at all but involves guesses on the part of the editor or someone else. This information is set out in the notes in a compressed and cryptic style, usually printed in very small letters, which makes them look even more forbidding. There is no need to read them if you are not a specialist, but for the reader who wants to know exactly what an ancient writer wrote in a particular passge, they can be invaluable.

Thanks to the work of many generations of palaeographers and textual critics we now have all the ancient texts in printed editions which are both easy to read and more correct than any of the surviving manuscripts. This is not, however, the case with texts from the Middle Ages, since there are many more of them and they have attracted much less interest from Latin specialists. Many of them, even ones that are well worth reading, have been published using only one manuscript that happened to be to hand, even though much better manuscripts may exist. Many more texts have not been published at all, but are waiting in libraries for someone to read them and prepare an edition. There is a limitless amount of valuable work waiting to be done by those who would like to devote themselves to Latin and the Middle Ages.

With this we now leave behind all questions about the language itself and how it was spoken and written, and move on to what people wrote in Latin after antiquity, quite a lot of which is worth reading or at least knowing something about.

Saints and heretics

Since the people who knew how to write belonged to the Church, it is natural that a lot of what they wrote concerned religious and ecclesiastical matters, and many of those texts are of no interest today. Works which commented on and explained the various books of the Bible were, for example, very popular throughout the Middle Ages, and some very industrious individuals succeeded in writing commentaries on every single book of the Bible. Only the most dedicated modern scholars manage to read more than short sections of these works, although they sometimes contain, dotted here and there, very valuable nuggets of information about the period in which they were composed.

Somewhat more entertaining are the holy legends. Already in antiquity it was common to write biographies of prominent people. The Christians adopted that habit, although they obviously preferred to write about holy men and women, especially if they had died for their faith and thereby become martyrs. These legends usually contain a description of the life of the person in question, to the extent that it was known, but first and foremost they are accounts of the remarkable deeds and miracles which earned the saint his or her halo. One of the earliest and best known legends concerns St Martin of Tours and starts with a famous tale. While Martin was still doing his military service, he was out riding in the winter and happened upon a poor man who had no warm clothes to protect him from the cold. Martin had already given all his money away to other poor people, so what could he do? He took his sword and cut his cloak in two halves, and gave one half to the poor man. This story may well be authentic as the writer, Sulpicius Severus, was a contemporary of Martin's and knew him. Even so, it is not easy to swallow the miracles that ensue, with Martin raising several people from the dead, curing lepers, and a good deal more in that vein.

But *Vita Sancti Martini* 'The Life of Saint Martin' set a trend. There are thousands of lives of saints in Latin, all containing edifying descriptions of the good deeds and miracles performed by the saints. Some are well written, and some contain a quantity of interesting information about the period, but most of them are simply tedious. There were a great many saints, as every region wanted at least one, and it was very often not known what in fact the saint had done. Still, there had to be a life, not least so that it could be read aloud on the saint's designated day in the calendar. If the author did not know anything about the saint, he had to invent some miracles and pious acts or borrow episodes from other lives, with the result that one saint's life is often not easily distinguishable from another.

Sometimes too the author embellished the story. St Denis is the patron saint of France. He is supposed to have been the first bishop of Paris and to have suffered martyrdom through being beheaded. According to legend, he immediately stood up and walked a good distance, carrying his head in his hands, to the place where the church which bears his name is now situated, a little to the north of Paris. This was miraculous enough, you would have thought, but there are ways to improve on it. In later lives there are saints who do exactly the same thing, but walk even further or are accompanied by other beheaded martyrs also carrying their own heads. In fact this motif became so common that the experts have invented a special name for this kind of saint: *cephalophores*. This is from Greek, and of course means 'headbearers'.

But the saints were not always such shadowy figures to whom anything could be attributed. There is a long line of real historical personages, who left behind them their own writings, and who were canonized after their deaths. One such is Pope Gregory the Great, who lived around the year 600. He left a large collection of letters which document his struggle to achieve Rome's supremacy over all the churches in western Europe, and how he set in motion the conversion of England by sending the Roman monk Augustine to Kent to become the first archbishop of Canterbury. Letters between Gregory and Augustine are still extant, and there is even a letter from the Pope to King Ethelbert of Kent.

Several hundred years later, in the middle of the twelfth century, the most important man in the whole Church was an organizer and mystic by the name of Bernard of Clairvaux. He was the driving force behind the enormous extension of the Cistercian order; several monasteries were founded even as far away as Sweden. He was also a very prolific writer. The edition of his collected works, which contains sermons, theological treatises, letters, and a good deal more, every word in Latin, runs to nine volumes.

The most famous British saint, Thomas Becket, was hardly known for his saintly habits in the early part of his life. He was a learned and very energetic ecclesiastic who rose to the position of chancellor to

King Henry II. However, when he was appointed Archbishop of Canterbury by his friend the king, he changed his way of life dramatically and devoted himself to furthering the cause of the Church. This infuriated the king, and their subsequent lengthy conflict ended with Thomas being murdered in his own cathedral. He was soon declared a saint, and large numbers of people made pilgrimages to his tomb throughout the Middle Ages. One such journey provides the setting for Chaucer's *Canterbury Tales*.

These three saints are just some examples of the very many writers who wrote important works within the Church during the Middle Ages. Most of it is really not light reading but a good percentage of these works are invaluable sources for scholars who are interested in the history, ideas, and ways of thinking in a period which is very different from our own.

The same obviously also goes for those at the other end of the religious spectrum, the people who were condemned as heretics. At several points in its history movements developed which sought to reform the Church or compete with it. One of the most important groups were those who in Latin were called *cathari*. The word comes from Greek and means 'the clean'. This, it goes without saying, was their own term for themselves, and is appropriate insofar as they lived a much more ascetic life than most of the monks in the monasteries. They were principally to be found in southern France from the eleventh until the fourteenth century, and they had both their own theology and their own organization. They had considerable support, but the Catholic Church finally managed to wipe out the whole movement. This was the job of the courts of the Inquisition. Strangely enough, in one case the detailed reports of the interrogations compiled by one of the judges, in Latin of course, has formed the basis of one of the best modern books about the late Middle Ages: *Montaillou*, by the French historian E. Le Roy Ladurie. He has succeeded in recreating life in a small town in the fourteenth century, from the methods of sheep-farming and the gossip through to the villagers' view of the afterlife. It is ironic that through this work the inquisitor has unintentionally ensured that the poor Cathars in Montaillou are more alive for posterity than any of their contemporaries. One thing which Le Roy Ladurie has made clear is that Latin, the language of the Church, was more or less unknown in Montaillou. No more than a couple of people out of the town's 250 inhabitants had any knowledge of it. That tells us something about the distance between the people and the Church and its court, which took down the whole proceedings in a language virtually none of them knew.

Another person who was also regarded as a heretic by the Catholic Church was Martin Luther. As is well known, his definitive break with Rome came when he nailed his ninety-five theses to the church door in Wittenberg in 1517. These theses, which were naturally written in Latin, are about whether it is possible to gain exemption from the punishment (*poena*) which all mortals had to face in purgatory (*purgatorium*). Luther did not believe that anyone had the power to grant such relief, and certainly not in a way that was connected to *thesauri ecclésiae* 'the wealth of the Church'. It was not possible, in other words, to buy oneself off. Since this was exactly the practice the Church had introduced as part of its new business plan, a conflict arose which led to Luther and his supporters breaking with Rome and to the establishment of Protestant Churches. The position of Latin was weakened at the same time. Luther was a keen supporter of the idea that Christians should hear the sermons and read the Bible in their own languages. This idea was not a new one; earlier reformers, especially John Wyclif, had had a similar attitude. But Luther was responsible for introducing it into Protestant Germany, among other things by translating the whole Bible himself from the original languages. Something very similar gradually took place in all the other Protestant Churches of northern and western Europe.

Nonetheless, Latin survived for a long time as the language of the educated even within the Protestant Churches. Education had Latin as its foundation, as we have already seen, and theological works of all kinds were written in that language for several hundred years to come. This also held true for people who were critical of the established Church or were strangers to it. One of the most famous dissidents was the poet John Milton. Nowadays Milton is remembered chiefly for

Paradise Lost, an epic poem about Satan's rebellion against God and about Adam and Eve in Paradise. He was not only a poet, however, but also a vigorous participant in the religious and political battles of his time. He took the side of the Puritans, and became a member of Cromwell's government. He was the secretary in charge of correspondence in Latin relating to foreign affairs, a task for which he was well qualified by his extraordinary command of the language. His most important writings in that language were pamphlets in support of the Puritan cause, one of which is *Pro Populo Anglicano Defensio*, 'A Defence of the English People', published in 1651. It was widely read abroad and caused considerable indignation; in Paris it was burned publicly. Similar works that he published in English had no such effect in other countries—a nice illustration of the fact that in the seventeenth century Latin was still the truly international language of Europe.

The Catholic Church continued to have Latin as its only language for even longer. The flow of religious texts did, however, decrease and by the nineteenth century even Catholic theologians had started writing in the modern languages, for the very good reason that they wanted to be read. However, the service in Catholic churches was in principle always administered in Latin until the 1960s. The Church's central administration in the Vatican, and its communication with daughter churches all over the world, was also conducted in Latin until the same period.

The guardians of the heritage

That we know quite a lot about what happened in antiquity is largely due to the writings of Livy, Tacitus, and others, who chronicled the history of the society they lived in. The idea of history writing was never forgotten, and in consequence in Europe every century has yielded its share of historical works. Most of what I have written above about the Middle Ages concerns things we know because they have been mentioned in a historical work of some kind.

There have always been historians who have compiled accounts spanning many centuries. In the Middle Ages, for example, it was fashionable to write histories of the world which started with the Creation about 6000 BCE. However, what is of interest to posterity is almost always what a writer has to say concerning things he knows about better than anyone else, things that involve his own region or people or epoch. These are the works, or parts of works, which modern historians use as their sources. There are many of them, but the new situation after the fall of the Western empire led to a complete change of perspective from that adopted by Roman historians. Historians never live in a vacuum, but work in a specific country under a specific regime, and it is often the history of that country or regime that occasions their interest. Roman historians like Tacitus and Livy lived at the centre of an empire, and they wrote the history of that empire.

After the fifth century that empire no longer existed, and historians lived in significantly smaller domains or kingdoms. They belonged to the Church, just like everyone else who could write. Hence they wrote the histories of different kingdoms or churches. One of the earliest and one of the most entertaining is Gregory of Tours, who narrated the history of the Franks, from their invasion of the Roman province of Gaul until his own time at the end of the sixth century. Gregory was bishop of Tours and an influential figure who knew most of the people he wrote about personally. The most important of these were the kings and queens of the Franks and their many relatives from the Merovingian dynasty. The things Gregory writes about are dreadful. The Merovingians seem mainly to have devoted their energies to trying to kill each other, when they were not at war with the rest of the world around them. This is how it reads when King Childebert's messenger comes to King Guntramn to ask him to hand over the Queen Mother Fredegunda:

Redde homicidam, quae amitam meam suggillavit, quae patrem interfecit et patruum, quae ipsus consobrinus meus gladio interemit

Hand back the murderess, who had my aunt's eyes put out, who killed both her father and uncle, and who had my cousins stabbed to death.

Note how the Latin allows more precision than English in identifying the victims of these atrocities. *Ámita,* from which comes English *aunt,* means specifically a paternal aunt, and *pátruus* is a paternal uncle. The corresponding maternal relations were *matértera* and *avúnculus* (whence via French the English word *uncle*). These genealogical niceties could be of crucial importance in such a murderous age, and it is by no means impossible that Fredegunda should have done everything that is stated here. Her husband was no better. When he died, Gregory described him as *Chilpericus, Nero nostri témporis et Herodes* 'Chilperic, the Nero and Herod of our age'. He ransacked and burned his own country, hated the poor, and had the eyes put out of anyone who did not do what he wanted them to.

This kind of narrative is more readable than tales of nice people who live out their lives in quiet affluence. Gregory of Tours has always had a large readership, both because the people he wrote about were as they were and because he is a highly gifted writer. He has probably also contributed in some measure to our image of the Middle Ages as a period of decline and decay. The people he describes really cannot be called civilized. He also writes differently from the classical authors. His Latin is vivid and easy to read, but he does not know how to distinguish between the different endings of the nouns, a fact of which he is all too painfully aware himself, and his spelling is atrocious. In the passage quoted, *ipsus consobrinus meus* looks as if it has the nominative singular ending in *-us*, which makes no sense. What is clearly intended is the accusative plural, which is correctly spelled *ipsos consobrinos meos*.

But what is called the Middle Ages is a thousand years of European history, and the Merovingian rule is just an episode of a couple of hundred years in one of the Continent's many regions. Culture and politics differed from country to country and from age to age. There are long periods of prosperity, just as there are moments of deep and difficult crisis. Indeed, not much remained constant in Europe throughout the medieval period. Everyone was Christian and Latin was used everywhere; apart from that, most things varied considerably. As a result, other historians from this era are very different from Gregory of Tours even though they all write in Latin. Unlike him, most of them write a very correct kind of Latin, and many even do so with elegance and according to the ancient rhetorical principles. And there are hundreds of them!

In the twelfth century in particular the writing of history flourished, as in fact did many other kinds of literary activity. There is, for example, William of Malmesbury, who wrote a history of England (*Gesta regum Anglorum* 'Deeds of the English Kings'), or William, bishop of Tyre in present-day Lebanon, who produced an excellent history of the Crusades (*Historia rerum in pártibus transmarínis gestárum* 'History of matters that have passed in the lands beyond the sea'). A much more fanciful view of the past was provided by Geoffrey of Monmouth in his *Historia regum Britanniae* 'History of the Kings of Britain'. He asserts that in fact he has just translated *Britannici sermonis librum* 'a book in the British (i.e. Celtic) language'; however, there is no other trace of that work. Geoffrey tells the story of the Britons from their first origin, which was in his opinion Troy. This of course made them the equals of the Romans, who also believed that they came from that city through Aeneas and his followers. The narrative carries on to the eighth century CE, when the Britons finally lost the wars against the Anglo-Saxons. Geoffrey's eventful work became immensely popular, and for good reason. It includes a great number of good stories that have been retold many times by others. The plot of King Lear is there, for example, but above all the work constitutes the starting point for the whole cycle of literature about the magician Merlin, King Arthur, his sword Excalibur and his famous followers. Geoffrey presents the first written version of the Arthurian legend; in that way, he is the first in an enormous tradition of romance and fantasy. This kind of literary production remains as popular as ever, as witness *The Lord of the Rings* and the Harry Potter books. However, romance was an area in which people soon started to use other languages. There are works of this kind both in French and in English soon after Geoffrey, and Latin did not play any important role in the subsequent tradition. For ordinary history, however, Latin remained in use for several centuries to come.

But it is not only the great historians who communicate knowledge about history. More modest writers who write about what happens around them or produce documents like letters or contracts are often much more reliable sources for the historians of today, and material of this kind can be found in very large quantities. The supply varies a good deal from place to place and period to period, but in general more has been preserved from the later than from the earlier periods. Historical sources of this kind are almost always in Latin throughout Europe until the thirteenth century. After that it varies, but it is common to find Latin sources up to and including the seventeenth century. Almost all of the history of Europe was written in Latin from the moment when the Romans themselves started writing history some time before the birth of Christ down until the fourteenth century. And for the following 300 or 400 years Latin was still in frequent use. Anyone who wants to study the history of Europe and read the sources will either have to learn Latin or limit their attention to the last 250–300 years.

Poetry after antiquity

All through the Middle Ages people continued to use Latin even for writing poetry. Much was written in the same style and the same metres as the great poets of antiquity had adopted. That tradition did not end with the Middle Ages either. If anything it increased during the Renaissance, and in the sixteenth and seventeenth centuries enormous amounts of Latin poetry were produced, including a number of verse epics in the style of Virgil. Writers followed this tradition throughout Europe, from England alone in this period there are hundreds of Latin poems. But probably only very few people ever read them. They were already for the most part learned exercises even at the time when they were written, but they still contain a good deal which is of interest to historians of culture and society.

It was certainly not only second-class writers who wrote in Latin in the classical style. For example, in the fourteenth century the great Italian humanist poet Petrarch wrote a fine epic in Latin with the title *Africa*. It is about the second Punic war between the Romans and the Carthaginians and was very justly celebrated in its time, but no one reads it today. Petrarch's love poems, which are written in Italian, are by contrast still very much alive and widely read. The same goes for John Milton, who composed a substantial quantity of poetry in Latin which is now known only to a handful of specialists. *Paradise Lost*, on the other hand, is firmly established as an English classic. Yet Latin poetry after antiquity is not just an imitation of the ancient texts. During the early Middle Ages a new kind of Latin poem developed, which was completely different both in content and form. This new content came with Christianity. The greater part of the poetry which was written in the Middle Ages revolved around Christian themes, which was natural enough, as most of the people who learnt Latin belonged to the Church. Above all there were hymns, simple texts which the congregation would be able to sing, but there were also many other kinds of poems in praise of God and the saints, or which urged people on to a better life.

The ancient metres were based on an alternation between long and short syllables, as we have already seen. But Latin changed, and in late antiquity that distinction did not exist in the spoken language any more. In Christian poetry another principle was then introduced, namely that of a line based on fixed stresses and a certain number of syllables. More or less the same basic principle is to be found in early English poetry and is still used (more or less successfully) in the lyrics of popular music.

Medieval texts came to resemble modern ones even more closely as a result of a new device which was introduced about a thousand years ago. In antiquity there had been no practice of systematically letting the last words of each line rhyme, but this technique was invented and gradually developed during the early Middle Ages, both in Latin and in the new national languages like French,

German, and Provençal. The habit of rhyming seems to have spread from Latin to the new written languages, although it was in the latter that it was to continue for hundreds of years. As an example of these new Latin poetic techniques using syllable count, fixed accents, and rhymes let us take one of the best-known Christian hymns, written in the thirteenth century by a man named Thomas of Celano. This is not exactly a light-hearted piece, painting as it does a terrible picture of the Last Judgement. Although it is not to be found in modern hymn books, it is often heard even today, set to music, since it forms part of the Requiem Mass. This translation is by the English vicar and hymn-writer William Josiah Irons and was published in 1848.

> Day of wrath and doom impending,
> David's word with Sibyl's blending!
> Heaven and earth in ashes ending!
>
> O what fear man's bosom rendeth
> When from heaven the Judge descendeth,
> On whose sentence all dependeth!
>
> Wondrous sound the trumpet flingeth,
> Through earth's sepulchres it ringeth,
> All before the throne it bringeth.

This translation sticks fairly closely to the line and rhyme pattern of the original, as quickly becomes clear when we compare it with the original Latin:

> *Dies irae, dies illa*
> *solvet saeclum in favilla*
> *teste David cum Sibylla.*
>
> *Quantus tremor est futurus*
> *quando index est venturus*
> *cuncta stricte discussurus.*
>
> *Tuba, mirum spargens sonum*
> *per sepulchra regionum,*
> *coget omnes ante thronum.*

It is easy to read the Latin; you just follow the same rhythm as in the English translation. The letter *y* is pronounced [i], so the rhyme is perfect even in the first stanza.

Let us use the Latin text of this rather sombre hymn as the basis of a little language exercise. Irons's translation is not entirely literal, since otherwise he would not have been able to create the necessary rhymes and get the right number of syllables in each line. Here is the poem again with a completely literal translation:

Dies irae, dies illa	The day of wrath, that day
solvet saeclum in favilla	will reduce the world to ashes
teste David cum Sibylla.	as witness David with the Sybil.
Quantus tremor est futurus	How great will the terror be
quando iudex est venturus	when the judge comes
cuncta stricte discussurus.	to judge everything harshly.
Tuba, mirum spargens sonum	The trumpet, spreading its wonderful
per sepulchra regionum,	sound through the graves of the
coget omnes ante thronum.	lands, will summon everyone before
	the throne.

In general the text has been translated word for word, although with differences in the word order, as in the first line, where Latin allows a demonstrative like *illa* to either precede or follow the noun, but where only the order *that day* is possible in English. Similarly, in line 7 English does not allow the noun *sonum* 'sound' and the adjective *mirum* 'wonderful' to be separated from each other as in the Latin.

Many words in the text can be recognised from English and/or French. *Saeculum* literally means 'a lifetime' or 'a generation', and is the source of the modern French word *siècle* 'century'. What is meant here is time itself, which together with the world will come to an end when the trumpets sound at the Last Judgement. Time, in other words, is synonymous with the world, which is a common motif in Christian Latin, and is reflected in our loanword *secular*, which means 'worldly' or 'non-religious', as when we speak of secular authorities. The word *sonum* (*sonus* in the nominative) is to be found in several English words such as *resonance*, whose original meaning was 'echo', *dissonance* (when sounds clash), *sonata* (a piece of music which comes via the Italian verb *sonare* 'to make sounds, to play (an instrument)'), and *consonant* (which literally means 'sounding with', since consonants were thought of as sounds which accompanied vowels).

In the Church and especially in the Catholic Church, Latin was used actively for a longer period than in other contexts, and the Christian poems in Latin became the ones that lasted longest. Early church music often consists of settings of Latin texts. If you want to hear what Latin sounds like, one way is to listen to masses and choral music by Bach. But medieval Latin poetry was not just religious. Even at that time people's minds turned to many other things apart from prayers and God's judgement, such as spring and love. These had been the subject of many poems already in antiquity, but during the early Middle Ages few poets wrote about such frivolous matters. From the twelfth century the spirit of the age changed, and people started writing and singing love poems in many languages, in the beginning especially in Provençal, German, and French. In Provence people talk of troubadour poetry, in Germany of *Minnesang*. At exactly the same time people also started writing love poems, drinking songs, poems about nature, and all sorts of non-religious poems in Latin. That did not happen by chance, of course, as everybody who knew Latin obviously also knew at least one of the spoken languages, and sometimes a writer was able to write in several languages. There are even mixed poems partly in Latin, partly in German or French.

This period was the first great Golden Age of poetry in the modern European languages. Even so, this does not mean that the Latin poems were imitations of the ones written in the national languages. In the beginning it may have been the other way round. Poetry and the art of versification in Latin was a model for the pioneers of the new languages. Gradually the poetry in the new languages grew away from those models. The authors of this new kind of poetry in the twelfth and thirteenth centuries were for the most part students, who tended to move from school to school, especially if their studies were not going well or if they had not paid their tuition bills. Quite a lot of this poetry has survived, but most of the poems are anonymous, and in several cases they were written down in extensive manuscript anthologies. One such manuscript is particularly famous. It was originally kept in a monastery in Benediktbeuren in Germany, south of Munich, and so the collection is called *Carmina Burana* which means 'songs from Benediktbeuren'. This collection has become particularly well known because the composer Carl Orff set a number of the Latin and German poems in it to music and created a great choral work called precisely *Carmina Burana*. One of the poems he includes is a very beautiful paean to spring and love which starts like this

Ecce gratum et optatum	Behold, the pleasant and longed-for
ver reducit gaudia:	spring brings back joy:
purpuratum floret pratum,	the meadow blossoms with violet flowers,
sol serenat omnia.	the sun makes everything bright.

Compare the word-for-word translation above with a somewhat less literal, but nonetheless quite close, translation which aims to reproduce something of the rhyme and rhythm of the Latin:

> Welcome, season,
> with good reason:
> spring restores our old delight:
> violets grow
> by the hedgerow,
> sunshine renders all things bright.

To a modern poet these rhymes might seem somewhat banal but this is not the fault of the translator, who has made a fine job of imitating the poetic devices of the original. Rather, after hundreds of years of this kind of poetry, virtually all rhymes have been exhausted and the rhythms have become commonplace; but when these poems were first written, the forms were fresh, unknown and intoxicating, just like spring itself to a twenty-year-old student.

Abelard and Héloïse

One of the most remarkable students and poets ever to come to Paris was called Petrus Abelardus. Or at least that was how he wrote his name in Latin; in English he is usually called simply Abelard. We know a good deal about his life through his own writings, in particular an autobiographical work which he wrote when he was a little over fifty called *Historia calamitatum*, 'History of calamities'. The title could not be more apt: he had more than his fair share of hardship and disaster.

Abelard was born in 1079 in what is today Brittany, close to the mouth of the Loire. From an early age it was evident that he was exceptionally talented, and it was not long before he went to Paris, which was beginning to gain a reputation as an important centre of learning. Abelard quickly came to realize that he was a better logician than the man who was the most prominent teacher there and the head of the cathedral school. The two men fell out and Abelard established himself as a teacher on the left bank of the Seine, just a few hundred metres from the cathedral school which was situated where Notre-Dame still stands to this day. Abelard's school was the first on the spot where the Sorbonne has been for the last 900 years, so in a sense he could be considered the founder of the University of Paris. He was a brilliant teacher: knowledgeable, charming, and inspirational. Students flocked to hear him, and he achieved one success after another. When he was about thirty, he took over the headship of the cathedral school, so obtaining a very prominent position in the city of Paris. At this moment, when he was at the pinnacle of his career, there occurred the biggest and most crucial disaster in his life; he fell in love.

He caught sight of a young girl called Héloïse. Abelard says: *per faciem non erat ínfima, per abundántiam litterárum erat suprema* 'in beauty she was not the last, in learning she was the first'. He decided to seduce her. That plan too was a success. He managed to rent a room in her uncle's house, where she lived, and the rest was very simple. But things probably did not turn out quite the way Abelard had intended. Not because Héloïse herself presented any obstacle to his designs, on the contrary. It all just became so much more serious than he had obviously planned. They fell passionately in love, devoted themselves to each other and their love. For the first time in his life Abelard neglected his teaching and his studies, and instead spent his time writing love poems, which became very popular and were widely circulated. Unfortunately they have not survived. Eventually their love affair became public knowledge, and at last the inevitable happened: even the naïve Fulbert, Héloïse's uncle, realized what was going on. The situation was difficult. Fulbert insisted that Abelard and Héloïse should get married, especially as she was pregnant. But Abelard belonged to the priesthood, and it would be the end of his whole career if he were to marry. Unable to decide, he hummed and hawed for several months. Finally they married in secret, but afterwards Abelard refused to acknowledge the marriage. Fulbert and his relatives concluded that Abelard had intended to deceive Héloïse all along, and decided to take their revenge. They broke into his house at night and castrated him.

At that point Abelard decided to become a monk. He took his vows in the monastery of Saint-Denis shortly after he had been attacked, and he ordered Héloïse to do the same, which she did in the convent of Argenteuil. Her nearest relatives tried to dissuade her: she was only nineteen years old. But she was calm and quoted from the ancient poet Lucan the words which Pompey's wife is supposed to have uttered immediately before she committed suicide: *Cur ímpia nupsi, si míserum factura fui?* 'Why did I marry against God's wish if I was only to make him unhappy?' With these words, Abelard writes, she hurried to the altar, received the nun's veil from the bishop, and took her vows. On the surface that is the end of the love story between Abelard and Héloïse. Physical love was no longer possible, and they remained bound by their vows for the rest of their lives. And yet the most interesting part of the story is still to come.

The events we have just narrated took place in about 1117 to 1119, when Abelard was thirty-eight or thirty-nine and Héloïse eighteen or nineteen. Abelard wrote his *Historia calamitatum* some fifteen years later, probably in 1134, when he was fifty-five. There he gives a detailed account of what happened to him during those last fifteen years, which, like all of his life, were full of conflict. At that time he was abbot in a monastery, and Héloïse was abbess in a convent. From the same period in their lives a number of letters have come down to us. The first is from Héloïse to Abelard, and in it she explains that she has happened upon a copy of his *Historia calamitatum* and that, having read it, she feels constrained to write to him. There follows Abelard's answer, Héloïse's reply, and so on. The letters are some of the most widely read and discussed in world literature. In particular, the first two by Héloïse have fascinated and surprised readers throughout the centuries.

In these letters she begins by explaining her love for Abelard: *te semper, ut ómnibus patet, immoderato amóre complexa sum* 'I have always embraced you with unfettered love, as everyone knows'. Most of the time she calls him *unice* 'my only one'. Everything he does and thinks is higher and better than anything else; his genius and knowledge place him above kings and emperors; he was the most beautiful of all, could sing and write better than anyone, was desired by all women, married and unmarried alike. For her part she has always done what she has done out of love for him, not for any other reason. And that especially applies to her entry into the convent. *Tua me ad religiónis hábitum iússio, non divina traxit diléctio* 'It was your command which made me take a nun's vows, not my love for God'. And therefore, she continues, I do not have any real moral worth. Outwardly I live a pious life, but what really counts is the heart's desire, and in my heart only you mean anything to me.

Moreover, she says, I live in chastity and am considered virtuous. But I still remember all the times when we were together in the flesh, where we were, what we did, and I think of you again and again at every moment, even during holy Mass. I am worthless in the sight of God and my suffering is intense. The one person who can and should help me is you by writing to me and sending me words of comfort. Indeed it is your duty: you are my husband. Write to me and care for me!

Abelard's reply is markedly cool in comparison with Héloïse's violent fervour. He places himself more or less in the role of her confessor and tells her that her struggle is a struggle to reach God, and that it is the more noble the harder she has to fight. He has been relieved from lust himself, but then he does not acquire any merit from fighting it either, whereas she, on the other hand, wins a great victory by fighting her physical desires. This thought probably did not altogether comfort Héloïse. At the beginning of her third letter she simply remarks that she will stop writing about this since that is what he tells her to do, but that she is not in command of her own feelings. *Nihil enim minus in nostra est potestate quam ánimus* 'For nothing is less under our own control than our heart'. After that there is no more about feelings; the correspondence goes on to talk instead about what form the rules of conduct in Héloïse's convent should take.

The story of Abelard and Héloïse is one of Europe's great love stories. The letters have been translated into many languages, and several writers have taken up and retold the story. This is hardly surprising, since it contains violent emotions and violent deeds, heroism and deceit, and lifelong love in spite of everything. It does not make it any less interesting that both parties were celebrities in their day. In particular, as we shall see, Abelard's pioneering contribution to philosophy and theology means that he has an important position in the history of European ideas.

Nonetheless, probably the most remarkable thing about this whole story is that they both wrote it down. Above all, how was the abbess Héloïse able to reveal her innermost feelings so nakedly? Is this really plausible? Many have believed that the whole correspondence is a forgery from a later period. But by studying the Latin of the letters, scholars have in fact been able to prove that they must have been written at Abelard's and Héloïse's time, and in all probability by them themselves. In other words, a man and a woman in the twelfth century really did express their innermost feelings to each other in letters written in a Latin which for the most part completely follows the classical rules. They wrote as people spoke a thousand years earlier and did so with great elegance. In such circumstances it is not possible to have uncontrolled outbursts, but that does not make the letters seem cold. On the contrary, the feelings come across all the more strongly because the writers express themselves in such a restrained but precise way, without any hint of sentimentality.

The thinkers

As we have said, Abelard played an important role in the development of European philosophy, a field where advances were closely bound up with the knowledge and use of language. Indeed, philosophy is arguably the most demanding way of using language. Throughout antiquity it was the Greek philosophers and their ideas who had held sway, even among the Romans. Only two Latin writers were widely read, Cicero and Seneca, and for the most part they produced popularized versions of Greek ideas. Some Christian thinkers were more independent and innovative, particularly Augustine, but even he had derived many of his ideas from Greek philosophers and theologians. In late antiquity knowledge of Greek became increasingly rare, and writers like Cassiodorus collected parts of the wisdom of the Greeks into short Latin compendia. One of Cassiodorus' contemporaries translated a number of important original works by Aristotle and commentaries on them into Latin, a contribution which proved to be of great value for hundreds of years to come. His name was Boethius, and he was remarkable both as a man and a philosopher.

Boethius came from an old and distinguished Roman family, and he became one of the most important officials of the Ostrogothic king Theoderic, who ruled from Ravenna. But after many years in which he wielded great power he fell into disfavour, was sent to prison in 523 and executed in 524. While he was awaiting his verdict, he wrote a beautiful work entitled *De consolatione philosophiae* 'The Consolation of Philosophy'. Philosophy, in the shape of a woman, comes to visit him in his cell and discusses his misfortune with him. He tells her how he has acted for the good and protected the weak, and how the powerful and evil have harmed him. She answers that he has had a good life in spite of that, and that the evil are worse off than him. The whole thing turns into a dialogue about the definition of good and evil, and is interleaved with short reflective poems. One begins like this:

> *Felix qui potuit boni*
> *fontem visere lúcidam,*
> *felix qui potuit gravis*
> *terrae sólvere víncula.*

> Happy, the one who can see
> the clear source of good,
> happy, the one who can release
> the chains of heavy earth.

Boethius was able to wait calmly for his death sentence and write beautiful poetry in the meantime. The ideas which gave him peace of mind came from the classical Greek philosophers, above all from Plato.

After him almost nobody in western Europe read Plato in the original for the best part of a thousand years, and only one of Plato's dialogues had been translated into Latin. There was more by Aristotle, Plato's apprentice, mainly as a result of Boethius' efforts. The most important Greek philosophers were almost unknown in western Europe from the seventh until the twelfth century, and in that period philosophy was more like an annexe of theology. The most important philosophical question was how to prove logically the existence of God.

Petrus Abelard was one of the people who revived philosophy, above all by daring to ask uncomfortable questions. He was a very talented logician, and with inexorable rigour of argument he called attention to the contradictions and obscurities in Christian teachings. As a result, he became something of an embarassment to the Church authorities, who accused and convicted him of heresy in his old age. But his ideas proved impossible to conceal. On the contrary, it became increasingly important to reconcile Christianity on the one hand with the demands of logic and on the other with the general world picture that was the legacy of the ancient philosophers. This whole set of questions acquired renewed urgency once Aristotle's works became more widely available in Latin translation in the twelfth and thirteenth centuries.

Strange as it may seem, they had not been translated directly from the Greek originals but from Arabic. This in turn was due to the meeting of Arabic and Latin cultures in central and southern Spain, which had been under Muslim rule since the eighth century. Aristotle was very important to Muslim philosophers, who had access to translations from Greek into Arabic. The philosopher who in Europe is called Averroes wrote important commentaries on the works of Aristotle in Spain in the twelfth century. Both Aristotle and Averroes were translated into Latin and attracted a great deal of attention.

The Church did not really have anything which was equivalent to this cogent and coherent philosophy, and the questions which Abelard had begun to raise came to seem even more problematic. Gradually the solution which emerged was a fusion or synthesis of Christian doctrine and an Arabized version of ancient philosophy. The person who was finally responsible for bringing this about was a certain Thomas from Aquino in Italy, hence the name by which he has become known to posterity, Thomas Aquinas. He was an intellectual giant who lived in the thirteenth century and produced vast numbers of theological texts. One of his main works is called *Summa theologiae* 'Summation of Theology', another one is called *Summa contra gentiles* 'On the truth of the Catholic faith against the Gentiles'. In these works he very systematically and thoroughly settles all the questions about what to believe and how to live as a Christian.

Thomas was enormously successful. He was not only canonized, but was commonly called *doctor angélicus* 'the angelic teacher'. Little by little his understanding of Christianity became the official line of the Catholic Church, as indeed it still is to this day. Numerous theologians followed in his footsteps. They are called Thomists, and the theological movement associated with his work is called Thomism. In principle the Catholic Church has had the same official philosophy for the last 800 years. This has not completely prevented continous philosophical activity even within the Church, while in Europe at large philosophy and theology have slowly but surely gone their separate ways.

For several hundred years after the time of Thomas it goes without saying that all philosophers in Europe wrote in Latin. It was the only language which had a fully developed terminology, except for Greek, which hardly anyone knew. It is not until the sixteenth century that philosophical works start to appear in the vernacular. One of the first to write in his national language was the Frenchman Montaigne, something he was able to do partly because he was not concerned with logical and metaphysical subtleties, but instead wrote essays on important topics rooted in everyday life.

His countryman Descartes, called Cartesius in Latin, used Latin for some of his writings and French for others. It was at his time, during the seventeenth century, that Latin started losing ground even among scholars. Descartes used Latin for texts which involved formal and technical reasoning, but French for texts which were intended to be accessible to a wider public. His most famous principle is known in its Latin form, and emerged while he was struggling to find a foundation for his view of the world, something which he could regard as absolutely certain. He found it in the proposition *cógito, ergo sum* 'I think, therefore I am', and he built his theory of the nature of the world on this basis.

Since the eighteenth century philosophers have generally written in their native languages. This obviously has great advantages, not least that they can be read by their countrymen, and that they can express themselves in an unfettered way in the one language which they know better than any other. But it also results in certain problems. As long as Latin was the common language of philosophers, it did not matter much which country a philosopher happened to come from. European philosophers discussed things with each other all over Europe. During the nineteenth century, and even more so in the twentieth, different philosophical schools have been established in different countries, so that for instance Anglo-American philosophy has become very different from French or German philosophy. Although the various traditions do not exist inside completely watertight compartments, it is nonetheless true that the different languages have made it more difficult for philosophers to understand each other than it was when they all wrote in Latin.

The Renaissance

For half a millennium, the history of Europe has usually been seen as a sequence of three periods: antiquity, the Middle Ages, and the modern era. The modern era starts with something called the Renaissance, and the clear implication is that antiquity was a period of high civilisation, while the Middle Ages was a time of decline which was finally brought to an end by the Renaissance, that is by the rebirth of classical culture and values. Not surprisingly, this view was invented and propagated by leading representatives of the Renaissance movement, who were mainly Italian writers, artists, and other intellectuals living in the fourteenth, fifteenth, and sixteenth centuries. There is no doubt, of course, about the extraordinary cultural achievements in Italy during this period; it is enough to mention names like Petrarch and Boccaccio in literature, and Leonardo da Vinci and Raphael in painting. Whether these people became so great because of their demonstrably ardent interest in classical antiquity is quite another matter, but we can safely leave that larger question aside here.

As far as the extent to which Latin was used, the Renaissance does not represent a clear break or constitute a particular turning point. In most domains, the changes were slow and gradual but almost always to the detriment of Latin from the thirteenth right through to the twentieth century, as we have already seen. What did come with the Renaissance, though, was a different attitude to correctness. During the many centuries that had elapsed since antiquity, Latin vocabulary had considerably expanded and new habits of style and usage had developed. Several leading figures in the Renaissance were learned humanists, convinced that the literary texts from classical antiquity were of supreme importance, both for their content and for their exemplary language, so they worked hard to eliminate non-classical words and expressions, and generally to improve the standards of written (and spoken) Latin in their own time.

This was not an entirely new idea. We have seen how, in the early ninth century, people such as Alcuin at the court of Charlemagne very consciously went back to the ancient models, and a trend in the same direction is quite evident in the twelfth century. Modern historians have accordingly coined the expressions 'the Carolingian renaissance' and 'the twelfth-century renaissance'.

But in the Renaissance proper, this trend became much stronger, and was also grounded in a partly different ideology. The earlier movements were mainly concerned with achieving a better knowledge of Latin and generally higher standards in education and learning. In the Renaissance, leading thinkers pursued much more lofty goals, such as allowing men (and to a lesser degree women!) to realize their full potential, and liberating them from the burden of superstition and ignorance that had accumulated after the brilliance of antiquity, during the *media aetas*, the Middle Ages. Reform in the use of the Latin language was one of the ways towards this goal. But precisely because of the very high ambitions, the results were not quite what might have been expected.

There is no doubt that the standards of written Latin rose considerably as a consequence of the Renaissance, first in Italy and later on in most of Europe. Brilliant humanists such as Coluccio Salutati unearthed forgotten manuscripts of important texts from antiquity, for example the letters of Cicero. They studied the language and style of the classical texts in great detail and produced manuals for their contemporaries, so that they would be able to write truly Ciceronian Latin. The most famous of these works was the *Elegantiae Linguae Latinae* (1471) by Lorenzo Valla.

An important northern European classicist and thinker who learnt much from Valla and his contemporaries about how to edit classical texts was Gerhard Gerhards, better known by his Latin pen name Desiderius and best of all by his Greek one, Erasmus of Rotterdam. His output was prodigious: in addition to original works, all written in Latin of course, he oversaw editions of works by many of the authors mentioned in this book, including Terence, Livy, Pliny, and Seneca. He also produced editions of the writings of several of the great Christian Fathers such as Jerome, Augustine, and Ambrose. Probably his most famous original composition is *Moriae Encomium* 'In Praise of Folly' (1511). He also published a book entitled *Adagia* 'Proverbs', a collection of thousands of Latin and Greek sayings, some of which are still with us, such as *mortuum flagellas* 'you are flogging a dead (horse)' and *inter caecos regnat strabus* 'in the kingdom of the blind the one-eyed man is king' (literally: 'among the blind reigns the one-eyed man').

Many people actually achieved such a mastery of Latin that they were able to compose poems and orations that met all the classical standards of language and stylistic expression. We have already mentioned Petrarch, from the very early Renaissance, and John Milton, who lived in the wake of the Renaissance movement. In the centuries that separate them, hundreds of writers produced countless artistic works in impeccable Latin. Unfortunately, much Renaissance literature in Latin suffered from a common weakness: content rarely matched form. Too many of these works are derivative, dull school exercises. Most were never widely read, and are nowadays taken off the library shelves only by a few specialists. There are exceptions, of course. In addition to the works we have already mentioned, we should not forget Thomas More's *Utopia* (1516), an extremely influential work by a truly original thinker. Nevertheless, the real literary landmarks of the Renaissance were written in the new languages of Europe, first in Italian, and later in French, English and other languages. The great collective effort spent on learning perfect classical Latin did not for the most part pay off in the form of original literary works in the language.

As for the daily use of Latin in the church, administration, and many other domains, it was affected by Renaissance ideals in two ways. On the one hand, the formal standard of written Latin rose in almost all contexts, which was certainly an improvement. On the other hand, the higher requirements of stylistic elegance meant that life became harder for writers. It became more difficult than before to attain the standard necessary to produce an official letter or a will, for example. In the long run, this problem reinforced the tendency for such documents to be drawn up in the national languages instead. Once it had become more complicated to write Latin, the language became less useful for practical purposes.

On the whole, then, the Renaissance did not mean a return to a wider use of Latin in Europe, in spite of the fact that the leading protagonists really loved the language and worked hard to promote it. To the extent that the movement had any effect, it may actually have been to accelerate the trend towards the abandonment of Latin and the shift to the national languages.

Doctors and their language

How often have you been to the doctor and been told: 'It's just a virus. Come and see me again in a few days if it hasn't cleared up'? Or maybe you are unlucky and the doctor says: 'I think you've got appendicitis and need an operation straightaway.' Or perhaps your doctor diagnoses neuralgia of some kind and prescribes some analgesics. Embedded in these and a hundred other such remarks which are heard daily in hospitals and surgeries are thousands of words which derive from the classical languages. *Virus* comes from Latin, where it means an animal poison such as a snake's or scorpion's venom or any animal or plant secretion to which magical or medicinal qualities are attributed. Pliny, for example, reports that people believed wolves secreted a *virus amatorium* or 'love juice'. *Appendix* means simply 'appendage' and is related to the verb *appendo* 'hang' but in a medical context now refers specifically to that rather useless organ that can become inflamed, cause great pain and require surgical removal. *Neuralgia*, which means 'nerve pain', comes from the Greek words *neuron* 'nerve' and *algia* 'pain', and in Greek the prefix *a-/an-* marks a negative, as in *amoral*, so an analgesic is something that takes away pain. In fact, almost all our medical terms come from Latin or Greek. Of course this is also true within many other areas of science, as we shall see, but medicine is special because there are so many completely unchanged Latin words such as *appendix* and *virus*. Until recently it was even common for doctors to write their diagnoses in pure Latin, using expressions like *deméntia senilis* 'senile dementia'. *Senilis* in Latin is simply an adjective referring to old age and could be used positively or negatively, but once doctors shifted from Latin to an anglicized form of Latin like *senile dementia* there was the problem of the negative connotations that the English adjective *senile* had acquired over the years. As a result the expression is largely avoided these days.

The fact that medical doctors in particular stuck so doggedly to Latin for such a long time has a simple historical explanation. We have already mentioned that the Romans were no innovators when it came to medicine, for the most part producing Latin compendia of what the Greeks had discovered. Greek medicine during antiquity, on the other hand, was very impressive: any Roman who could afford it had a Greek doctor. The Emperor Marcus Aurelius had one such, a personal physician by the name of Galen, who became a very important figure in the history of medicine. He wrote a number of works in Greek, which were exceptionally influential over a very long period. Within certain areas of medicine he was the leading authority until the beginning of the nineteenth century. One of the foundations of

Galen's teaching was the theory of the four bodily fluids. The general idea was that a person's health depends on which fluid is dominant in the body. The theory is often called 'the pathology of the humours': *humor* means precisely 'fluid' and pathology is the 'theory of diseases', from the Greek word *pathos* meaning suffering or illness.

Nowadays the word *humour* means something completely different in English, but its modern meaning comes from the idea of bodily fluids. If you have the right balance of fluids in your body, you have a propitious temperament and can make jokes and be happy. The bodily fluids which formed part of Galen's account were blood (*sanguis* in Latin), phlegm (*phlegma*), yellow bile (*chole*), and black bile (*melaina chole*). The last three names are Greek and were used as loanwords in Latin. Parts of the theory still live on today in the idea that different people have different temperaments: there are the sanguine types, optimistic people dominated by blood; the phlegmatic types, languid people who are dominated by phlegm; the choleric types, hot-tempered people ruled by bile; and the melancholic types, gloomy individuals who have to live with the black bile. Medicine in western Europe during the early Middle Ages was not very impressive, but towards 1100 real medical training started, first of all in Salerno in Italy. The impulse came partly from Byzantium in the east, partly from the Arabs, who were leading figures in this field as in many other areas of medieval science. Teachers in Salerno built on Galen, whose writings had been translated into Latin and had begun the western tradition of medicine.

For several centuries not a lot more happened, but the doctors added a few finishing touches to the ideas of their Greek predecessors, and in the process developed an elaborate Latin terminology, which also included a great number of words which were originally Greek, obviously due to the influence of Galen and other Greek writers. One consequence of this is that there are sometimes two words for the same thing in Latin, both the original word and the one which has been borrowed from Greek. For example 'nerve' is *nervus* in Latin and the English word is a loanword from that. The three-part facial nerve is therefore in Latin called *nervus trigéminus*. In Greek 'nerve' is called *neuron,* and from that Latin acquired words like *neurosis, neurasthenia,* and *neuralgia,* which have passed directly into English.

Unfortunately a rich panoply of terms and a good knowledge of Latin are not always of much help to the patients. It was a recurring complaint about doctors, even as late as the eighteenth century, that they were very learned and tended to lard their speech with elegant theoretical disquisitions, but that they were not able to do much about diseases. And that is indeed how it was. Things began to change once doctors gave up the belief that the ancient authorities knew best and started to conduct their own systematic research. A pioneer in this respect was the Belgian Vesalius, who in the sixteenth century started to use dissections as a way of investigating human anatomy. In the seventeenth century the Englishman William Harvey discovered how the circulation of the blood works and published his discovery in a document with the grand title *Exercitátio anatómica de motu cordis et sánguinis in animálibus* 'An anatomical disquisition on the movement of the heart and blood in animals'. Thereafter further discoveries were made in quick succession, and gradually, though with a long delay, these led to new ways of treating sick people.

This new development did not lead to a change of language. The innovators wrote and discussed matters in Latin just as their predecessors had done, as indeed was necessary if their ideas were to become widely known amongst their international peers. It was also difficult to translate medical terminology into the national languages. The learned academic tradition is and always has been very strong among doctors, and so they stuck to Latin as their professional language for a very long time. Until the eighteenth century it was very common for doctors to speak Latin to each other, and in Britain it was only in the mid-twentieth century that it ceased to be necessary to have a knowledge of Latin to be accepted as a student of medicine.

Things are obviously different these days, but medical language is just as full of Latin and Greek words as it ever was. Hence doctors and other health workers have to learn hundreds or thousands of special terms which have no connection with their native language.

This may be hard work, but it has its advantages. Any specialized discipline has to have its own terminology, and a doctor for example needs to have names for all the muscles in the body. Everyone in the world has the same muscles whatever their language, and for most muscles it is only doctors and other specialists who ever have reason to refer to them by name. The words are never used in everyday language. Hence it would be both impractical and unwise to invent completely new names for them in each language. A common international terminology serves to avoid misunderstandings and confusion.

It is not of course necessary that these terms come from Latin and Greek, but because of the way medicine developed over the centuries, that is what we have, and there is no reason to change things now. Indeed, one advantage is that neither Latin nor Ancient Greek are spoken languages today, which means that no country has priority in the sense that its language is the basis of the international terminology. Contrast the position of English, which forms the basis of international usage in a more recent discipline such as computer science.

It is obviously an advantage for people who have to learn these terms if they know a bit of Latin. Even the small doses that can be found in this book will probably make it easier to understand quite a few words. If you know that *natus* means 'born' and that *prae* means 'before', it is not difficult to guess that prenatal damage is damage that occurs before the child is born. However, it would take a book of its own to explain medical vocabulary in full. Such books do exist, and we cannot go into more detail here. But in the vocabulary of medicine Latin (and Ancient Greek) are still very much alive and will continue to be so for the foreseeable future. The same is true in many other fields.

Linnaeus and Latin

Your heart may lift when you come upon a glade full of *Anemóne nemorósa*. You may 'twitch' at the sight of a *Motacilla alba*, but if against all the odds you come across an *Ursus arctos,* you had better get out of the way at once.

These are the Latin names for the wood anemone, the wagtail, and the brown bear respectively. In botany and zoology every species has its established Latin name. Today we seldom use these names in ordinary English texts like the above, but in any circumstance in which zoologists or botanists communicate with each other, they use the Latin terms for the species. It is not just the name which is in Latin; each species is also required to have an official description in Latin. Anyone who discovers a new species has to write and publish such a description. Within these sciences Latin still has an important practical use.

The historical explanation for this state of affairs has much to do with the tradition of medicine, which we have already discussed. For many years within European universities and academies the natural sciences took a back seat. Animals and plants were only really studied by doctors for their possible applications in medicine and related fields. The tradition of using Latin therefore became as strong within these sciences as it was in medicine.

During the eighteenth century, however, the natural sciences came on apace and gradually acquired their own identity independent of medicine. One of the pioneers was Carl von Linné, a Swede whose name, usually and very appropriately in its Latin form, *Linnaeus,* is known all over the world, at least by those who are interested in his field. Linnaeus was the son of a vicar from Småland in southern Sweden, and he studied in Lund and Uppsala before venturing abroad. In 1735 he went to Holland, where he became a doctor of medicine but also published in quick succession a number of pioneering works on botany. All these books were in Latin. Apart from Swedish that was the only language which Linnaeus had mastered, and just as for any scientist of his day it formed a necessary foundation for his career. He did not need any other languages, since he could take it for granted that people who had chosen to devote themselves to any kind of science would be able to read Latin.

Linnaeus was a great systematizer. He endeavoured to sort all living species into a coherent hierarchical classification. A number of species are grouped together to form a *genus* (plural *genera*, which literally means 'kind' or' sort'). A group of *genera* are then united into a larger group called an 'order' (in Latin *ordo*), a group of orders yields a 'class' (*classis*), and finally several classes make up a kingdom (*regnum*). Every species is allocated its place in this overarching system, which we still use to this day for both animals and plants (although obviously the details have been modified since Linnaeus' time). For instance, the species of great tits (*Parus major*) belongs to the genus Titmice (*Paridae*), which is part of the order Passeriformes, which is a subgroup of the class of birds (*Aves*), which in turn belong to the larger class of Vertebrates. At the top stands the kingdom of animals (*regnum animalium*). Linnaeus was not the only person to have developed a scheme of this kind, but he was a great classifier and namer, and it was his system that gained wide acceptance.

When it comes to plants, his great achievement was the so-called sexual system. The idea was to classify plants according to the appearance of their reproductive organs, more precisely according to how many stamens and pistils the flower has. These were clear and simple criteria, which brought order to the mess of different classifications which botanists had used before his time. Today the sexual system has been abandoned, as over the years it has been shown to bring together plants with quite different characteristics in an arbitrary way. The introduction of other criteria has been accepted. Furthermore, the whole of the present system of classification is tottering, as scientists have started measuring the degree of similarity among the DNA of a variety of species, with results that differ considerably from the established truths.

Nonetheless many of Linnaeus' achievements live on, most importantly his system of naming, which remains unchallenged. Before Linnaeus it was not at all clear how different plants and animals should be named, and the concept of species was also controversial. Linnaeus was convinced that every living creature belonged to a separate species, and one of the goals he set himself was to give each and every one of the species an unambiguous name. In the 1750s he published Latin descriptions with names of all the plants and animals which were known at that time, and with few exceptions those names are still valid. Of course many new species have been discovered since then, but they have always been named according to Linnaeus' principles. These require that the name must be in Latin, and that it must consist of two words, the so-called 'binomial' system. The first word is a noun which is usually common for all the species within the family which the species belongs to (called the 'generic name'). Wherever possible Linnaeus used existing Latin words: *ursus* means 'bear' in Latin, and *motacilla* means 'wagtail'. The word *anemone* is a Latinized form of the Greek word for that flower. The second word is a qualifier of the first and is called the 'specific name'. Very often it is a Latin adjective, as in *Motacilla alba*, literally 'white wagtail'. The qualifier distinguishes the name of the wagtail from its relatives, such as the yellow wagtail, *Motacilla flava*, literally 'yellow wagtail', and the grey wagtail, *Motacilla cinérea*, literally 'ash-coloured wagtail'.

It is the same with the name of the wood anemone, *Anemone nemorosa*, literally 'grove anemone'. The adjective *nemorosus* comes from *nemus* 'grove', and means 'belonging to grove' or simply 'grove' as an attributive. The qualifier distinguishes it from, for example, the *Anemone sylvestris*, literally 'wood anemone' (the adjective *sylvestris*, also spelled *silvestris*, comes from *silva*, 'wood'), which in English is sometimes called 'snowdrop anemone'. The potential confusion that arises from popular names, which differ from place to place, make a clear and consistent naming system essential. A famous example is the word *robin*, which refers to *Erithacus rubicula* in Britain and to *Turdus migratorius* in the United States.

In the case of the brown bear, the second name is also a noun, *arctos*, which is quite simply the Latin form of the Greek word for bear. The name *Ursus arctos* actually means 'bear bear'. Not particularly informative, you might think, but the specific name still serves a purpose in the sense that it distinguishes the brown bear from other species of bears such as for example *Ursus Americanus*, the American black bear.

Names like this clearly have their own intrinsic meaning, but quite a few names of species are in fact almost arbitrary, like the ones that were constructed from the name of the discoverer or some place. They may be modern and non-Latin in origin but they must still always have a Latin form. An example is the group of plants called *woodsia* in English. This is the Latin name derived from the name of the nineteenth-century British botanist Joseph Woods, who first identified the plant. One species of this plant, called in English the Rusty or Fragrant Woodsia, has as its Latin name *Woodsia ilvensis*. The specific name is an adjective meaning 'coming from Elba', which we presume is where he first identified it. This species is slightly different from the Northern Woodsia, which is called *Woodsia alpina* in Latin.

These examples are enough to show how the Latin names are constructed. Formally they are always Latin words with correct Latin endings. Sometimes the word stems also come from Latin, but very often they are Greek, and not infrequently from a completely different language. There are even a few words which are sheer nonsense and do not mean anything at all. But whatever the source of the individual words, in the domains of botany and zoology Latin is a language which guarantees that the terminology is correct and consistent. The system which Linnaeus introduced has turned out to be so good that it does not just live on but is continuously being extended and added to. For Linnaeus, as we have seen, it was a matter of course to use Latin for his names, as it was the only scientific language available in his day. Latin may have disappeared from most other sciences, but when it comes to the naming of species it is most probably going to stay for the foreseeable future. There is simply nothing else that works as well.

Physicists, chemists, and others

Arithmetic, geometry, and astronomy were three of the *artes liberales* which formed part of the curriculum in the Middle Ages.

For a long time this involved nothing more than handing on a portion of the knowledge that had been acquired in classical times. It was not until the thirteenth century that an interest in more advanced mathematics and physics was rekindled, and the truly spectacular advances only came in the seventeenth century. The greatest upheaval took place in astronomy. The Greeks and Romans in fact knew a great deal about celestial phenomena and obviously had names for what they saw. Even today we still use the same names the Romans used for the planets Mercury, Venus, Mars, Jupiter, Saturn, all of which are names of the Roman gods. The three planets which have been discovered in modern times have likewise been named after other Roman gods: Uranus, Neptune, and Pluto. The ancients also grouped the stars into constellations to which they gave names, and many of these are still in use today such as Leo ('lion') and Gémini ('twins').

In antiquity everyone thought that the earth was the centre of the universe, and that the sun, the moon, and all the other celestial bodies revolved around it. Careful observation and precise mathematical calculation gradually led to the conclusion that it was the earth that orbited the sun rather than vice versa. This idea, first developed by Copernicus in the early sixteenth century, was set against the traditional, so-called geocentric view in a famous book, *Dialogue Concerning the Two Chief World Systems,* published by the Italian astronomer Galileo Galilei in 1632. As is well known, this book caused a furore. The Church declared Galileo's views to be heretical, and he had to spend the rest of his life under house arrest.

One of the reasons why Galileo was dangerous from the Church's point of view had to do with language. He did not always write in Latin, as almost all other scholars did at that time. His *Dialogue* is written in Italian, and moreover in a relatively accessible style, exploiting, as the title indicates, the then popular dialogue form in which the argument is presented as a conversation between advocates of the two opposing positions. He was read by many people, even outside the universities. When ordinary people in Italy were able to read things that went against the claims of the Church, the Pope and his men struck hard, and prohibited the book's circulation. That did not help in the long run. The book was soon known all over Europe. It was speedily translated into Latin and became accessible to educated people everywhere.

The fact that the translation was made shows that Latin was still the most important language of science at that time. On the other hand Galileo heralded a new era precisely by writing in his own language. The great mathematicians, physicists, and astronomers who continued the scientific revolution after Galileo often published their writings both in their native language and in Latin. We have already mentioned the philosopher Descartes, who wrote both in French and in Latin, as did Leibniz, who in addition sometimes used his native language, German. The greatest of them all, Isaac Newton, wrote in both English and Latin. One of the things he used Latin for was his most famous book, about gravitation, *Philosophiae naturalis principia mathemática* 'Mathematical Principles of Natural Philosophy', which was published in 1687. After his time it became increasingly unusual for important works in physics and mathematics to be written in Latin, though one of the most famous mathematical treatises of the twentieth century—the *Principia Mathematica* (1910) by Whitehead and Russell—does at least retain Latin in the title as a homage to Newton's masterpiece. The transition to national languages came much earlier within these subjects than in medicine and biology, where it is still not complete, as we have seen. There are likely to have been several reasons for this.

By writing in Italian Galileo set an example to his successors. Moreover these subjects did not have the same solid tradition in the universities as medicine. New ideas developed very rapidly, and the people who were engaged in developing them were probably some-what more revolutionary and correspondingly less respectful of tradition. But above all they were eager to have a wide readership and not just amongst academics at universities. This was obviously even more the case with people who were concerned with practical applications of mathematics and physics, from surveyors to statisticians and mechanical engineers. These disciplines did not traditionally belong in universities, and a good deal of technology and applied science was developed in other parts of the community by people who had little or no knowledge of Latin. Not surprisingly, therefore, we find very little in these domains which is written in Latin.

Chemistry is different again. During antiquity and the Middle Ages interest was largely confined to what was called alchemy, which we will look at in more detail in the next section. Modern chemistry did not really come into existence until the eighteenth century, when people began to understand the nature of combustion, and it became clear that there was a set of elements out of which all other compounds are made. The founder of this new science was Antoine Laurent de Lavoisier, who published pioneering work in the 1780s. By that date Latin's time as the language of scholarship was more or less over, and Lavoisier only wrote in his native language, French. One of his famous works is called *Méthode de nomenclature chimique*, 'Method of Scientific Nomenclature', which provided the foundation for the language of chemistry.

Chemistry, then, came onto the scene so late that Latin was never really relevant. The same goes for most applied science and for a number of other disciplines, such as economics, which in its modern form starts more or less in the eighteenth century. In these fields modern scientists have few or no predecessors who wrote in Latin. But that certainly does not mean that Latin is not found within these areas. On the contrary, a great many of the terms which are used come from Latin or from Greek via Latin, even within these subjects and within many others which the Greeks and the Romans had no conception of, and which did not exist in the medieval universities. The reason lies in the need for a special terminology. Within all sciences and technical subjects new terms are continually needed for concepts or topics which nobody has spoken or written about before. Latin provides a ready supply of such terms which are conveniently different from those which are used in everyday language. The creators of these terms like words with an old and distinguished ring to them and prefer to borrow word parts from Latin and Greek rather than from their own language. This process is still going on today, and we can usefully look in a bit more detail about the way it happens. First, however, a word about magic and related matters.

Alchemy, witchcraft, and Harry Potter

Although chemistry in its modern form appeared as late as a few hundred years ago, it had an important precursor that stemmed from antiquity. The ancient Egyptians possessed remarkable skills in metalwork, and the Greeks could never quite figure out their secret procedures. Many tried, though, and this seems to have constituted the beginnings of the very long tradition of alchemy. A main object-ive was to produce gold from less valuable substances, obviously a potentially profitable business. There was nothing absurd in the idea itself as long as the basic difference between elements and other substances had not been made clear, which did not happen until around 1800. The Greeks in Hellenistic times invested a great deal of time and energy on this question, and while they were naturally never able to reach their ultimate goal, they learnt plenty about the properties of chemical substances and their reactions along the way. However, the attitude of people who worked in this field was very different from that of other Greek natural scientists. They believed that their art was inspired by ancient gods or famous figures from the distant past, such as Moses or the Pharaoh Cheops, and they included in their work ideas from astrology, common superstition, and a variety of other sources. From the beginning, then, alchemy was a rather ill-behaved cousin of science.

The alchemist tradition was not much pursued by the Romans, and these ideas were carried into medieval Europe along the same route as the philosophy of Aristotle, via the Arabs. Around 1200 there appeared a number of Latin treatises on alchemy, containing the precepts of famous Arab specialists. From that time on, alchemy became part and parcel of the intellectual heritage of Europe. Many famous men spent time on it, including individuals of the stature of

Thomas Aquinas, Roger Bacon, and Isaac Newton. However, real progress was minimal.

The main goal remained to find a way of making gold, but the means to reach it was seen more and more to be the possession of a mystic substance that could effect that transformation and also possessed other extraordinary powers such as conferring eternal life. This substance was given many names in Latin, which was the language of most treatises on alchemy: for example, it was called *lapis philosophi* 'the philosopher's stone' or *magisterium* 'mastery, control'. It was repeatedly rumoured that someone had found the stone and/or had made gold, but as no such rumour ever turned out to be true, the reputation of alchemy eventually waned.

The founders of modern chemistry in the late eighteenth century did not use Latin, as we have already discussed. In addition to the obvious fact that the language was already in retreat at this time, an additional reason may well have been that in this way they severed any connection with alchemy, which was mainly embodied in thousands of Latin texts.

While alchemy can be seen as wayward science, magic is for many an aberrant form of religion. It was much in favour in Rome from the very beginning, or so it seems. Cato in his book about agriculture included tips for handling various situations. One concerns what to do about a sprain or a fracture: one part of the treatment is to chant a spell: *Motas uaeta daries dardares astaries dissunapiter.* The words look a little like Latin, in fact the first one is a genuine Latin word meaning 'moved', but the whole thing is just meaningless gibberish. Or rather, it has no meaning for the uninitiated, whereas the powers to which it is addressed are supposed to understand it very well. In this way, magic words may be even more meaningful than ordinary ones. Cato's spell does not seem to have prospered, but over the centuries some magic words and phrases occur again and again in various texts. A couple of familiar ones are *abracadabra*, known already from Greek and Latin antiquity, and *hocus pocus*, first attested in the sixteenth century.

Pronouncing magic words is one of the chief activities of wizards (*magi* in Latin), who practise the art of magic or *ars magica*. Ancient

Latin literature is full of references to wizards and witches, who could sometimes heal people but who could also put spells on them so that they became ill or even died. They sometimes used herbs and concoctions, but in other cases just uttered the appropriate magic words. Some of them were also able to transfigure living creatures. The only complete novel in Latin from antiquity that is preserved bears the title *Metamorphoses,* and the plot is about a young man, Lucius, who is transformed into an ass by an evil witch. The work is replete with accounts of all sorts of sorcery; its author, Apuleius, was reputed to be a magician himself.

The magical powers were seen to be connected in different ways with fabulous creatures such as werewolves and dragons, who were usually evil, as well as centaurs and unicorns, who were beneficial. The whole sphere of magic is interwoven with themes from fable and myth, so that it is not always easy to say what should be called magic and what is merely fanciful storytelling.

With the rise of Christianity, the practitioners of witchcraft met with fierce hostility. The Christian authorities believed that miracles could only be performed by true Christians and in the name of Christ. Supernatural events of other kinds could only emanate from the Devil. In principle, the Christian Church did not accept any witchcraft at all. This did not prevent people from believing in wizardry and practising it throughout the history of Europe. Over the centuries, new ideas were added to those inherited from antiquity. An important source was old Celtic lore, which became popular all over Europe from the twelfth century and on. It was transmitted to a larger public through the already mentioned *Historia regum Britanniae* by the Welshman Geoffrey of Monmouth, a work in which the wizard Merlin occupies an important place.

In practice, for long periods the church authorities were to some degree tolerant of witchcraft, but the fifteenth century saw the beginning of the era of the great witch hunts: thousands of people, mainly women, were burned as witches and allies of the powers of evil. The ideological basis for this activity was a book called *Malleolus maleficarum* 'The witch-hammer', written by two members of the papal Inquisition. But even such cruelty on the part of the churches could not eradicate the popular belief in magic. Interest in the magical arts persisted.

In more recent times, advances in science and a general trend toward rationalism have eroded some of the support for magic. Those who deal in it often combine it with ideas from alchemy, astrology, and other disciplines that have been relegated from the sphere of respectable science and scholarship. However, it would be a great mistake to conclude that magic is no longer of interest.

A proof to the contrary is the astonishing success of the Harry Potter books. To date, five volumes have been published, and literally hundreds of millions of copies have been sold. The author of the books, J. K. Rowling, has studied Latin, and it is worth having a look at how she makes use of that knowledge in her books. It even has some significance for the general status of the language, for very few books with any Latin in them have reached anything like this number of people. On the title page of each book there is a coat of arms with the motto *Draco dormiens nunquam titillandus*, which is perfectly good Latin and means 'A sleeping dragon should never be tickled'. The Latin phrase and the blazon evoke thoughts about the medieval roots of wizardry and of Hogwarts School, where most of the action takes place. Within the books, there is not a lot of Latin, but it is used in a very special way.

Several of the characters have first names that are Latin words which hint at their qualities. Albus ('White') Dumbledore is a pure spirit and a force for good, while Draco ('Dragon') Malfoy and Severus ('Strict') Snape come across as mean and unpleasant; Sirius ("Dogstar") Black sometimes appears in the guise of a large black dog. The names convey a secret message to those who know some Latin.

Mainly, though, the language is used for magic. The spells and curses that abound are often in Latin. Several are ordinary Latin verbs with the ending *-o*, denoting first person, such as *Accio!* 'I summon!' or *Reparo!* 'I repair' (used to mend a broken piece of china or a pair of glasses). Others are nouns, such as *Impedimenta!* 'Impediments' when something is to be obstructed, or adjectives such as *Impervius!* 'Impervious' (to make Harry's spectacles repel water). There are even some short sentences, such as *Expecto Patronum* 'I wait for the Patronus', where a Patronus is a benevolent power with a Latin name. But many spells, such as *Reducio!* (used to shrink a spider), look like Latin forms, but actually are not. This one is obviously connected with the English word 'reduce', and ulti- mately with the Latin word *reduco*; but that means 'I lead back', which does not fit the sense of the spell. So this spell is pseudo-Latin, really based on English.

As a matter of fact, the spells, whether in Latin or pseudo-Latin, are usually more or less understandable for an imaginative reader who knows English (and preferably a little French). They are made up from word stems that are found in Latin as well as English, and some Latin ending is attached. For example, the spell to disarm your opponent is *Expelliarmus!*, which contains Latin *expelli*/English 'expel', Latin *arma*/English 'arms', and the Latin ending *-us*. The Latin in the Harry Potter novels, then, turns out to be mostly English in disguise. The author's purpose seems to be the same as that of old Cato, to use magical words that provide suitable associa- tions but are not actually fully understandable. There are two good reasons to use Latin in this way. In the first place, it remains a lan- guage of prestige, especially in the context of arcane knowledge found in old books. Secondly, Latin word stems are mostly more or less understandable to speakers of English. This last fact is a very interesting one, which brings us back from the murky realm of sor- cery to the general influence of Latin in modern life, an important aspect of which is that English and other European languages clearly contain thousands of Latin words.

Loanwords and neologisms

English and all the other modern European languages have many words that come from Latin and from Greek via Latin. They have entered the language at different times and via different routes. You might think that most of these words would have come in a long time ago when more people spoke Latin, but in fact the opposite is true. In the last hundred years or so we have taken in more words from this source than ever before. If anything, the rate seems to be increasing rather than decreasing.

Do we want our digital TV channels via satellite or via cable? That is a question of current interest in the year 2004. Twenty years ago there was no digital broadcasting, fifty years ago there were no satellites, and a hundred years ago we did not even have the word *television*. The whole question would have been completely incomprehensible a century ago, but the words with which it is framed would have been partly understood by anyone who had learnt Latin.

Digital is formed from the Latin word *digitus* 'finger', which had over time acquired the secondary meaning 'digit', as witness the English word *digit* which is a loan from Latin and which only has the secondary sense. The link here is obviously the fact that we use our fingers for counting. A digital transmission involves transmitting ones and noughts instead of continuously changing waves. The word *television* consists of the stem of the Latin word *vísio* 'sight' prefixed by the Greek word *tele* 'far away, distant'. The word *satellite* was quite uncommon in English before the 1950s, being used used only by astronomers for the moons which orbit some of the planets and by the odd science fiction writer. Since we have managed to launch objects into space and make them orbit the earth, the term, which comes from Latin *satelles* (*satéllitis* in the genitive) meaning 'attendant', has been charged with a new meaning.

All the key terms in our question have their origins in Latin. The same goes for the word *channel*. This has existed in English for many hundred years, but actually it originally comes from Latin *canalis* via French (as opposed to *canal*, which comes directly from Latin). The giveaway here is the initial *cha* as opposed to *ca*. Many Latin words which began *ca* were changed in Old French so that they had the initial sound which we spell *ch*. In many cases it is the French form which ends up in English, e.g. *chapel, chart, chapter* beside

Latin *capella* 'chapel', *charta* 'document', *capitulum* 'heading', but sometimes we end up with both as in the case of *channel* and *canal*, or *enchant* beside *incantation*, both, from *in* 'in' + *cantare* 'sing'.

It's the same in field after field. If you are on a diet and are careful about your intake of proteins and calories, you are also using ancient words in disguise. *Diaeta* 'manner of living as prescribed by a physician' is an old Latin medical term which originally comes from Greek. The word 'calorie' was created at the beginning of the nineteenth century from the Latin word *calor* 'heat', in the first place as a unit for measuring energy. The word *protein* has been formed from a Greek word *proteion* 'the beginning' and a Latin suffix,-*in*, which is found in many names for substances. The great Swedish chemist Jons Jacob Berzelius seems to have been the first to use this term in the 1830s to refer to a class of substances which are of vital importance in living organisms. The word exists in all major European languages (and probably in many other languages too), where in one sense it could be seen as a loanword from Swedish. It belongs to a large group of modern scientific words which, once coined, spread rapidly from country to country, and which are truly international, simply because the word stems are from Latin or Greek and not from any of the languages which are spoken today.

Quite a few words of this kind have become so common in everyday usage that they have been abbreviated beyond recognition. A *bus* takes its name from the Latin word *omnibus* which means 'for all'. It would have seemed a very strange way to abbreviate the word to a Roman, since -*ibus* is the case ending of the dative plural and was shared by literally thousands of words in the language. A bicycle has two wheels, so the name *bi-* 'two' -*cycle* 'rotation' is transparent, but that transparency is lost in the abbreviated form *bike*. A recent coining in English is *burb*, used first as an abbreviation of *suburb* and later to mean a region or a space, especially on the internet, where numerous special interest groups have established burbs to exchange news and thoughts. *Suburb* is a transparent Latinism from *sub* 'under' and *urbs* 'city', but the truncated form *burb* adds the last consonant of the prefix to the stem to create an entirely opaque form that can then itself be prefixed, as in the 1980s coinage *technoburb*.

Once the need arises, such abbreviations often catch on very fast. A recent example is *mobile telephone*, which literally means something like 'moving distant sound' (*phone* means 'sound' in Greek). But the expression is long, and practically nobody says anything more than *mobile* nowadays.

These are just a few examples of the thousands of modern words in English which come from Latin or Greek. It would take a pretty large book to list them all. Anyone who is interested in the origin of a given word can look it up in the etymological dictionaries. If you do not know the ancient languages, it can often be difficult to work out the origin of a word, but there are certain characteristics which can give you a clue. Loans from Latin very often start with a prefix, like *in-* 'in-', *de-* 'from', *ex-* 'out', and *con-* 'with', so it is easy to see that words like *consume* or *industry* come from Latin. And very often they end with a suffix that derives from Latin such as *-(at)ion*, *-ant* or *-ent*, and *-(at)or*: e.g. *explosion, gestation, mutant, absorbent, vector, generator*, and many more. Words that come from Greek can sometimes be recognized by sounds or combinations of sounds which are not common in Latin or in English. Foreign words which contain *y* or start with *ps* often come from Greek, like *psychology* (the study of the *psyke* 'mind, soul'), or *analysis* from *ana* 'up' and *lysis* 'detaching'. (Interestingly, in English we use the other end of the scale when we talk of breaking something *down* into its constituent parts.) They can also be recognized by prefixes like *epi-* 'on', *en-* 'in', or *peri-* 'around', as in *epigraphic, entropy* or *periphery*.

You can find out quite a bit about the background of English words by studying the list of Latin words at the back of this book, where I have included many of the most common word stems and prefixes and suffixes. If you want to acquire a more detailed understanding of how words are formed, there are handbooks on the subject, but to consult these you will also have to learn the fundamentals of Latin properly and preferably also quite a bit of Greek.

So far we have talked about all the modern European languages together, but there are in fact interesting differences between them in the way they adopt loanwords, as will emerge in the next section.

Latin and German

Whereas English in general has been fairly susceptible to borrowing foreign words of all kinds and hence has adopted modern scientific terminology in something very close to the original Latin and Greek form, other languages have often been more resistant, and have resorted to coining words for the new concepts from their own resources. Where English has *television* German has *Fernsehen*, which is made up of *fern* 'far' and *sehen* 'see'. Nonetheless the structure of the German word is copied from the structure of its Greco-Latin model. This process is known as loan translation or calquing. Another domain where we can see the same process at work is in the names of the basic scientific elements. In English we have *oxygen* and *hydrogen*, which have been taken over directly from the French names coined by Lavoisier. The first parts are Greek roots meaning 'acid' and 'water' respectively and *-gen* means 'give birth, produce' (as in *generate, congenital,* etc.). In German the names follow the same idea, but using native ingredients: *Sauerstoff* 'acid material' and *Wasserstoff* 'water material'.

All of which is not to say that German does not have any scientific Latin and Greek loans. For example, the first part of *nitrogen* can be used as a prefix as in the name of the explosive *nitroglycerine* and for this purpose German too uses *nitro-*, whence *Nitroglyzerin*. And the German for 'molecule' is *Molekül*, from Latin *molécula* 'small mass'. German too, like most other European languages, has its share of more specialist vocabulary derived from Latin such as mathematical concepts like *Summe* 'sum', *Prozent* 'percent', or terms of politics and administration like *Nation* 'nation', *Kanzler* 'Chancellor', and *Kongress* 'congress'.

Less immediately detectable are the words that entered German during or immediately after the imperial period. We have already seen how *Kaiser*, the German word for 'emperor', is simply the name *Caesar* preserved in something very close to its original pronunciation. Other German words that stem from this era are *Keller* 'cellar' and *Kirsche* 'cherry'. They, too, preserve the [k] pronunciation of the original Latin words *cellárium* and *cerásea*. In fact, this pronunciation of very early loanwords into German proves very nicely that the Romans of antiquity must have pronounced such words with an initial [k]. In other instances German has the sound [ts], as in *Zelle* 'cell' from Latin *cella* and *Zins* 'tax', from Latin *census* 'register, census' (since the compiling of a register of the population was a necessary concomitant of the levying of taxes). This suggests that these words came into the language at a somewhat later period, when the change from [k] to [ts] had already taken place.

The Roman presence in Germany can be traced too in the etymologies of place names. Augustus conducted military campaigns in the area and sought to reorganize its administrative boundaries. Settlements established in his time often had the word *Augusta* as the first part of their name. This has survived in different forms as in the Swiss village of Augst, the Italian city of Aosta, or the first part of German Augsburg, which was earlier called Augusta Vindelicorum, literally 'the Augustan city of the Vindelici'. Another similarly named town, Augusta Treverorum, instead lost the first part of its name to become modern Trier. An emperor might also name a settlement after a member of his family, as when Claudius founded a colony of veterans and called it Colonia Agrippinensis after his wife, Agrippina. Her name has, however, been erased by history and the modern place is simply called Köln. In English we call this city Cologne, which is the French version of the Latin name for a German town!

Latin and French

The origin of the French language is Latin, so you might think that anyone who has mastered Latin would be able to recognize all the words in French. This is not so. First, all languages have a certain turnover of words: some words lose their currency, and new ones enter the language either as loanwords from other languages or as newly created words. Second, the original words change gradually, both in form and meaning, so that in the end it may be difficult or impossible to recognize them.

In French some very significant sound changes have taken place since the time of Latin, and as a result the French words are much more different from their Latin ancestors than are their counterparts in Spanish and Italian. For instance 'sing' is *cantare* in Latin, *cantare* in Italian, *cantar* in Spanish, but *chanter* in French. The word for 'night' is *noctem* (the accusative) in Latin, *notte* in Italian, *noche* in Spanish, and *nuit* in French. The word for 'father' is *patrem* (the accusative) in Latin, *padre* in Italian and Spanish, and *père* in French. If you know French, you will notice that the spelling of the words more closely reflects the Latin sounds than the pronunciation does. For one thing there is an *-r* in *chanter*, a *-t* in *nuit* and an *-e* in *père* only in the spelling, not in the pronunciation. Those final sounds were heard when the present French spelling system was introduced several hundred years ago, but they are no longer pronounced.

French words that have come directly from Latin have managed to change so much that specialist knowledge is often needed in order to be able to see the connection. But French is nevertheless full of words which are very much like Latin words. An example is the word *cantique*, which means 'canticle' and comes from the Latin *canticum* 'song' (it is mainly used about religious hymns, and about the Song of Songs in the Bible). Similarly, the word *nocturne*, literally meaning 'nocturnal, by night' from the Latin *nocturnum*, which has the same meaning. And the French *paternel* 'fatherly, paternal' comes from the Latin *paternalem* and also has not changed its meaning.

You might conclude that sound changes only affect some words and not others, since the same stem in Latin can lead to completely different results: *noct-* becomes *nui(t)* in one word but remains unchanged in another. But it is not like that. Sound changes in a language generally affect all the words in a language. The true explanation must therefore be sought elsewhere, namely in the fact that words like *nocturne* and *cantique* have not existed in French right from the beginning. In particular, they were not part of French at all during the many centuries when the sound changes took place.

Where did they come from? Well, they were obviously borrowed from Latin, which was the language of the educated. French has great numbers of words which have been adopted as loans from the scholarly Latin of many different periods, from as early as the twelfth century and right down to our own day. Those words have not undergone the sound changes from Latin to French, but have by and large preserved their Latin form. Often these words also exist in English in a very similar form.

This difference between original words and later loans from Latin is important for everybody who studies French thoroughly. The French call a word like *nocturne* a *mot savant* 'learned word', whereas a word like *père* is a *mot populaire* 'popular word'. The learned words can often be recognized from English or from other modern European languages or from Latin, since they belong to Europe's common international vocabulary. As far as the popular, inherited words are concerned, it is only sometimes possible to associate them with a word in other languages.

Even so, French learned words did not completely turn out like the Latin ones. In some cases French uses its own endings. Consider for instance the French word *importer*, which is obviously a learned word that comes from the Latin *importare* 'to matter'. As you can see the French infinitive ending *-er* has been added to the word. In Italian, by contrast, the word has preserved the form *importare*. A case like this shows how the Latin words can be made to seem more French, and there are many more examples. What happened in French had a certain impact on most European languages, as French had a great influence. But today it is English which is the most influential language, and, in some respects at least, it has other ways of dealing with Latin words.

Latin and English

English was a written language already in the seventh century, but the oldest English texts cannot be understood by someone who only knows modern English. One of the reasons is that the vocabulary was very different. In the beginning English was a purely Germanic language, and contained very few loans from other languages. Many of those old Germanic words have now disappeared, or have changed so much that it is no longer possible to recognize them.

After 1066 the situation changed completely. William the Conqueror and his French-speaking Normans occupied the country. The only written languages they used were Latin and French, and they took over important functions in society including the ownership of most of the big estates. For several centuries French was the common spoken language among all the rich and powerful people in England (and to a lesser extent in Wales and Scotland). English was the spoken language of the masses, but it was hardly used in writing at all.

By the fifteenth century English had once again become the spoken language for almost everyone, and it had broken through as a written language in many domains. But during the centuries when French was dominant, English had changed radically. Among other things a large number of all kinds of words were adopted from French, both learned words that had come quite recently from Latin and 'popular' words. Furthermore, English borrowed lots of words directly from Latin, which was the language of the learned even in Britain. Learned loans from Latin and Greek continued to enter the language in the following centuries, with the result that English has gradually developed a very large vocabulary. The Germanic words, which have been in the language since the beginning, are now just a small minority of all the words in an English dictionary. The words that come from Latin or Greek, either directly or via French, are the great majority. Estimates vary between three quarters and nine tenths. At most the original Germanic words constitute no more than about twenty per cent.

English is a Germanic language which mainly consists of words that are not Germanic. Certainly the most common words—such as *have, sister, come,* and *go*—are usually Germanic and resemble the corresponding item in German or the Scandinavian languages. But the majority have been borrowed during the last thousand years. This state of affairs has many advantages. One of them is that there are many opportunities to vary the language with synonyms and to express fine distinctions with different words. Quite often there is a Germanic and a Latin or a French word for approximately the same thing. We have pairs such as the following, where the first is Germanic and the second is Latin: *get/obtain, come/arrive, warder/guard, hug/embrace,* and many more. The implications of this circumstance should probably not be exaggerated, since there are other ways of creating words with similar meanings in languages like French and German; but there is no doubt that English has ended up with a very rich stock of words as a result of its history.

Sometimes the learned words from Latin are identical in their written form in English and French (although the pronunciation is almost always more or less different). In both languages we have *influence,* from a medieval Latin word, *influentia,* which has exactly the same meaning as the English and the French words. This in turn is made up of *in-* 'in' and *fluere* 'flow', so an influence is something that literally flows into one place from another.

However, for the most part the French and the English forms differ to some extent. The French word *importer,* for instance, corresponds to English *import.* This reflects a general difference: the English verbs do not have an equivalent of the Latin ending and are therefore shorter than the French ones. We find *permit* and *inform* in English, but *permettre* and *informer* in French beside *permíttere* and *informáre* in Latin. This difference derives from the fact that French verbs are conjugated in many forms precisely as in Latin and to a large extent with endings that have been inherited from Latin. 'We permit' for example is *nous permettons* in French, with a verb form which is relatively similar to the Latin equivalent *permittimus*. In English there are many fewer verb endings, and they have nothing to do with Latin. In other words, when English borrows, it borrows the stem but not the ending.

The English words that come from Latin obviously belong to several word classes. Latin has a verb *admirári*, which becomes *admire* in English. The adjective *admirábilis* becomes *admirable*, and the noun *admirátio* becomes *admiration*, and it is easy to see that the Latin adjective and noun have been formed from the verb. In English there are thousands of adjectives and nouns that have been formed in a similar way. That applies to most of the words that end in *-ion* and *-ble*. Some random examples are *presentation, combination, delegation, probable, considerable, notable*.

These patterns have become so common in English that an ending like *-able* can now be added to other stems than the Latin ones. There are words like *likeable*, which has been formed from the English *like* and the ending *-able*. There are even instances where *-able* has been added to a whole phrase, as when we say a novel is *unputdownable* or a place is *ungetatable*. Such words cannot be called loanwords, since the stem is English, but they are not domestic either since the ending is from Latin. They represent a new resource which English has developed through its numerous loans, which have created a model for the indigenous words to follow.

Latin and us

The first part of this book deals with Latin as the native language of the Romans, a function which it served for slightly more than a millennium. It became the vehicle of a culture which in various ways was superior to everything that had preceded it, and which still fascinates many of us two thousand years later.

There are not many people left today who see the ancient Romans as models, which is perhaps just as well, but in many ways they are our immediate predecessors, both for good and for evil. At the same time their world is so remote from ours that much of it remains strange, even alien to us. Ancient Rome bears some similarities to today's New York, Washington, or Paris, but in other respects it is more like the Tenochtitlán of the Aztecs. Yet we can trace most of our institutions, ways of thinking, and cultural traditions back to Rome. Like it or not, we will always have a link with antiquity, and it is primarily the Latin language which allows us to investigate that aspect of our heritage should we choose to do so.

The second part of the book is about the Europe which had Latin as its common language. The language was no longer anyone's native language, but instead it acquired other functions. For several centuries it was more than anything the language of the victorious Christian religion, and it retained that status for a very long time. But at the same time Latin represented a link back to antiquity and its non-Christian world, which was a source of knowledge and skills otherwise unknown in the later period. Little by little, religion and the Church became less dominant. A new tradition of thinking and literature and science developed out of what had been written in Latin in antiquity, but that tradition gradually became more and more independent and turned into the new European way of thinking, writing, and conducting research. In the beginning Latin was almost the only language of that tradition. Writers gradually started using the new national languages, at first in imaginative literature, much later in philosophy and the increasing number of new sciences. Even so, within certain areas, such as botany and zoology, Latin is to some extent still used as a language of communication.

The history and cultural history of Europe after antiquity was written almost entirely in Latin until the thirteenth century, thereafter decreasingly so. In this way the European states have a very recent shared linguistic and cultural background. After antiquity

Latin was the international language which made it possible for western Europe to preserve and establish bonds right across the Continent. Although people stopped using spoken and written Latin in discipline after discipline, that did not mean that the language disappeared completely. The useful words, of which there were many, were transferred to the new languages. Their number is increasing, and they exist in most European languages and now also in many languages in other parts of the world.

Latin has, or has had, three distinct roles. It was the native language of the Romans in antiquity; it was Europe's international language until two or three hundred years ago; and it is the language from which the modern European languages have drawn the majority of their loanwords. That means that there are three good reasons for knowing something about Latin, and hopefully this book contains a little useful information about each of these areas. Some of you may even be inspired to go further and really learn the language. It takes time and a lot of effort, but it can be very rewarding.

So far we have almost only looked backwards, which is natural, as you mainly devote yourself to Latin if you are interested in history. But what does the future hold? Will knowledge of Latin and antiquity die? Or will the interest be revived? Might people start using Latin as a supranational language again? I have no answer to those questions. Personally I do not believe that people will go back to writing their memos or debating in Latin, even if it is not impossible that someone might suggest the idea. On the other hand, I do not believe either that interest in antiquity and the long history of Europe will disappear. And anyone who is really interested in those periods, which apart from a few centuries at the end constitute the whole of our history and culture to date, will have to learn Latin too. And that considerable portion of the world's population who speak a European language will have to use Latin words every day and every hour for as long as one can see into the future. That is how Latin will live on.

Part III
About the Grammar

Introduction

This part of the book offers a very brief survey of the grammar of Latin, or rather of those parts of the grammar which are different from English and present the English-speaking learner with difficulties. The idea is that, if you are interested, you will be able to identify the forms of the words that occur in this book and be able to understand how simple sentences are constructed in Latin. Most space is devoted to a short summary of the morphology of Latin, that is to say the rules for building words and the regular patterns of inflection. Inevitably many exceptions and irregular patterns, which do not occur in the passages cited in this book, have had to be left out. I have tried to make the treatment readable even for people who have not done much grammar before.

Pronunciation and stress

We have already covered the pronunciation of Latin sounds in antiquity at the beginning of the book (pp. 4–6). In the section entitled 'Speaking and spelling' (pp. 107–15) we dealt with pronunciation and spelling in the Middle Ages and after. Here I will look at some points which were not covered in the earlier discussion.

Right from the beginning Latin had five simple vowels: *i, e, a, o*, and *u*, each of which could be either long or short. By long and short we mean just that: an extra degree of phonetic length coupled with a small difference in the way the vowel is articulated, much as in the contrast between *bit* and *beat* in English. Something similar existed in Chaucer's time for all the pairs of vowels in English too, but changes since then mean we often apply the term 'long' to vowels which have substantially altered their phonetic quality and have become diphthongs. So people often talk of English *mane* having a long vowel and primary school teachers introduce their children to the magic 'e' which turns the short vowel in *man* into the long vowel of *mane*, when in fact phonetically the difference is between a short vowel [æ] and a diphthong [ei].

In principle the correct length has to be learnt for every vowel in every word, so Latin dictionaries usually have a small sign over each vowel. A small line over the vowel, technically called a *macron* (from the Greek word for 'large'), indicates a long vowel, e.g. *ā*, *ē*. A small semi-circle or *breve* (from the Latin word for 'short') over the vowel indicates a short vowel: *ă*, *ĕ*, *etc*. The word for 'woman' in the nominative case can be written *fēmĭnă*, while 'woman' in the ablative case is *fēmĭnā*. This notation, which is typographically rather untidy, is often used in Latin dictionaries and word lists, not least because pairs of words may difffer only as to the length of the vowel, as with *mālum* 'apple' beside *mălum* 'evil' or *ēdo* 'I give out' beside *ĕdo* 'I eat'.

There certainly are some contexts in which it is good to know exactly which vowels are long and which are short, one being the rules for assigning stress to Latin words. We have already mentioned that most Latin words have the stress on the second last syllable, which in Latin is called the *(syllaba) paenúltima*. But quite a few words are stressed on the syllable before the second last syllable, the *(syllaba) antepaenúltima*. The key rule is that the penultimate syllable is stressed if it is long; otherwise the stress falls on the antepenultimate syllable.

The rule then refers to the length of the penultimate syllable. If the vowel in a syllable is long, the syllable is also said to be long, so we need to know the length of the vowel. For example, the word *monstratus* has a long vowel in the penultimate syllable and is stressed *monstrátus*. However, if the vowel is short, things are a bit different. If a short vowel is followed by no more than one consonant, as in *civitas*, then the syllable is also short, and the stress falls on the preceding syllable: *cívitas*. But if the short vowel is followed by two or more consonants, the syllable is still long (in most cases). In *perfectus* the vowel in the penultimate syllable is short, but since it is followed by two consonants, the syllable is long and receives the stress: *perféctus*. There is a quite complex interconnection between the length of the vowels and the stress of the words. It is for this reason that I have chosen not to show vowel length in the word list at the back of this book but to indicate the position of the stress instead.

The other context where it is useful to know the length of the syllable is poetry. Ancient Latin poetry followed very strict metrical rules, but the rhythm is created not, as in English poetry, through an alternation between stressed and unstressed syllables but through an alternation between long and short syllables. In order to understand and appreciate the metre in a classical Latin poem, you have to learn which syllables are long and which are short in all words and in all positions, not just in the penultimate syllable. As we have seen, this means both knowing the length of the vowels and being able to apply the rules which determine syllablic length. This, however, is a topic which lies outside the scope of this book.

In teaching children to read—and, believe it or not, up until the mid-twentieth century in some British schools also to write—Latin verse, a technique called 'scansion' was used. This involves stressing the syllables which are long and which also are considered to have a so-called 'strong' position in the line. This can lead to words being stressed differently in poetry and in prose. Here, for example, is the first line of Virgil's *Aeneid* with its scansion indicated by the accent marks:

Árma virúmque canó, Troiáe qui primus ab óris . . .

The words *cano* and *Troiae* are stressed here on the last syllable, which does not accord with the normal rules for word stress in Latin.

How poetry really sounded in antiquity when the Romans read it aloud we do not know, but we do know that they could perceive differences between long and short vowels both in stressed and unstressed syllables. English speakers on the other hand often have difficulty maintaining differences in vowel quality in unstressed syllables, where vowels tend to be reduced to a short indiscriminate sound often called schwa.

Note that in this book I have not made any changes to reflect the practice of scansion. Even in the poetic passages which occur in the word list I have indicated the normal prose stress of a word.

Sentences, verbs, and nouns

Here is a simple Latin sentence:

Fémina amícum videt.

The woman sees the friend.

In Latin, as in English and other languages, a sentence usually contains a verb form and one or more nouns, with the nouns having different roles in relation to the verb. In this sentence it is the woman who sees, and her role is said to be that of subject, the one who carries out the activity indicated by the verb. The friend is called the object, the one who is the goal of the verb's activity. All sentences can be described in this way, and such descriptions make up the core of the grammar. One way of putting it is to say that each sentence constitutes a mini-drama, and grammar is the analysis of what happens in the play and how the roles are shared out amongst the actors.

When it is our own language, we mostly do not need to pay attention to the grammar, since we know what the sentences mean. However, when it comes to learning another language, where the means of showing the action and the actors are different from those we are used to, it is often very useful to learn the grammatical rules, at least to the extent that they differ from those we are familiar with. The Latin sentence we have been considering differs from its English translation in the order of the words. In the English the expected word order is 'subject-verb-object', but in Latin it is 'subject-object-verb'. This is part of a larger structural difference between the two languages. Although the subject comes first in both—contrast a language like Welsh, where the subject comes second—in Latin the verb follows everything else such as the object, the indirect object, and any expressions like *today* and *through the window*. In English, on the other hand, all these follow the verb. Compare:

Femina amicum per fenestram bene videt.

The woman sees the friend through the window well.

By the same principle, auxiliary verbs precede the main verb in English, so we say *The woman can see her friend,* but follow it in Latin, where the equivalent sentence would be *Femina amicum videre potest.* Of course both in Latin and in English there is quite a bit of freedom to move words around, usually in order to emphasize them, but in most cases things work according to this basic rule.

Another difference between Latin and English is that the roles and the action of the sentence in Latin are indicated by the endings of the words to a much greater extent than in English. Each noun consists of a stem and an ending, and the ending shows the role of the word in the sentence. Each verb also consists of a stem and an ending, with the ending, among other things, telling us who the subject is and the time of the action. In order properly to understand the meaning of a Latin sentence, therefore, it is essential to learn a large number of endings for nouns and verbs, and indeed for other classes of words such as adjectives and pronouns. It takes time, systematic training, and practice to handle these endings speedily and with confidence. In the remainder of this chapter I have given a synopsis of all the most common, regular forms. With the aid of this information and the word list at the back, the reader who wants to do so should be able to identify all the forms that occur in this book.

Words and word classes

Usually most of the words in a language are nouns, that is to say words for living creatures, things, or ideas like *homo* 'man', *mensa* 'table', or *amor* 'love'. The second biggest group is verbs, like *monstrare* 'to show' or *esse* 'to be'. The third main group is adjectives, which express properties like *bonus* 'good' or *brevis* 'short'. An adjective usually goes together with a noun. Nouns, verbs, and adjectives are the three most important word classes, and they are often called 'open' classes because there is no real limit to how many words there can be in each class. It is always possible to create new members of these classes if the need arises and if speakers show the required imagination. If you leaf through a word list or dictionary of any language, the majority of entries will be for words that belong to one of these classes. This means that any time you want to do anything with a Latin word, such as look it up in a dictionary or compare it to a modern word, you have to know something about how these word classes differ. In order to understand the meanings, you have to be able to recognize the forms. For this reason, I shall need to go into a bit of detail about the endings or inflections of these word classes in particular.

Not that they are the only ones. Other word classes include prepositions (*ad* 'to', *cum* 'with', etc.), pronouns (*ego* 'I', *qui* 'who, which', etc.) and adverbs, this last being a very mixed bag of words which mostly do not seem to fit into any of the other classes. These word classes contain relatively few members, apart that is from the kind of adverb which can be formed freely from almost any adjective (think of English *free, freely, happy, happily*, etc.). On the other hand, and not by chance, they are all very common words, for which you have to learn special rules if you are to be able to use them properly. Only a small selection of these rules are to be found in this book.

Nouns

In English nouns have different forms in the singular and the plural, for example *friend* in the singular and *friends* in the plural. In Latin it is the same, hence the singular *amicus* 'friend' beside the plural *amici* 'friends'. These grammatical terms in fact almost always come from Latin. The English words 'singular' and 'plural' come from the Latin terms *singuláris* and *plurális*. The former is connected with *síngulus* 'alone', which is also the origin of the word *single*. The word *pluralis* is related to *plus*, which means 'more'.

For singular and plural, then, both English and Latin use the same basic device to distinguish between the forms, namely endings, or suffixes, attached to the stem of the word. However, the English system is much less complex than the Latin one. In the first place, there are only endings in the plural, while the singular form consists just of the stem. In the second place, the plural ending is almost always *-s* or *-es*, as in *friend-s, ax-es*. The few exceptions, such as *ox-en*, are actually remnants of an earlier system, which was rather more like the Latin one. In Latin there is not just one plural ending, but a number of different ones. Moreover, there are endings in the singular too, so that a Latin noun almost always consists of a stem and an ending, and there are as many different endings for the singular as there are for the plural.

However, a given noun can only take one set of endings. There are five different sets of endings, also called declensions. One set is the group of words which behave like *femin-a* 'woman', *femin-ae* 'women' or *serv-a* 'female slave', *serv-ae* 'female slaves'. Latin has a number of such words which end in *-a* in the singular and *-ae* in the plural. This inflection class is called the first declension.

There are also a great many words which end in *-us* in the singular and *-i* in the plural: words like *amic-us* 'friend', *amic-i* 'friends' or *serv-us* 'slave', *serv-i* 'slaves', a pattern which is called the second declension.

So far the system bears some similarity to what we find in English. However, in Latin there are several more forms for each noun, which certainly creates difficulties when it comes to learning the language. The reason is that Latin nouns have different forms for the different roles in the sentence which we mentioned above. They are usually called 'cases', and English only has this sort of system to a very limited degree. The nearest we come to a separate case for every noun in English is in the expression of possession, where in principle each noun has a corresponding form with an -*s* attached. The spelling requires an apostrophe between the noun and the ending, *girl's*, but in the pronunciation the [s] sound is attached directly to the word stem, and the form of the noun thus created could be called the 'genitive' case as in *the girl's bicycle*, although the situation is complicated by examples like *the bishop of London's bicycle*, where the '*s* attaches to *London* and not *bishop*.

In Latin the ending always attaches directly to the noun it relates to, but things are complicated in a different way in that there are different genitive endings for each declension and number: *femina* 'woman', *feminae* 'woman's', *feminae* 'women', *feminarum* 'women's' and *amicus* 'friend', *amici* 'friend's', *amici* 'friends', *amicorum* 'friends''. There is no particular reason why the forms which mean 'woman's' and 'women' are exactly the same; it just happens to be that way, just as *sheep* in English is both singular and plural. This apart, you can see that there is a certain symmetry between the forms of *femina* and those of *amicus*, although unfortunately it is not perfect. If you want to know the forms, there is no alternative to learning the declension.

The genitive is generally used as in English to show that one noun qualifies another, for example *amicus feminae* 'the woman's friend' or *vita feminarum* 'the life of women'.

We have now seen so many forms for each word that it is possible to make a table for each declension, as we have done in Table 1 (below). In the table the stem is in plain type and the ending in bold. You can see that in fact there are not just forms for two cases but for five different ones. Since there is a singular and a plural form for each case, that in turn means ten different forms for each noun.

The case form which I have indicated as the basic form of the nouns, for example *femina* and *amicus*, is called the nominative. This is used for the subject of the sentence, which is normally the doer or agent of the action, so *femina videt* means 'the woman sees' and *amicus videt* 'the friend sees'.

A third case is called the accusative, and the endings are most often -*m* in the singular and -*s* in the plural (see Table 1). The accusative indicates the object of the verb, that is the person or thing which receives or is the goal of the action. An example is *femina amicum videt* 'the woman sees the friend'. In this sentence *femina* is the nominative and *amicum* the accusative. To say the opposite you have to change the cases, for example, *amicus feminam videt* means 'the friend sees the woman'.

The difference between the nominative (the case of the subject) and the accusative (the case of the object) also exists in English, but not for ordinary nouns, only for a small group of words called personal pronouns, such as *I* and *we*. Forms like *the woman* and *the friend* can be both subject and object, but *I* and *we* can only be the subject. The object form of *I* is *me* and of *we*, *us*, precisely as the object form of *amicus* is *amicum*. One says *I see the friend* but *The friend sees me*.

In Latin there are even more cases. The dative is used for what is called the indirect object. An example is: *femina amico viam monstrat* 'the woman shows the friend the way'. The form *amico* is in the dative. In the translation I have just given, the corresponding English is simply the expression *the friend*, but it is also possible to say 'the woman shows the way to the friend', where the dative is translated by the preposition *to*. Elsewhere the best English translation is *for*: *femina amico togam emit* 'the woman buys her friend a toga' or 'buys a toga for her friend'. It is often like that when you translate from Latin (or indeed from any other language). A particular pattern in Latin, here the dative case, does not just have one corresponding pattern in English; you may have to choose between several alternatives. Different languages work in different ways and exact translation is not always possible.

This is even more true when we come to the remaining case, the ablative, since that can be used for an even wider variety of functions. The most common use is after certain prepositions, such as *in* 'in, on' and *cum* 'with', for example *in via* 'on the road', *cum amico* 'with a friend'. But it is also used to express a means or an instrument, for instance *femina digito viam monstrat* 'the woman shows the way with her finger' in which *digito* 'with (her) finger' is the ablative. It can also be used to indicate time, as in *anno Domini* 'in the year of our Lord' where *anno* is in the ablative and *Domini* is in the genitive.

So far we have mentioned two declensions but there are in fact three more, making a total of five. The third declension is very common, as are the first and the second, whereas the fourth and the fifth are only used for a very few words each. The safest way to find out which declension a word belongs to is to look at the form of the genitive singular, and that form is therefore mentioned for each word in the word list. Starting from the genitive you can search in the tables to find any other form, as we shall see. Before that though a word about another nominal category, gender.

Latin is like languages such as French and German and unlike English in that each noun has its own intrinsic gender. The Latin term for this is *genus*, which can mean either 'family' or 'sort, kind'. In Latin there are three genders, which are traditionally called *masculínum* 'masculine', *femininum* 'feminine', and *néutrum* 'neuter'. There is some link with meaning in that most, but not all, words denoting males are masculine and similarly most words for females are feminine. Etymologically, 'neuter' means 'neither the one nor the other', and indeed most words that are neuter refer to inanimate things such as *lac* 'milk' and *ebur* 'ivory' and abstract concepts such as *bellum* 'war' and *nomen* 'name'. However, the word *animal* 'animal' is also neuter, and many, perhaps most, words that refer to objects and ideas are either masculine (e.g. *gladius* 'sword', *sol* 'sun') or feminine (e.g. *machina* 'machine', *luna* 'moon'), so most of the time the gender of a word is just an arbitrary fact about it which has to be learnt. That is why dictionaries for languages like Latin, French, or German always indicate a noun's gender.

Similarly, the word list at the back of this book shows the gender for each noun. This is needed for a number of reasons. The pronoun a word is replaced with depends on gender, very much as in English, where the word *girl* is replaced by *she* or *her* and *boy* by *he* or *him*. Adjectives also vary their inflection according to the gender of the noun they go with, a pattern which we do not have in English but which readers who know French, Spanish, or Italian will readily recognize. We have *luna magna* 'large moon' but *sol magnus* 'large sun'. Nouns which are neuter are declined slightly differently from the others, as you can see from Table 2.

You can use Tables 1 and 2 to identify a form from a text. First you find the word in the word list, which gives the form the word takes

Table 1. *Noun, masculine and feminine*

Declension	1	2	3	4	5
Meaning	'woman'	'friend'	'city'	'fruit'	'day'
Gender	feminine	masculine	feminine	masculine	masculine
Nominative sg.	fémina	amícus	urbs	fructus	dies
Genitive sg.	féminae	amíci	urbis	fructus	diéi
Dative sg.	féminae	amíco	urbi	frúctui	diéi
Accusative sg.	féminam	amícum	urbem	fructum	diem
Ablative sg.	fémina	amíco	urbe	fructu	die
Nominative pl.	féminae	amíci	urbes	fructus	dies
Genitive pl.	feminárum	amicórum	úrbium	frúctuum	diérum
Dative pl.	féminis	amícis	úrbibus	frúctibus	diébus
Accusative pl.	féminas	amícos	urbes	fructus	dies
Ablative pl.	féminis	amícis	úrbibus	frúctibus	diébus

Table 2. *Noun, neuter*

Declension	2	3	4
Meaning	'temple'	'sea'	'horn'
Gender	neuter	neuter	neuter
Nominative sg.	templum	mare	cornu
Genitive sg.	templi	maris	cornus
Dative sg.	templo	mari	córnui
Accusative sg.	templum	mare	cornu
Ablative sg.	templo	mari	cornu
Nominative pl.	templa	mária	córnua
Genitive pl.	templórum	márium	córnuum
Dative pl.	templis	máribus	córnibus
Accusative pl.	templa	mária	córnua
Ablative pl.	templis	máribus	córnibus

in the nominative and in the genitive singular, and its gender. The genitive singular endings are: *-ae, -i, -is, -us,* and *-ei.* If the word is masculine or feminine, then look in Table 1 for the corresponding ending in the genitive singular row. Then look in the column you are now in for the form with the ending that you are looking for. If the word is neuter, you do the same in Table 2.

There is one more case, the vocative, which is used when you address someone, as in *Brute* 'Brutus!'. The specific ending *-e* for the vocative is used for masculine singular nouns belonging to the second declension. Otherwise the vocative is always identical to the nominative.

Some forms deviate from the pattern set out in Table 1. In the first instance we find this with the nominative singular. To begin with there are words in the second declension whose stems end in *-r,* and which have no ending in the nominative singular. An example is *vir* 'man' (nominative singular) beside *viri* (genitive singular or nominative plural). There are several other kinds of irregularity in the nominative singular in the third declension. Words like *urbs* in Table 1 have a nominative ending *-s,* but if the stem ends in a *c* or a *g* instead of the expected sequence *cs* or *gs,* we find the letter *x,* pronounced [ks]. The word meaning 'peace' is *pacis* in the genitive and *pax* in the nominative, and 'king' is *regis* in the genitive and *rex* in the nominative.

There are also words in the third declension which have no ending in the nominative singular. A large group of this kind is made up of words with a stem ending in *-or* such as *orátor, oratóris* 'orator'. Another is words whose stem ends in *-on-,* which lose their *-n-* in the nominative singular: for example *nátio, natiónis* 'nation'. Then there are words like *civis, civis* 'citizen' whose nominative singular ending is *-is,* the same as the genitive. Because of these kinds of irregularity both the nominative singular and genitive singular are given in the word list. The genitive is always regular, and the ending of that form tells you which declension a noun belongs to. The material that precedes the genitive ending is the stem, to which the endings are added for all the cases, except, as we have said, for some nominative singulars.

The other case forms are almost always as they are to be found in Table 1. The only exceptions are that in the third declension the ending of the ablative singular is -*i* instead of -*e* for some masculine and feminine words (the neuter is always in -*i*), and the ending of the genitive plural is -*um* and not -*ium* for certain words. We have *regum* 'of kings' beside *urbium* 'of cities'.

Adjectives

Adjectives are used to qualify or modify nouns, and have endings which show case and number and which reflect the gender of the noun they accompany. This means that in principle each adjective must have a form for each of the five cases, both singular and plural, and in the three genders. That means 5 × 2 × 3, or a total of 30 forms.

This is not as difficult as it seems, since the endings are the same as the endings for nouns. Indeed the adjective often has the same ending as the noun: *femina clara* 'a famous woman', *feminae clarae* 'famous women', *amicus clarus* 'a famous friend', *amici clari* 'famous friends', *templum clarum* 'a famous temple', *templa clara* 'famous temples'. That is how things work out when the noun belongs to either the first or second declension and the adjective is one of the most common ones, which are called in the grammars 'adjectives of the first and second declension' (see Table 3).

If the noun belongs to another declension it obviously has different endings. The word *rex* 'king' is masculine and *urbs* 'town' is feminine and both belong to the third declension. We have *urbs clara* 'a famous town', *urbes clarae* 'famous towns', *rex clarus* 'a famous king', *reges clari* 'famous kings'.

There is also another type of adjective which has the endings of the third declension, for example *brevis* 'short' (see Table 4). This yields combinations such as *femina brevis* 'a short woman', *feminae*

Table 3. *Adjective, declension 1 and 2*

| Meaning | 'famous' | | |
Gender	masculine	feminine	neuter
Nominative sg.	clar**us**	clar**a**	clar**um**
Genitive sg.	clar**i**	clar**ae**	clar**i**
Dative sg.	clar**o**	clar**ae**	clar**o**
Accusative sg.	clar**um**	clar**am**	clar**um**
Ablative sg.	clar**o**	clar**a**	clar**o**
Nominative pl.	clar**i**	clar**ae**	clar**a**
Genitive pl.	clar**órum**	clar**árum**	clar**órum**
Dative pl.	clar**is**	clar**is**	clar**is**
Accusative pl.	clar**os**	clar**as**	clar**a**
Ablative pl.	clar**is**	clar**is**	clar**is**

Table 4. *Adjective, declension 3*

| Meaning | 'short' | |
Gender	masculine, feminine	neuter
Nominative sg.	brev**is**	brev**e**
Genitive sg.	brev**is**	brev**is**
Dative sg.	brev**i**	brev**i**
Accusative sg.	brev**em**	brev**e**
Ablative sg.	brev**i**	brev**i**
Nominative pl.	brev**es**	brév**ia**
Genitive pl.	brév**ium**	brév**ium**
Dative pl.	brév**ibus**	brév**ibus**
Accusative pl.	brev**es**	brév**ia**
Ablative pl.	brév**ibus**	brév**ibus**

breves 'short women', *rex brevis* 'a short king', *reges breves* 'short kings'.

An important group which is declined according to this pattern comprises the past participles of verbs, such as *monstratus, monstrata, monstratum* 'shown'.

As with the third-declension nouns, there are several different forms of the nominative singular in this class. A very small group of

Table 5. *Present participle*

| Meaning | 'showing' | |
Gender	masculine, feminine	neuter
Nominative sg.	mónstrans	mónstrans
Genitive sg.	monstrántis	monstrántis
Dative sg.	monstránti	monstránti
Accusative sg.	monstrántem	mónstrans
Ablative sg.	monstránti, monstránte	monstránti, monstránte
Nominative pl.	monstrántes	monstrántia
Genitive pl.	monstrántium	monstrántium
Dative pl.	monstrántibus	monstrántibus
Accusative pl.	monstrántes	monstrántia
Ablative pl.	monstrántibus	monstrántibus

words have different forms for masculine and feminine precisely in the nominative singular, as for instance *acer* (masculine), *acris* (feminine) and *acre* (neuter) 'sharp'. At the other extreme, quite a lot of words have a single form in the nominative singular across all genders, as *íngens* (nominative), *ingéntis* (genitive) 'huge, powerful'. Here the nominative ending is *-s* and the *-t-* of the stem disappears before it, just as happens with a noun like *mens, mentis* 'mind'. An important group of words which are declined according to this pattern are the present participles of verbs: *monstrans* 'showing'. As Table 5 shows, these items otherwise differ very little from other adjectives belonging to the third declension.

In the word list the three forms of the nominative in the masculine, feminine, and neuter are indicated for most adjectives, but for those where there is only one form for the three genders, I have given that form followed by the genitive.

In Latin, as in English, adjectives have comparative and superlative forms. Beside English *clear, clearer, clearest* we find Latin *clarus, clárior, claríssimus*. The superlative is formed by adding *-issim-* to the stem of the positive. To that you then add the normal adjectival endings following the pattern in Table 3. To make the comparative, you add *-ior* to the same stem. The comparative for most forms is declined like third-declension adjectives (Table 4 above). For example the genitive singular is *clarióris*. In the nominative singular there is no case ending, so for both masculine and feminine we get the form *clárior*. In the neuter, on the other hand, a different ending, *-ius*, is added, so the form for both the nominative and accusative singular (which are never distinct for neuter nouns and adjectives) is *clárius*.

Pronouns

The personal pronouns 'I, you (singular), we, you (plural)' have the forms shown in Table 6. There is an important difference between English and Latin in the use of pronouns. In Latin the form of the verb already indicates the person of the subject, so an unstressed pronoun is not needed (see below when we discuss the verb). Pronouns like *ego* 'I' and *tu* 'you (singular)' are only used when there is a particular need to emphasize them, so Latin really has no exact equivalent of the English unstressed pronouns such as 'he, she, it, they'. Even so, there are pronouns in Latin which are often rendered as 'he', 'she', 'it', etc. in English. One of them is, in the

Table 6. *Personal pronouns*

	Form	Meaning	Form	Meaning
Nominative	ego	'I'	tu	'you'
Dative	mihi	'(to) me'	tibi	'(to) you'
Accusative	me	'me'	te	'you'
Ablative	me	'(with) me'	te	'(with) you'
Nominative	nos	'we'	vos	'you'
Dative	nobis	'(to) us'	vobis	'(to) you'
Accusative	nos	'us'	vos	'you'
Ablative	nobis	'(with) us'	vobis	'(with) you'

masculine singular nominative, *is* 'he'. The corresponding feminine form is *ea* 'she' and the neuter *id* 'it'. The word is declined more or less like an adjective of the first and second declension, albeit with several irregular forms (see Table 7).

There are pronouns which behave similarly. The most important are *hic* 'this' (Table 8) and *ille* 'that' (Table 9).

The relative pronoun *qui* 'who, which' is in principle also declined like an adjective, as is the interrogative pronoun 'which, who'. Just as

Table 7. *Demonstrative pronoun* is *'he, that'*

Gender	masculine	feminine	neuter
Nominative sg.	is	ea	id
Genitive sg.	eius	eius	eius
Dative sg.	ei	ei	ei
Accusative sg.	eum	eam	id
Ablative sg.	eo	ea	eo
Nominative pl.	ei, ii	eae	ea
Genitive pl.	eórum	eárum	eórum
Dative pl.	eis, iis	eis, iis	eis, iis
Accusative pl.	eos	eas	ea
Ablative pl.	eis, iis	eis, iis	eis, iis

Table 8. *Demonstrative pronoun* hic *'this'*

Gender	masculine	feminine	neuter
Nominative sg.	hic	haec	hoc
Genitive sg.	huius	huius	huius
Dative sg.	huic	huic	huic
Accusative sg.	hunc	hanc	hoc
Ablative sg.	hoc	hac	hoc
Nominative pl.	hi	hae	haec
Genitive pl.	horum	harum	horum
Dative pl.	his	his	his
Accusative pl.	hos	has	haec
Ablative pl.	his	his	his

Table 9. *Demonstrative pronoun* ille *'that'*

Gender	masculine	feminine	neuter
Nominative sg.	ille	illa	illud
Genitive sg.	illíus	illíus	illíus
Dative sg.	illi	illi	illi
Accusative sg.	illum	illam	illud
Ablative sg.	illo	illa	illo
Nominative pl.	illi	illae	illa
Genitive pl.	illórum	illárum	illórum
Dative pl.	illis	illis	illis
Accusative pl.	illos	illas	illa
Ablative pl.	illis	illis	illis

Table 10. *Relative and interrogative pronouns 'who, which'*

Gender	masculine	feminine	neuter
Nominative sg.	qui/quis	quae	quod/quid
Genitive sg.	cuius	cuius	cuius
Dative sg.	cui	cui	cui
Accusative sg.	quem	quam	quod/quid
Ablative sg.	quo	qua	quo
Nominative pl.	qui	quae	quae
Genitive pl.	quorum	quarum	quorum
Dative pl.	quibus	quibus	quibus
Accusative pl.	quos	quas	quae
Ablative pl.	quibus	quibus	quibus

in English, the two pronouns usually have the same forms, although the latter sometimes has the form *quis* for the nominative singular masculine and *quid* for the neuter nominative and accusative (Table 10).

A number of other pronouns are in the main declined in the same way as adjectives, though some have special forms. The word *aliquis* 'someone' goes like *quis* in Table 10, as does *quisque* 'each, every' except that this has -*que* added on after the inflectional endings: *quisque, quemque, cuiusque,* etc. The word *idem, éadem, idem* 'same' is similar in that -*dem* is added after the inflections and induces certain adjustments in the sounds, so that the -*s* is omitted in the masculine nominative singular and the forms that would otherwise end in -*m* change to -*n,* so accommodating to the pronunciation of the following [d], so that we have *eandem, earundem,* etc. The emphatic pronoun *ipse, ipsa, ipsum* 'self, same' is also declined as an adjective following the pattern in Table 3 (above), except that like the other pronouns it has the endings -*ius* in the genitive singular and -*i* in the dative singular for all genders. The same endings are also found in a number of other words such as *unus* 'one', *alter* 'other', *totus* 'whole'.

The forms of the verb

Verbs are obviously important words in Latin, as they are in other languages. Latin verbs also form the basis of literally thousands of English loanwords, so it will be useful and interesting to become acquainted with the most familiar of them. Unfortunately, it is not always easy to recognize them, whether in Latin texts or as loanwords, since each verb has a huge variety of different forms, principally as a result of the different endings a verb can have. This variety is in turn dictated by the fact that a verb has a good deal of work to do within the sentence. In the first place, the verb always tells you the person of the subject, so there are different forms corresponding to 'I', 'you (singular)', 'he/she/it', 'we', 'you (plural)' and 'they'. For the verb 'show' these forms are respectively: *monstro, monstras, monstrat, monstrámus, monstrátis, monstrant.* (You can see here the base of the English verb *demonstrate.*) In compensation, there is no need for a separate word for 'I', etc.: the verb form does the job very nicely by itself. For example, 'I show the way' is *viam monstro* and 'they show the way' is *viam monstrant.* The endings are in effect

Table 11. *Latin tense forms*

Latin form	Name	Meaning
mónstro	present	'I show'
monstrábam	imperfect	'I showed'
monstrávi	perfect	'I have shown/I showed'
monstráveram	pluperfect	'I had shown'
monstrábo	future	'I will show'
monstrávero	future perfect	'I will have shown'

equivalent to the pronouns, and so a Latin verb has six forms where an English verb has only two: *show, shows.*

Second, the verb is responsible for indicating the time of the action. To some extent this is also true in English, but in many circumstances we indicate the time through an extra verb, a so-called auxiliary verb, which in general Latin does not use. In the English forms *I show, I showed, I have shown, I had shown, I shall show,* the difference between the first two is like Latin in being conveyed by an ending, but in the others the job is done by the auxiliaries *have, had,* and *shall.* Latin has a separate form for each of these meanings, and indeed for one more in which English has recourse to a combination of auxiliaries, namely *I shall have shown.* Each tense has its own name, as set out in Table 11. There are six tense forms for each Latin verb, each of which obviously has six variants according to the person, so for example: *monstrábas* 'you (singular) showed' and *monstraverátis* 'you (plural) had shown'. Altogether, then, that makes thirty-six forms for each verb so far.

That may seem a lot, but it is not in fact necessary to learn each form individually since there is a system. Each form consists of three parts. The form *monstrabas,* for example, can be divided into *monstra-ba-s.* The last bit is equivalent to our personal pronoun: *-s* indicates 'you (singular)'. The bit in the middle shows the tense, here *-ba-* for the past or imperfect tense. The first part indicates the basic meaning of the verb and is called the stem, so the form in its entirety means 'you (singular) showed'.

In principle, you only have to learn the six person endings and the six tense markers in order to know all thirty-six forms. In practice things are a bit more complicated than that, since the person endings are not always the same in each tense group, and there can be differences in the verb stem in different tenses. However, once you have grasped the general principle that there are three parts to a verb form, you will mostly get it right. In fact, there are yet more verb forms beyond the thirty-six, but they too can be broken down in the same way. The so-called subjunctive forms indicate that something might happen, should happen, or should have happened, or sometimes simply signal the fact that the sentence containing this verb form constitutes a subordinate clause. There are four different subjunctive series: *monstrem* 'I (may) show', *monstrárem* 'I might show, I showed', *monstráverim* 'I (may) have showed', *monstrávissem* 'I might have showed, I had showed'. What distinguishes these subjunctive forms from the other more common ones (called the 'indicative' in grammatical terminology) is the middle part. Compare *monstra-re-s* 'you (singular) showed (subjunctive)' and *monstra-ba-s* 'you (singular) showed (indicative)'.

Each of the forms we have seen so far also has a passive equivalent. In English the passive is obtained through the use of another auxiliary verb, this time the verb *be*, so beside I *show* we have I *am shown*, beside *you will show* we have *you will be shown* and so on. Something similar happens in Latin when you come to make the passive of the perfects, but for the most part passives are another context in which Latin has different endings where English uses an auxiliary verb. Since passive changes the role of the person from subject to object, it is perhaps not surprising that what distinguishes the passive is a different set of person endings. For example, we have *mónstratur* 'he is shown', *monstrábatur* 'he was shown' both with -*atur* instead of the active ending -*at*, and so on.

Just to make life really tough, some verbs have passive forms even though they do not have passive meanings! 'I encourage' is *hortor* (cf. English *exhort*) and 'I use' is *utor*, both with the same -*or* ending as *monstror*. Such verbs obviously only have passive forms in the word list, as they have no sets of forms for the active. Verbs of this type are called 'deponent'. One that has an English correspondent is *nascor* 'I am born' which is paralleled in Latin but not in English by the similarly deponent *morior* 'I die'.

For each verb, then, there are altogether 120 different forms which indicate person and tense differences. In addition, there are quite a few other forms, such as the infinitive *monstráre* 'to show', participles like *monstrans* 'showing' and *monstrátus* 'shown', the imperative *monstra* 'show!', and a few others. The participles have many forms since they decline like adjectives, as we have already seen. If you take all these forms into account, the conclusion is that a Latin verb can occur in some 300 different forms. Put like that, it sounds an awful lot. But you have to remember that almost every form has a direct equivalent in English. The difference is that we use many separate words, as in 'you might have shown' where Latin has only one: *monstravisses*, which of course consists of parts with different meanings. It is not really that difficult to have to learn that an ending -*s* means 'you (singular)' or that -*isse*- before the ending means 'should/might' when used in combination with -*v*- which expresses the perfect.

It is unfortunate that not all Latin verbs are inflected or, as grammarians say, conjugated in quite the same way. Most of them belong to one of four (or five) main types, which are called conjugations. Table 12 shows the patterns for each conjugation. With the aid of this table you can identify almost all forms of almost all verbs, but you do need to know how to go from the word list to the table. In the word list there are mostly four forms for each verb, for example: *monstro, monstrávi, monstrátus, monstráre*. The first form is the first person singular present indicative 'I show'; the second is the first person singular perfect indicative 'I have shown/I showed'; the third is the perfect participle in the nominative singular masculine 'shown' (if there is no masculine form the neuter is given); and the fourth is the present infinitive 'to show'.

These four forms have been chosen because together they show you how the stem of the verb—to which the endings are attached—appears in the different sets of forms. The second form shows what the stem looks like for all the members of the perfect, the pluperfect, and the future perfect series and some other forms given in Table 13. You just remove the ending -*i* and you have what is called the perfect stem, which in this case is *monstrav-*. To that you add the endings according to the table, so, for example, you can arrive at forms like *monstráverat* 'he had shown'. Other verbs can have perfect stems which look completely different. For instance, the second form of the verb *video* is *vidi*, as you can discover from the word list, and its perfect stem is *vid-*. The second form of the verb *sum* 'be' is *fui* and hence has a perfect stem *fu-*. On these stems you can build forms like *viderat* 'he had seen' and *fuerat* 'he had been'.

The third form of a verb in the word list is the perfect participle, which has the ending -*us*. The material before the ending constitutes the participle stem, to which you add the endings for the adjectives as in Table 3 (above). For the verb *monstro* we have, for example, *monstratus* 'shown (masculine singular nominative)', *monstrati* 'shown (masculine plural nominative)', etc. and for the verb *video* 'see' we have *visus* 'seen (masculine singular nominative)', *visi* 'seen (masculine plural nominative)', etc. The perfect participle has many uses in Latin, one being to help make the passive forms for the perfect, pluperfect, and future perfect. If for instance you want to say 'he had been shown', there is actually no simple verb for that in Latin, and you would have to use instead the expression *monstratus erat*, which may of course also mean 'he was shown'.

The forms that we have mentioned so far have exactly the same endings for all verbs, so that, as long as you know the stem, you will know what all the forms will look like. The remaining forms are the present, the imperfect, and the future, both active and passive. The forms are shown in Tables 12a, and 12b, which each have five columns, one for each of the five conjugations. To know which conjugation a verb belongs to, you have to look at the infinitive, which is the last form given in the word list, and compare it with the forms in the row 'Infinitive' at the beginning of Table 12a or 12b. The first conjugation has an infinitive in -*áre*, the second in -*ére*, the third in unstressed -*ere*,

Table 12a. *Verb formation, present stem forms: active*

Tense, mood	Form meaning	Conjugations					
		1 'show'	2 'see'	3a 'rule'	3b 'take'	4 'hear'
Infinitive	'to show' etc.	monstráre	vidére	régere	cápere	audíre
Present participle (see Table 5)	'showing' etc.	mónstrans, gen. monstrántis	vídens, gen. vidéntis	régens, gen. regéntis	cápiens, gen. capiéntis	aúdiens, gen. audiéntis
Imperative singular	'show!' etc.	mónstra	víde	rége	cápe	aúdi
Imperative plural	'show!' etc.	monstráte	vidéte	régite	cápite	audíte
Present indicative	'I show' etc.	mónstro	vídeo	régo	cápio	aúdio
	'you show' etc.	mónstras	vídes	régis	cápis	aúdis
	'he/she/it shows' etc.	mónstrat	vídet	régit	cápit	aúdit
	'we show' etc.	monstrámus	vidémus	régimus	cápimus	audímus
	'you show' etc.	monstrátis	vidétis	régitis	cápitis	audítis
	'they show' etc.	mónstrant	vídent	régunt	cápiunt	aúdiunt
Imperfect indicative	'I showed' etc.	monstrábam	vidébam	regébam	capiébam	audiébam
	'you'	monstrábas	vidébas	regébas	capiébas	audiébas

	monstro	video	rego	capio	audio
'he/she/it'	monstrábat	vidébat	regébat	capiébat	audiébat
'we'	monstrabámus	videbámus	regebámus	capiebámus	audiebámus
'you'	monstrabátis	videbátis	regebátis	capiebátis	audiebátis
'they'	monstrábant	vidébant	regébant	capiébant	audiébant
Future 'I will show' etc.	monstrábo	vidébo	régam	cápiam	aúdiam
'you'	monstrábis	vidébis	réges	cápies	aúdies
'he/she/it'	monstrábit	vidébit	réget	cápiet	aúdiet
'we'	monstrábimus	vidébimus	regémus	capiémus	audiémus
'you'	monstrábitis	vidébitis	regétis	capiétis	audiétis
'they'	monstrábunt	vidébunt	régent	cápient	aúdient
Present subjunctive 'I show/may show' etc.	mónstrem	videam	régam	cápiam	aúdiam
'you'	mónstres	videas	régas	cápias	aúdias
'he/she/it'	mónstret	videat	régat	cápiat	aúdiat
'we'	monstrémus	videámus	regámus	capiámus	audiámus
'you'	monstrétis	videátis	regátis	capiátis	audiátis
'they'	mónstrent	videant	régant	cápiant	aúdiant
Imperfect subjunctive 'I showed/might show' etc.	monstrárem	vidérem	régerem	cáperem	audírem
'you'	monstráres	vidéres	régeres	cáperes	audíres
'he/she/it'	monstráret	vidéret	régeret	cáperet	audíret
'we'	monstrarémus	viderémus	regerémus	caperémus	audirémus
'you'	monstrarétis	viderétis	regerétis	caperétis	audirétis
'they'	monstrárent	vidérent	régerent	cáperent	audírent

Table 12b. *Verb formation, present stem forms: passive*

Tense , mood	Meaning	Conjugations				
		1 'be shown'	2 'be seen, seem'	3a 'be ruled'	3b 'be taken'	4 'be heard'
Infinitive	'to be shown' etc.	monstrári	vidéri	régi	cápi	audíri
Gerundive (forms as in Table 3)	'which should be shown/to show' etc.	monstrándus	vidéndus	regéndus	capiéndus	audiéndus
Present indicative	'I am shown' etc.	mónstror	vídeor	régor	cápior	aúdior
	'you'	monstráris	vidéris	régeris	cáperis	audíris
	'he/she/it'	monstrátur	vidétur	régitur	cápitur	audítur
	'we'	monstrámur	vidémur	régimur	cápimur	audímur
	'you'	monstrámini	vidémini	regímini	capímini	audímini
	'they'	monstrántur	vidéntur	regúntur	capiúntur	audiúntur
Imperfect indicative	'I was shown' etc.	monstrábar	vidébar	regébar	capiébar	audiébar
	'you'	monstrabáris	videbáris	regebáris	capiebáris	audiebáris
	'he/she/it'	monstrabátur	videbátur	regebátur	capiebátur	audiebátur
	'we'	monstrabámur	videbámur	regebámur	capiebámur	audiebámur
	'you'	monstrabámini	videbámini	regebámini	capiebámini	audiebámini
	'they'	monstrabántur	videbántur	regebántur	capiebántur	audiebántur

	monstrábor	vidébor	régar	cápiar	aúdiar
Future 'I will be shown etc.	monstrábor	vidébor	régar	cápiar	aúdiar
'you'	monstráberis	vidéberis	regéris	capiéris	audiéris
'he/she/it'	monstrábitur	vidébitur	regétur	capiétur	audiétur
'we'	monstrábimur	vidébimur	regémur	capiémur	audiémur
'you'	monstrabímini	videbímini	regémini	capiémini	audiémini
'they'	monstrabúntur	videbúntur	regéntur	capiéntur	audiéntur
Present subjunctive 'I am shown/ may be shown' etc.	mónstrer	vídear	régar	cápiar	aúdiar
'you'	monstréris	videáris	regáris	capiáris	audiáris
'he/she/it'	monstrétur	videátur	regátur	capiátur	audiátur
'we'	monstrémur	videámur	regámur	capiámur	audiámur
'you'	monstrémini	videámini	regámini	capiámini	audiámini
'they'	monstréntur	videántur	regántur	capiántur	audiántur
Imperfect subjunctive 'I was shown/ might be shown' etc.	monstrárer	vidérer	régerer	cáperer	audírer
'you'	monstraréris	videréris	regeréris	caperéris	audiréris
'he/she/it'	monstrarétur	viderétur	regerétur	caperétur	audirétur
'we'	monstrarémur	viderémur	regerémur	caperémur	audirémur
'you'	monstrarémini	viderémini	regerémini	caperémini	audirémini
'they'	monstraréntur	videréntur	regeréntur	caperéntur	audiréntur

Table 13. *Verb formation, perfect stem forms*

Tense and mood	Meaning	Form
Infinitive	to have shown	monstravísse
Perfect indicative	'I have shown/showed'	monstrávi
	'you have shown/showed'	monstravísti
	'he/she has shown/showed'	monstrávit
	'we have shown/showed'	monstrávimus
	'you have shown/showed'	monstravístis
	'they have shown/showed'	monstravérunt
Pluperfect indicative	'I had shown'	monstráveram
	'you had shown'	monstráveras
	'he/she had shown'	monstráverat
	'we had shown'	monstraverámus
	'you had shown'	monstraverátis
	'they had shown'	monstráverant
Future perfect	'I will have shown'	monstrávero
	'you will have shown'	monstráveris
	'he/she will have shown'	monstráverit
	'we will have shown'	monstravérimus
	'you will have shown'	monstravéritis
	'they will have shown'	monstráverint
Perfect subjunctive	'I have shown/show'	monstraverim
	'you have shown/show'	monstráveris
	'he/she has shown/shows'	monstráverit
	'we have shown/show'	monstravérimus
	'you have shown/show'	monstravéritis
	'they have shown/show'	monstráverint
Pluperfect subjunctive	'I might have shown'	monstravíssem
	'you might have shown'	monstravísses
	'he/she might have shown'	monstravísset
	'we might have shown'	monstravissémus
	'you might have shown'	monstravissétis
	'they might have shown'	monstravíssent

and the fourth in –*íre*. In the third conjugation there are two sub-groups, 3a and 3b. To decide which group a verb belongs to, look at the first form given in the word list. If that ends in -*io*, like *facio* 'do', the verb belongs in 3b; if it ends in -*o*, like *mitto* 'send', it belongs in 3a.

When you have established which conjugation a verb belongs to, you know which column in Table 12a or 12b you need to look in to find the forms of the verb. Each form consists of a stem plus a suffix which indicates tense and mood (for example the imperfect subjunctive) plus a person ending. In *monstra-bi-t* 'he/she will show', -*t* indicates third person singular, -*bi*- the future indicative active, and *monstra*- is the stem meaning to show. The stem is in principle what comes before -*re* in the infinitive, but there are quite a number of complications, especially in the third conjugation. To be certain about a given form you have to either look it up in the table or learn the table by heart.

The present participle, for example *mónstrans* 'showing', contains the present stem, and the inflection for this class is given in Table 5 (above) in the section on adjectives (since the participle is a verbal adjective). The genitive of this word is *monstrántis*, and from that it is clear that the stem to which the adjectival endings are attached is *monstrant*-. That stem in turn consists of the present stem plus -*nt*-, although there are some discrepancies in some of the conjugations.

The stem ends in a long -*a*- in the first conjugation, a long -*e*- in the second, and a long -*i*- in the fourth. The third conjugation contains both words with a stem ending in a short -*i*- and words with a stem ending in a consonant, and the forms of the sub-types have influenced each other in various ways that need not concern us here.

Finally, there are also verb forms called gerundives. These have a stem which is similar to that of the present participle, but with the addition of -*nd*- instead of -*nt*-. To the -*nd*- stem are attached the adjectival endings from Table 3 (above), for instance *monstrándus*. This form means, among other things, 'which should be shown'. We discuss it in more detail in the following section.

A few Latin verbs have irregular forms, the most important being the verb *esse* 'be', which is conjugated in the present as shown

Table 14. *The verb* sum *in the present stem forms*

Tense and mood	Meaning	Form
Infinitive	'to be'	esse
Present indicative	'I am'	sum
	'you are'	es
	'he/she/it is'	est
	'we are'	súmus
	'you are'	éstis
	'they are'	sunt
Imperfect indicative	'I was'	éram
	'you were'	éras
	'he/she/it was'	érat
	'we were'	erámus
	'you were'	erátis
	'they were'	érant
Future	'I will be'	éro
	'you will be'	éris
	'he/she/it will be'	érit
	'we will be'	érimus
	'you will be'	éritis
	'they will be'	érunt
Present subjunctive	'I am/may be'	sim
	'you are/may be'	sis
	'he/she/it is/may be'	sit
	'we are/may be'	símus
	'you are/may be'	sítis
	'they are/may be'	sint
Imperfect subjunctive	'I were/might be'	éssem
	'you were/might be'	ésses
	'he/she/it were/might be'	ésset
	'we were/might be'	essémus
	'you were/might be'	essétis
	'they were/might be'	éssent

in Table 14. Forms of *esse* are often used in combination with a perfect partciple as in *Gallia divisa est* 'Gaul is divided'. The combination *esse* + perfect participle is also used to express the passive correspondents of the perfect active stem (see above, p. 201).

Amandi *and* Amanda

These are verb forms that contain -*nd*- followed by an ending, as in the title *Ars amandi* 'the art of loving' and Cato's famous words *Praetérea cénseo Cartháginem esse deléndam* 'Moreover I am of the opinion that Carthage should be destroyed'. These forms have confusingly similar names; the first is called the gerund and is quite close in function to the English -*ing* form in expressions like *the art of loving* (not to be confused with the participial -*ing* as in *a loving child*), while the second is called the gerundive and has no real equivalent in English.

In many respects the gerund is very like an infinitive, and indeed the two forms in English can sometimes be substituted for each other. Compare *Winning the battle will be hard* and the virtually synonymous *To win the battle will be hard*. In Latin, by contrast, the two forms are complementary in their occurrence. When the action of the verb is subject we find the infinitive as in *errare humanum est* 'to err is human'. Unlike the infinitive, the gerund has a case ending, which means that it can occur in contexts where a noun would normally be required and where the infinitive would not be allowed. In the form *amandi* this is the final -*i*, which indicates the genitive, and hence *ars amandi* means 'the art of loving' just as *ars amatoris* means 'the art of the lover', with the genitive of the noun *amator* 'lover'.

Another example is *docendo discimus* 'we learn by teaching'. The form *docendo* is ablative and expresses the means by which something is achieved, just as the ablative does in a sentence like *gladio interfectus est* 'he was killed by a sword', where *gladio* 'sword (ablative)' is the instrument of murder.

Table 15. *The gerund*

Case	Form	Meaning
Genitive	amandi	'of loving'
Dative	amando	'to/for loving'
Accusative	amandum	'loving' (used only after a preposition)
Ablative	amando	'with/by loving'

The gerund, then, is a verbal noun which is used in circumstances where the meaning is verbal but where the form required is that of a noun. In other words the gerund provides the case forms of the infinitive. The forms themselves are those of a noun in the neuter singular, except that there is no nominative since that function is fulfilled by the infinitive. The declension of the gerund of the verb *amare* is set out in Table 15.

While the gerund is a noun, the gerundive is an adjective formed from the verb stem just as the present and perfect participles are. Its meaning is 'which should be done' or 'which is worth doing'. The form *amandus* for example means 'who should be loved' or 'who is worth loving' or quite simply 'lovable'. This form is masculine and refers to a man. The corresponding form for a woman is *amanda*. Both forms have been used as names in the past but only the feminine version is still in common use today.

A simple sentence with a form in the gerundive is *puella amanda est* 'the girl should be loved' or literally 'the girl is (one) who should be loved'. By the same token Cato's favourite refrain in the Senate *Praetérea cénseo Cartháginem esse deléndam* may be literally translated as 'Moreover I am of the opinion that Carthage is (a place) which should be destroyed'. These inelegant renderings show that it is not always possible to translate word for word from one language into another, especially when the grammatical constructions required are quite divergent.

There are further complications with the gerundive which mean that in other circumstances it too sometimes has to be translated as if it were an infinitive. I think it is best to let anyone who wants to study Latin grammar more thoroughly discover these mysteries for themselves.

What is probably worth reminding ourselves of is that the gerundive is in fact the only Latin word form for which English has no equivalent at all. In all other circumstances the Latin form can be represented quite well with one, two, three, or even on occasion more English words according to specific and quite simple rules. Although the languages may at first seem very different from each other, there is in most cases a direct match between them. It is only when there is not, as with the gerundive, that translation becomes really difficult.

How words are formed

Earlier we saw how Latin nouns, adjectives, and verbs can be divided into a stem and an ending. Sometimes the stems cannot be further broken down, as with *puer* 'child', but quite often the stem itself consists of smaller parts, as with *puer-il-is* 'childish'. The word *puerílis* has been formed from *puer* by adding a suffix to the stem, just as in English *childish* is formed from *child* and *-ish*. Both Latin and English have many such ways of forming words from other words. In the above instance, the suffix *-il-* is used to convert a noun into an adjective. Other examples of its use are: *civilis* 'civil' from *civis* 'citizen', *virílis* 'virile' from *vir* 'man', *senílis* 'concerning, like an old person' from *senex* 'old man'. In this example note how the meaning is not necessarily pejorative, unlike English *senile*, and how the noun's special nominative ending, *-ex*, is removed before the adjective is formed.

There is a huge variety of suffixes like this, and it is a good idea to remember them since that diminishes the amount of work one has to do to learn words. They are not just used to make adjectives out of nouns but for many different combinations. For instance, the suffix *-tas* works in the other direction, taking an adjective such as *liber* 'free' and turning it into the noun *libértas* 'freedom', genitive *libertátis*.

Table 16. *Nouns and adjectives referring to animals in Latin and English*

Latin noun	Latin adjective	English noun	English adjective
canis	caninus	dog	canine
equus	equinus	horse	equine
feles	felinus	cat	feline
bos	bovinus	cow	bovine
vulpes	vulpinus	fox	vulpine

You can even make a noun out of an adjective that comes from a noun, as in *puerílitas* 'childishness', where the English suffix *-ness* fulfils the same function.

Many of these suffixes have come into English via Latin loans, so that we have for example *virile, puerile, infantile*. Similarly, Latin nouns in *-tas* often have counterparts in English in *-ty* (where the English form of the suffix has been mediated by French): *liberty, quality, quantity, identity*, and the like. It is interesting too to note the way that English has often borrowed the derived word but not the base on which that word is built. Although we have *infant* beside *infantile*, we have not borrowed the other nouns that enter into the pattern with *-ilis*. Another example of this kind concerns adjectives relating to animals where the Latin suffix is *-inus*. Table 16 shows the pattern. This pattern comes about because adjectives of this kind are characteristic of learned, scientific language, where Latin borrowings were, as we have seen, common, while there were already perfectly good words for the animals themselves so the nouns did not need to be borrowed.

To provide a full treatment of word formation would require a book of its own, but before leaving the topic it is important to underscore one big difference between word formation and inflection. The inflection of words is in principle predictable: when you know which pattern of inflection to apply for a given word, you know all the forms of the words. But word formation is not regular in this sense. A given suffix is generally used in the same way in all the words in which it is used, but you cannot know in advance if a particular suffix can be used with a particular stem. That is true both of Latin and of English. For example, 'man' is *vir* and 'woman' is *mulier*. The adjective meaning 'relating to man' is *virílis* but the adjective which means 'relating to woman' is *muliébris*, which is formed with a completely different suffix. In English we have *gentlemanly* but *ladylike* with two different suffixes and in *boyish* and *girlish* we have a different suffix again. For these reasons, it is good to know what the most common ways of building words in Latin are, but it is not a good idea to try and form new words by simply extending the patterns.

So far we have only used examples with nouns and adjectives, but in fact verb stems are the ones most commonly deployed in the formation of new words. Latin verbs can very often be discerned in words in English and other modern European languages. The stem of the verb *video* 'see' is contained in *provide*, where the original Latin meaning was 'look ahead' hence 'make arrangements' or 'provide for' and thus 'supply', this last being the most common meaning in modern English. The same stem combined with a different prefix is found in *evident*, which comes from the present participle of a verb meaning 'seem, appear'. The verb *mitto* 'send' is at the heart of a number of modern English verbs such as *remit, omit, transmit, submit, commit,* and *permit,* and similar prefixes occur with the stem of the verb *capio* 'take' in *receive, conceive, perceive,* and *deceive.* In this last example, the fact that the stem -*ceive* is so altered with respect to its Latin ancestor is due to the fact that this set of verbs came into English via French.

The meaning of a verb with a prefix can sometimes be radically different from the meaning of the original simple verb both in Latin and in English. If we take the -*mit* set as an example, we can see different degrees of transparency in the ways the parts combine together. Given that -*mit* means 'send' and *trans* means 'across', it is natural that *transmit* should mean what it does. In the case of *submit* the prefix *sub* means 'under', and *submit* means to give in or to fall under a greater force or authority. Similarly, if you submit an essay or an application, you are giving it to someone who for the purposes of assessment is higher than you on some scale of authority. With *permit* it is perhaps less obvious, but this originally meant 'to send, let through', a sense which survives most directly in expressions like *work permit* and *residence permit*. From this it is a short step to the meaning 'allow'. There are many more examples in English with stems like -*pose* 'put', -*fer* 'carry', and -*mote* 'move'. With the aid of a good dictionary you should be able to puzzle out the way the modern meanings have arisen.

The items that do all the work in the above examples are the prefixes *trans-, sub-, per-, pro-, con-,* etc. All of these also exist as independent prepositions in Latin, and in this respect the formations here are similar to the combinations you find in English with a verb and a particle, as in *give in/out/up/over/*etc or *take in/out/away/over,*etc. Once again the meanings are sometimes fairly self-evident—a take-away meal is one that goes away from the place where it was made—and in other instances pretty obscure. How does *take in* come to mean 'deceive', for example? In other instances in English, too, verb and preposition have become fused, often with a meaning that is no longer transparent, e.g. *understand, withstand, outdo, forgo, undergo.*

From these scattered examples, you can see that new words can be formed from Latin verb stems in several different ways, and in order to understand the connection you will often need to look at the different parts of the verb as given in the word list. In particular, words derived from verbs are often built on the third form in the list, the past participle. From *visus* 'seen' we have *visio* 'sight', whose accusative form *visiónem* ultimately gives English *vision*, and *visíbilis*, borrowed into English as *visible*. A compound built on this same stem is *revísio, revisiónis*, from which we have acquired *revision*. English has then created a verb out of this, namely *revise*.

Words of this latter kind are particularly common among the loanwords in modern European languages. English has many hundreds of words in -*ion* and pretty well all of them are formed from the past participle stem of a Latin verb. A few examples are: *information, tradition, organization, illustration* and *mission*. The different shapes of the stem in question can be found by consulting the entries for *informo, trado, organizo, illustro,* and *mitto* in the word list.

There are many other ways of building words. For instance, it is obviously possible to make verbs from nouns. A case in point is the Latin verb *finire* 'end', which is formed from the noun *finis* 'end' just as the English verb *to end* comes from the English noun *end*.

Part IV
Basic Vocabulary

Lists of words, phrases and quotations

The following wordlist includes all the Latin words that occur in this book. Where a word receives particular discussion or explanation in the text, its entry is followed by a reference to the relevant page(s). The list also gives some basic Latin vocabulary. In choosing the words for inclusion here I have given priority to those which have left frequent traces in modern languages.

In all the words or forms with more than two syllables an accent indicates the position of the stress. Two-syllable words are always stressed on the first syllable. It is important to remember that these accents are meant as an aid to the user of this list and are not employed in ordinary Latin spelling.

The stress indicated is in principle the one which was used in classical times; in most cases this is also the stress which has been used throughout the word's subsequent history. However, for a certain group of words I have preferred to give an alternative stress, which was the one adopted in the Middle Ages. The words in question are Greek loans ending in -*ia*, such as *philosophía*. In Latin as it has been spoken since antiquity such words are stressed in the same way as in Greek, namely on the penultimate syllable, but in classical Latin the stress fell on the antepenultimate syllable, thus *philosóphia*.

In the grammar section above I have explained which inflected forms are indicated in the wordlist for nouns, adjectives and verbs. For nouns gender is shown by the abbreviations m. for masculine, f. for feminine and n. for neuter.

The wordlist is followed by a compilation of some 500 more or less well-known Latin phrases, expressions and quotations with translations. After each genuine quotation the name of the author or source is indicated in a parenthesis. In the many cases where a well-known expression can be traced back to a rather different wording by a particular writer, the author's name is generally not given. All the words which occur in the phrases and quotations can also be found as separate entries in the wordlist. Where the phrase is discussed in the body of the book, the entry is followed by a reference to the appropriate page(s).

Basic vocabulary

a, ab   from, by
abbas   *abbátis* m. abbot
ábdico   *abdicávi abdicátus abdicáre* renounce, abdicate
abdómen   *abdóminis* n. abdomen
abdúco   *abdúxi abdúctus abdúcere* take or bring away
ábeo   *ábii abíre* go away, disappear
abício   *abiéci abiéctus abícere* throw away
ábies   *abíetis* f. fir
ablátus   *abláta ablátum* carried away
abnórmis   *abnórmis abnórme* irregular, abnormal
abóleo   *abolévi abólitus abolére* efface, destroy
abomínábilis   *abomínábilis abomínábile* abominable
abóminor   *abominátus abominári* deprecate, detest
aborígines   *aboríginum* m. original inhabitants, especially
   the ancestors of the Romans
abórtio   *abortiónis* f. miscarriage, abortion
abrúmpo   *abrúpi abrúptus abrúmpere* break off, sever
abrúptus   *abrúpta abrúptum* interrupted, steep, sudden
ábsens   gen. *abséntis* absent
abséntia   *abséntiae* f. absence
absínthium   *absínthii* n. wormwood
absolútus   *absolúta absolútum* perfect, complete
absólvo   *absólvi absolútus absólvere* complete; acquit
absórbeo   *absórbui absorbére* drink up, swallow
ábstinens   gen. *abstinéntis* abstinent
abstinéntia   *abstinéntiae* f. abstinence
abstíneo   *abstínui abstinére* abstain
abstráctus   *abstrácta abstráctum* withdrawn, abstract
ábstraho   *abstráxi abstráctus abstráhere* drag away, withdraw
absum   *áfui abésse* be away, be absent
absúrde   absurdly
absúrdus   *absúrda absúrdum* absurd, unreasonable
abundántia   *abundántiae* f., abundance, richness
abúndo   *abundávi abundáre* overflow

Basic vocabulary

abúsus *abúsus* m. misuse, waste (noun)
abútor *abúsus abúti* misuse, consume
ac and
accédo *accéssi accéssum accédere* approach
accéndo *accéndi accénsus accéndere* light
áccido 1 *áccidi accídere* happen
accído 2 *accídi accísus accídere* cut down, cut off
áccio *accívi accítus accíre* call, summon 163
accípio *accépi accéptus accípere* receive, accept 113
accúso *accusávi accusátus accusáre* accuse
acer *acris acre* sharp 193
actum *acti* n. act
actus 1 *acta actum* done, transacted
actus 2 *actus* m. motion, performance
acus *acus* f. needle
ad to
adagium *adagii* n. proverb, adage
addo *áddidi ádditus áddere* add
addénda things to be added (a list of things to be added and corrected
  is headed 'Addenda et corrigenda')
addúco *addúxi addúctus addúcere* lead to
ádeo 1 *ádii adíre* go to, approach
ádeo 2 so far, thus, indeed
adhíbeo *adhíbui adhíbitus adhibére* bring to, use
adhuc hitherto, still
adício *adiéci adiéctus adícere* add, place near
adiéctum *adiécti* n. addition
adiectívus *adiectíva adiectívum* placed beside, adjective 104
áditus *áditus* m. entrance
adiúngo *adiúnxi adiúnctus adiúngere* join, add
ádiuvo *adiúvi adiútus adiuváre* help
admirábilis *admirábilis admirábile* admirable 174
admirátio *admiratiónis* f. admiration 174
admíror *admirátus admirári* admire 174
admítto *admísi admíssus admíttere* admit, allow
admóneo *admónui admónitus admonére* admonish
adópto *adoptávi adoptátus adoptáre* adopt
adsum *áffui adésse* be present; help

aduléscens   *adulescéntis* m. adolescent
advénio   *advéni advéntum adveníre* come to, arrive at
advéntus   *advéntus* m. arrival
advérbium   *advérbii* n. adverb 104
advérsus   against
advocátus   *advocáti* m. legal counsellor, advocate
ádvoco   *advocávi advocátus advocáre* call to, summon
aedes   *aedis* f. building
aedífico   *aedificávi aedificátus aedificáre* build
Aegaeus *Aegaea Aegaeum*   Aegean
aeger   *aegra aegrum* ill
aegre   with difficulty
aemulátio   *aemulatiónis* f. emulation 48
aequális   *aequális aequále* equal
aequus   *aequa aequum* even, flat
aër   *áëris* m. air
aes   *aeris* n. copper, bronze
aestas   *aestátis* f. summer
aéstimo   *aestimávi aestimátus aestimáre* estimate, weigh
aetas   *aetátis* f. age
aetérnitas   *aeternitátis* f. eternity
aetérnus   *aetérna aetérnum* eternal
aether   *aétheris* m. ether, sky, heaven
aevum   *aevi* n. era, age
affício   *afféci afféctus affícere* influence
ager   *agri* m. field 13
aggrédior   *aggréssus ággredi* attack
aggréssio   *aggressiónis* f. attack
ágito   *agitávi agitátus agitáre* drive, stir up
agnus   *agni* m. lamb
ago   *egi actus ágere* drive, do
agréotio   *agréotio agróoto* having to do with the land
agrícola   *agrícolae* m. farmer 18
agricultúra   *agricultúrae* f. agriculture, farming 13, 18
Albáni   *Albanórum* m. the Albans
albus   *alba album* white 152, 155, 163
álea   *áleae* f. dice
álgeo   *alsi algére* feel cold

Basic vocabulary

álibi   somewhere else
aliénus   *aliéna aliénum* belonging to others, alien, strange, foreign
aliquándo   sometimes
áliquis   *áliqua áliquid/ áliquod* someone, something
   (Table 10) 69
áliquot   some, a few
áliter   in another way
álius   *ália áliud* other 36
almus   *alma almum* kind
alpínus   *alpína alpínum* alpine 155
altáre   *altáris* n. altar
alter   *áltera álterum* the other (of two) 197
altérnus   *altérna altérnum* by turns, alternate
altíssimus   *altíssima altíssimum* highest, deepest
áltius   higher, deeper
altus   *alta altum* high, deep
amábo   please 66
amátor   *amatóris* m. lover
amatórius   *amatória amatórium* concerning love
ámbulo   *ambulávi ambulátum ambuláre* walk, go around
americánus   *americána americánum* American 155
amica   *amicae* f. friend (female)
amicítia   *amicítiae* f. friendship
amícus   *amíci* m. friend (male)
ámita   *ámitae* f. paternal aunt 129
amo   *amávi amátus amáre* love (vb.) 22
amor   *amóris* m. love (noun) 22
amplus   *ampla amplum* large, ample
an   if, whether (in questions)
anatómicus   *anatómica anatómicum* anatomical
anemóne   *anemónes* f. anemone, windflower 150
angélicus   *angélica angélicum* angelic 144
ángelus   *ángeli* m. angel
anguis   *anguis* m., f. snake
ánima   *ánimae* f. soul, spirit
ánimal   *animális* n. animal
ánimus   *ánimi* m. heart, soul, mind
annus   *anni* m. year

ante   before 44

antepaenúltimus   *antepaenúltima antepaenúltimum*
antepenultimate 180

ánulus   *ánuli* m. ring

ánxius   *ánxia ánxium* uneasy, anxious

apério   *apérui apértus aperíre* open

appáreo   *appárui apparére* appear

appéllo   *appellávi appellátus appelláre* call

appéndix   *appéndicis* f. something which hangs down, appendage 149

appéndo   *appéndi appénsus appéndere* hang

ápprobo   *approbávi approbátus approbáre* approve

aptus   *apta aptum* fitting, suitable

apud   at, near

Apúlia   *Apúliae* f. Apulia

aqua   *aquae* f. water 6

Aquitánus   *Aquitáni* m. Aquitanian, a person from Aquitania
(a province in south-west France)

árbiter   *árbitri* m. judge, umpire

árbitror   *arbitrátus arbitrári* give a judgement, believe

arbor   *árboris* f. tree

árceo   *árcui arcére* enclose, keep away

architectúra   *architectúrae* f. architecture 64

árdeo   *arsi ardére* glow, burn

ardor   *ardóris* m. ardour, glow

árduus   *árdua árduum* difficult, arduous

arésco   *árui aréscere* dry (vb.)

argéntum   *argénti* n. silver 22

arguméntum   *arguménti* n. proof, reason, argument

arithmética   *arithméticae* f. arithmetic 102

arma   *armórum* n. arms, weapons

armo   *armávi armátus armáre* arm, equip

árrigo   *arréxi arréctus arrígere* raise, rouse

ars   *artis* f. art 33, 102

ártifex   *artíficis* m. artist

arx   *arcis* f. castle, fortress

ascéndo   *ascéndi ascénsum ascéndere* mount, ascend

ásinus   *ásini* m. ass, donkey

aspéctus   *aspéctus* m. sight

Basic vocabulary

asper *áspera ásperum* rough
aspício *aspéxi aspéctum aspícere* look at, look upon, see
assíduus *assídua assíduum* constant
astronomía *astronomíae* f. astronomy 103
astrum *astri* n. star
at but
ater *atra atrum* black
atque and
atrox gen. *atrocis* gloomy, hideous
aúctio *auctiónis* f. auction
auctor *auctóris* m. author, originator
auctóritas *auctoritátis* f. authority 17
audácia *audáciae* f. courage, bravery
audax gen. *audácis* daring, brave
aúdeo *ausus audére* dare
aúdio *audívi audítus audíre* hear
aúfero *ábstuli ablátus auférre* take away, remove
aúgeo *auxi auctus augére* increase
aula *aulae* f. hall; the royal court
aura *aurae* f. breeze, air
aúreus *aúrea aúreum* golden
auris *auris* f. ear
aurum *auri* n. gold 122
auspícium *auspícii* n. observing the flight of birds (as a way of telling
the future); chief command (in time of war only the commander-in-
chief had the right to take auspices in this way)
aut or
autem however
auxílium *auxílii* n. help, aid
avárus *avára avárum* avaricious, greedy
ave hail!
avérsio *aversiónis* f. aversion, loathing
avérto *avérti avérsus avértere* turn away from
avis *avis* f. bird
avúnculus *avúnculi* m. maternal uncle 129

baptízo *baptizávi baptizátus baptizáre* christen 80
bárbarus *bárbara bárbarum* barbarian

básium   *básii* n. kiss
beátus   *beáta beátum* happy, fortunate, blessed
Belga   *Belgae* m. Belgian
bellum   *belli* n. war
bene   well
benedíco   *benedíxi benedíctus benedícere* bless
benígne   benevolently
benígnus   *benígna benígnum* kind, benign
béstia   *béstiae* f. (wild) beast
bibo   *bibi bíbere* drink
bis   twice
biséxtilis   *biséxtilis biséxtile* double sixth 44
biséxtus   *biséxta biséxtum* double sixth 44
blandus   *blanda blandum* friendly, flattering
bónitas   *bonitátis* f. goodness
bonus   *bona bonum* good 18
bos   *bovis* m., f. bull, cow
brácchium   *brácchii* n. arm
brevis   *brevis breve* short 191
brévitas   *brevitátis* f. shortness
Brutus   *Bruti* m. Brutus

cadáver   *cadáveris* n. corpse, dead body
cado   *cécidi cádere* fall
caecus   *caeca caecum* blind
caedo   *cecídi caésus caédere* hit, kill
caeléstis   *caeléstis caeléste* celestial
caelum   *caeli* n. heaven
caerimónia   *caerimóniae* f. ceremony 12
Caesar   *Caésaris* m. Caesar 36, 114
calámitas   *calamitátis* f. misfortune 137
cálamus   *cálami* m. reed
caleo   *cálui calére* be warm, hot
calor   *calóris* m. warmth, heat
cámera   *cámerae* f. vault, room
campus   *campi* m. field
canális   *canális* m. channel, groove 165
cándidus   *cándida cándidum* white

Basic vocabulary

canis   *canis* m. dog
cano   *cécini cantum cánere* sing
cantátum   *cantáti* n. song, cantata
cánticum   *cántici* n. song
canto   *cantávi cantátus cantáre* sing 170
cantus   *cantus* m. song
cápio   *cepi captus cápere* take
capítulum   *capítuli* n. capital (of a column), chapter
capélla   *capéllae* f. chapel
cápsula   *cápsulae* f. capsule
captívus   *captíva captívum* captive
caput   *cápitis* n. head
carcer   *cárceris* m. prison
cáreo   *cárui carére* lack, be without
cáritas   *caritátis* f. love
carmen   *cárminis* n. song
caro   *carnis* f. meat
carpo   *carpsi carptus cárpere* pluck
Carthágo   *Cartháginis* f. Carthage
carus   *cara carum* dear
casa   *casae* f. hut 5
castéllum   *castélli* n. fort, fortress
cástitas   *castitátis* f. chastity
castus   *casta castum* chaste
casus   *casus* m. fall, cause
cátharus   *cáthari* m. cathar 125
cáthedra/cathédra   *cáthedrae/cathédrae* f. chair, teacher's desk
catíllus   *catílli* m. small bowl, plate
caupo   *caupónis* m. wine merchant, innkeeper 72
causa   *causae* f. cause, reason, legal case
cáveo   *cavi caútum cavére* beware of
cavo   *cavávi cavátus caváre* hollow out
cavus   *cava cavum* hollow
cedo   *cessi cessum cédere* yield, get out of the way
célebro   *celebrávi celebrátus celebráre* celebrate
celer   *céleris célere* rapid
cella   *cellae* f. chamber, closet 5, 111, 169
cellárium   *cellárii* n. cellar 169

celo *celávi celátus celáre* hide, conceal
Celta *Celtae* m. Celt
cena *cenae* f. meal, dinner
cénseo *cénsui censum censére* judge, advise, believe
censor *censóris* m. censor (a Roman magistrate)
centrum *centri* n. centre 113
centum hundred
cerásea *ceráseae* f. cherry 169
cerno *crevi cérnere* distinguish
certo *certávi certátus certáre* fight
certus *certa certum* certain
cervix *cervícis* f. neck
céteri *céterae cétera* the others
céterum but
chaos n. chaos
charta *chartae* f. leaf, document, letter
chorus *chori* m. choir, chorus
christiánus *christiána christiánum* Christian
cibus *cibi* m. food
Cícero *Cicerónis* m. Cicero 108
cinéreus *cinérea cinéreum* ash-grey 155
cingo *cinxi cinctus cíngere* gird, go around
cinis *cíneris* m. ashes
circa around, about
circénses *circénsium* m. circus games
círculus *círculi* m. circle
circum around, about
circumspício *circumspéxi circumspéctus circumspícere* look around
cítius faster, more quickly
cito 1 *citávi citátus citáre* urge, cite
cito 2 quickly
civílis *civílis civíle* pertaining to citizens, civil, civic 211
civílitas *civilitátis* f. politics
civis *civis* m. citizen 190
cívitas *civitátis* f. town 81, 180
clamo *clamávi clamátus clamáre* shout (vb.)
clamor *clamóris* m. shout (noun)

Basic vocabulary

clarus   *clara clarum* shining, famous 3
classis   *classis* f. class, fleet 154
claudo   *clausi clausus claúdere* close
claustrum   *claustri* n. monastery
clausus   *clausa clausum* closed
cleméntia   *cleméntiae* f. clemency, leniency
cléricus   *clérici* m. priest, clergyman
cóeo   *cóii coíre* go, come together
coepi   *coeptus, coepísse* begin
cogitátio   *cogitatiónis* f. thought
cógito   *cogitávi cogitátus cogitáre* think
cognítio   *cognitiónis* f. knowledge
cognómen   *cognóminis* n. surname, family name 40
cognósco   *cognóvi cógnitus cognóscere* learn, become acquainted
   with, know
cogo   *coégi coáctus cógere* drive, force
cohors   *cohórtis* f. cohort, contingent
cóitus   *cóitus* m. sexual intercourse
collis   *collis* m. hill
collum   *colli* n. neck
colo   *cólui cultus cólere* cultivate 13
colónia   *colóniae* f. colony 13, 169
colónus   *colóni* m. cultivator, farmer 13, 18
color   *colóris* m. colour
colúmna   *colúmnae* f. column, pillar
coma   *comae* f. hair
combinátio   *combinatiónis* f. combination
comméndo   *commendávi commendátus commendáre* recommend
commítto   *commísi commíssus commíttere* commit
cómmodus   *cómmoda cómmodum* suitable, convenient
commúnis   *commúnis commúne* common
cómparo   *comparávi comparátus comparáre* compare
compléctor   *compléxus complécti* embrace
compóno   *compósui compósitus compónere* compose, put together
concédo   *concéssi concéssus concédere* yield, grant, concede
concéptum   *concépti* n. concept, idea 108
concípio   *concépi concéptus concípere* conceive, understand
concórdia   *concórdiae* f. agreement, concord

concúrro   *concúrri concúrsum concúrrere* run together, compete
concúrsus   *concúrsus* m. assembly, concourse
condício   *condiciónis* f. condition
condo   *cóndidi cónditus cóndere* found
cónfero   *cóntuli collátus conférre* compare
conféssio   *confessiónis* f. confession
confício   *conféci conféctus confícere* complete, finish
confído   *confísus confídere* rely on
confíteor   *conféssus confitéri* confess, own 79
cóngrego   *congregávi congregátus congregáre* assemble
coniúnctio   *coniunctiónis* n. conjunction 104
conséntio   *consensi consensum consentíre* agree
consequéntia   *consequéntiae* f. consequence 114
cónsequor   *consecútus cónsequi* pursue, reach, attain
considerábilis   *considerábilis considerábile* deserving consideration
consídero   *considerávi considerátus consideráre* examine, consider
consílium   *consílii* n. advice, decision
consobrínus   *consobríni* m. male cousin
consobrína   *consobrínae* f. female cousin
consolátio   *consolatiónis* f. consolation, comfort
consors   *consórtis* m. partner
constítuo   *constítui constitútus constitúere* fix, settle
consto   *cónstiti constáre* stand fast, agree
consuésco   *consuévi consuétus consuéscere* to be accustomed
consuetúdo   *consuetúdinis* f. custom, habit
consul   *cónsulis* m. consul 8
consuláris   *consuláre* of a consul, consular
cónsulo   *consúlui consúltus consúlere* consult, decide
consúmo   *consúmpsi consúmptus consúmere* consume
contémno   *contémpsi contémptus contémnere* despise, hold in
   contempt
conténdo   *conténdi conténtus conténdere* contend against, compete
conténtus   *conténta conténtum* content
continéntia   *continéntiae* f. abstemiousness, continence
contíneo   *contínui conténtus continére* hold or keep together, contain
contíngo   *cóntigi contáctus contíngere* touch; happen
contra   against
contradíctio   *contradictiónis* f. contradiction

contrárius *contrária contrárium* opposite, contrary

convénio *convéni convéntum conveníre* come together, convene

convérto *convérti convérsus convértere* turn, convert

convíva *convívae* m. guest

cópia *cópiae* f. supply, abundance

cor *cordis* n. heart

cornu *cornus* n. horn

coróna *corónae* f. garland, crown (noun)

coróno *coronávi coronátus coronáre* crown (vb.), adorn with a garland

corpus *córporis* n. body 71

corrigénda mistakes (lit. 'things which must be corrected', cf. *addénda*)

córrigo *corréxi corréctus corrígere* correct

corrúmpo *corrúpi corrúptus corrúmpere* corrupt, destroy

cras tomorrow

creátor *creatóris* m. creator

credo *crédidi créditus crédere* believe

crédulus *crédula crédulum* trusting, gullible

creo *creávi creátus creáre* produce, create

cresco *crevi créscere* grow

crimen *críminis* n. charge, offence

crudélis *crudélis crudéle* cruel

crux *crucis* f. cross

cui for whom (from *qui*)

cuiúsque of each and every (from *quisque*)

culpa *culpae* f. fault 72

cultúra *cultúrae* f. cultivation, culture 13

cultus *cultus* m. cultivation, worship

cum 1 when

cum 2 with

cuncti *cunctae cuncta* all

cupído *cupídinis* f. desire

cur why

cura *curae* f. care, concern

curo *curávi curátus curáre* take care of

currículum *currículi* n. race

curro *cucúrri cursum cúrrere* run

cursus *cursus* m. run

custódio   *custodívi custodítus custodíre* watch, guard
custos   *custódis* m. guard
cycnus   *cycni* m. swan

da   give! (from *do*)
damno   *damnávi damnátus damnáre* judge, condemn
Dánai   *Danaórum* m. the Greeks
de   of, from, about 69
dea   *deae* f. goddess
debéllo   *debellávi debellátus debelláre* vanquish
débeo   *débui débitus debére* must, ought to
decem   ten 44
decérno   *decrévi decrétus decérnere* decide
decet   *décuit decére* be fitting
décimus   *décima décimum* tenth
decípio   *decépi decéptus decípere* deceive
declamátio   *declamatiónis* f. statement, declamation 161
decor   *decóris* m. ornament
décoro   *decorávi decorátus decoráre* decorate, adorn
deféndo   *deféndi defénsus deféndere* defend
defénsio   *defensiónis* f. defence
defénsor   *defensóris* m. defender
deínde   then
delécto   *delectávi delectátus delectáre* please, amuse
delegátio   *delegutiónis* f. delegation
déleo   *delévi delétus delére* destroy
delíctum   *delícti* n. crime
delíneo   *delineávi delineátus delineáre* draw, sketch, delineate
deméntia   *deméntiae* f. insanity, madness, folly 149
deménto   *dementávi dementátus dementáre* drive mad
demónstro   *demonstrávi demonstrátus demonstráre* show, demonstrate
demum   just
dens   *dentis* m. tooth
densus   *densa densum* thick, dense
deplóro   *deplorávi deplorátus deploráre* regret, deplore, feel sorry for, complain about
depóno   *depósui depósitus depónere* put down, deposit

Basic vocabulary

derídeo   *derísi derísus deridére* laugh at
derisor   *derisoris* m. someone who mocks or scoffs
descéndo   *descéndi descénsum descéndere* descend
descénsus   *descénsus* m. descent
désero   *desérui desértus desérere* abandon
desértum   *desérti* n. desert
desidérium   *desidérii* n. longing
desídero   *desiderávi desiderátus desideráre* wish, desire
désino   *désii désitus desínere* cease
desípio   *desípere* be a fool
despéro   *desperávi desperátus desperáre* despair, give up hope
desum   *défui deésse* be absent, fail, let down
detérior   *detérior detérius* worse
deus   *dei* m. god
di   m. gods (plural of *deus*)
diábolus   *diáboli* m. devil
diaéta   *diaétae* f. manner of living, diet 166
dialéctica   *dialécticae* f. dialectics, logic 102
dico   *dixi dictus dícere* say
dictátor   *dictatóris* m. dictator 15, 25
dies   *diéi* m., f. day 44, 133
differéntia   *differéntiae* f. difference
difficilis   *difficilis difficile* hard, difficult
diffúgio   *diffúgi diffúgere* disperse, scatter
dígitus   *dígiti* m. finger 165
dígnitas   *dignitátis* f. dignity
dignus   *digna dignum* worthy, deserving, fit
diléctio   *dilectiónis* f. love
díligens   gen. *diligéntis* diligent
díligo   *diléxi diléctus dilígere* love, esteem
dimídium   *dimídii* n. half
diplóma   *diplómatis* n. diploma, letter
dírigo   *diréxi diréctus dirígere* direct
dirus   *dira dirum* dire, terrible
disciplína   *disciplínae* f. learning, discipline
disco   *dídici díscere* learn
discórdia   *discórdiae* f. disagreement
discrímen   *discríminis* n. difference, turning point

discútio   *discússi discússus discútere* shatter
disiéctus   *disiécta disiéctum* spread around, scattered
dispóno   *dispósui dispósitus dispónere* set in order, arrange, dispose
dispósitio   *dispositiónis* f. ordering, disposition 34
dísputo   *disputávi disputátus disputáre* dispute, argue, discuss
diu   for a long time
divérsus   *divérsa divérsum* different, opposite
divídia   *divídiae* f. trouble
dívido   *divísi divísus divídere* divide
divínus   *divína divínum* divine
divísus   *divísa divísum* divided 136
divus   *diva divum* divine
dixi   see *dico*
do   *dedi datus dare* give
dóceo   *dócui doctus docére* teach
doctor   *doctóris* m. doctor 144
doctrína   *doctrínae* f. teaching
dóleo   *dólui dolére* be in pain, ache
dolor   *dolóris* m. pain
dolorósus   *dolorósa dolorósum* painful
domi   at home
dómina   *dóminae* f. lady
dóminor   *dominátus dominári* rule
dóminus   *dómini* m. master, lord 79
domus   *domus* f. house, home
domúsio   *domusiónis* f. domestic use
dono   *donávi donátus donáre* give, grant
donum   *doni* n. gift
dórmio   *dormívi dormíre* sleep
dormíto   *dormitávi dormitáre* sleep
draco   *dracónis* m. dragon
dúbito   *dubitávi dubitátus dubitáre* doubt
duco   *duxi ductus dúcere* lead
dulcis   *dulcis dulce* sweet, delightful
dum   while, when
duo   *duae duo* two

Basic vocabulary

durus   *dura durum* hard
dux   *ducis* m. leader

e   see *ex*
ebur   *éboris* n. ivory
ecce   behold, here is
ecclésia   *ecclésiae* f. church 80
edo 1   *edi esus édere* eat
edo 2   *édidi éditus* give out
éduco   *educávi educátus educáre* bring up, educate
éfficax   gen. *efficácis* efficient
effício   *efféci efféctus effícere* bring about
effrenátus   *effrenáta effrenátum* unbridled, unrestrained
egens   gen. *egéntis* needy, poor
egentíssimus   *egentíssima egentíssimum* very needy
egéstas   *egestátis* f. poverty
ego   I (Table 6) 194
égomet   I myself (expressing emphasis)
eheu   ah, alas
eius   his, hers, its (from *is*)
elegántia   *elegántiae* f. elegance, refinement 168
elocútio   *elocutiónis* f. oratorical delivery, phrasing of a speech 34
eloquéntia   *eloquéntiae* f. eloquence
elúdo   *elúsi elúsus elúdere* elude
eméritus   *emérita eméritum* having completed one's term of service
éminens   gen. *eminéntis* prominent, high, eminent 96
emítto   *emísi emíssus emíttere* send out
emo   *emi emptus émere* buy
encómium   *encómii* n. speech of praise
enim   indeed
eo 1   *ii itum ire* go
eo 2   with, by him/it (from *is*)
eo 3   there, thither
eódem   to the same place
epíscopus   *epíscopi* m. bishop
epístula   *epístulae* f. letter
eques   *équitis* m. knight, cavalryman 31
equus   *equi* m. horse

erat was (see *sum*)
ergo therefore
érigo *eréxi eréctus erígere* raise, erect
erro *errávi errátum erráre* err, make a mistake
erúmpo *erúpi erúptus erúmpere* break out
esse be (see *sum*)
est is (see *sum*)
este be! imperative plural of *sum*
esto be! imperative of *sum*
et and, also, even 25
étiam even, also
etsi although, but
eúndo by going (from *eo*)
evénio *evéni eveníre* come out; happen
ex, e out of, from
excédo *excéssi excéssus excédere* exceed
excélsior *excélsior excélsius* higher
excípio *excépi excéptus excípere* except
éxcito *excitávi excitátus excitáre* rouse
éxcolo *excólui excúltus excólere* ennoble, refine
excrúcio *excruciávi excruciátus excruciáre* torment
excúso *excusávi excusátus excusáre* excuse
exémplum *exémpli* n. example
exérceo *exércui exércitus exercére* practice, exercise
exercitátio *exercitatiónis* f. exercise
exercítium *exercítii* n. exercise
exércitus *exércitus* m. army
exitiábilis *exitiábilis exitiábile* fatal, deadly 77
éxitus *éxitus* m. exit, end
expéllo *éxpuli expúlsus expéllere* expel
expéndo *expéndi expénsus expéndere* weigh out, pay
expérior *expértus experíri* experience
expértus *expérta expértum* experienced
expóno *expósui expósitus expónere* put or set out, expose
exsísto *éxstiti exsístere* come into existence, be, exist
exspécto *exspectávi exspectátus exspectáre* wait for, expect
exstínguo *exstínxi exstínctus exstínguere* put out, extinguish, annihilate

exténdo   *exténdi exténsus exténdere* stretch out, extend
exténsus   *exténsa exténsum* stretched out, extended
extra   outside
extrémus   *extréma extrémum* furthest out
exul   *éxulis* m. banished, exile

faber   *fabri* m. craftsman, skilled workman
fábula   *fábulae* f. narrative, story
fácies   *faciéi* f. face
fácilis   *fácilis fácile* easy
facíllime   easiest
fácinus   *facínoris* n. deed, crime
fácio   *feci factus fácere* make, do
factum   *facti* n. fact, deed
fallo   *fefélli falsus fállere* deceive
falsus   *falsa falsum* false
fama   *famae* f. fame
fames   *famis* f. hunger
família   *famíliae* f. family
fatum   *fati* n. fate, destiny
fáveo   *favi faútum favére* favour
favílla   *favíllae* f. ashes
feci   see *fácio*
felix   gen. *felícis* happy
fémina   *féminae* f. woman 3, 180
femینínus   *feminína feminínum* feminine 188
fenéstra   *fenéstrae* f. window 12
fere   almost
ferens   gen. *feréntis* carrying
fero   *tuli latus ferre* carry
ferraméntum   *ferraménti* n. tool of iron
ferrum   *ferri* n. iron
ferus   *fera ferum* wild
fessus   *fessa fessum* tired
festíno   *festinávi festinátus festináre* hurry
festum   *festi* n. feast
festus   *festa festum* festive
fidélis   *fidélis fidéle* faithful

fides *fídei* f. faith
fido *fisus fídere* trust
fidus *fida fidum* faithful
fíeri happen (from *fio*)
figo *fixi fixus fígere* fix, fasten
figúra *figúrae* f. form, shape, figure
fili son! from *filius*
fília *fíliae* f. daughter
fílius *fílii* m. son
fingo *finxi fictus fíngere* form, shape
fínio *finívi finítus finíre* finish 215
finis *finis* m. end, border 215
fio *fíeri* happen, become, be done
firmaméntum *firmaménti* n. support, foundation
firmus *firma firmum* firm, stable
flagéllo *flagellávi flagellátus flagelláre* whip, lash
flagrans gen. *flagrántis* burning
flamma *flammae* f. flame
flavus *flava flavum* yellow 155
flecto *flexi flexus fléctere* bend
flóreo *flórui florére* flower (vb.)
flos *floris* m. flower (n.)
flúctuo *fluctuávi fluctuátus fluctuáre* move with the waves, fluctuate
fluo *fluxi flúere* flow
focus *foci* m. hearth, fireplace
foedus *foéderis* n. treaty, agreement
fólium *fólii* n. leaf
fons *fontis* m. spring, source
fore to be about to be (from *sum*)
foris outside
forma *formae* f. form, shape, beauty
forsan perhaps
fortásse perhaps
forte by chance, accidentally
fortis *fortis forte* strong 17
fórtiter strongly
fortitúdo *fortitúdinis* f. strength 17
fórtius stronger

fortúna   *fortúnae* f. fortune, destiny
forum   *fori* n. square 6
frango   *fregi fractus frángere* break
frater   *fratris* m. brother 11
fraus   *fraudis* f. fraud
frequens   gen. *frequéntis* numerous
frígidus   *frígida frígidum* cold
frons   *frontis* f. forehead
fructus   *fructus* m. fruit
fuga   *fugae* f. flight
fugax   gen. *fugácis* fleeting
fúgio   *fugi fúgere* flee, take flight
fui   (I) was, have been (from *sum*)
fúimus   (we) were, have been (from *sum*)
fúlgeo   *fulsi fulgére* flash, shine
fundo   *fundávi fundátus fundáre* found
funus   *fúneris* n. funeral
furca   *furcae* f. fork
furiósus   *furiósa furiósum* mad, raging
furor   *furóris* m. madness, rage
futúrus   *futúra futúrum* coming, future

gaúdeo   *gavísus gaudére* enjoy, rejoice
gaúdium   *gaúdii* n. joy
gaza   *gazae* f. treasure, riches
gémini   *geminórum* m. twins 157
gemma   *gemmae* f. jewel
gener   *generi* m. son-in-law
gens   *gentis* f. family, clan, people 40
gentílis   *gentílis* m. belonging to the same family
genu   *genus* n. knee
genus   *géneris* n. kin, kind, sort 154
geometría   *geometríae* f. geometry 102
gero   *gessi gestus gérere* bear, do
gesta   *gestórum* n. deeds, exploits 130
gladiátor   *gladiatóris* m. gladiator
gládius   *gládii* m. sword
glória   *glóriae* f. glory, honour, fame

gnatus *gnata gnatum* born
gradus *gradus* m. step
Graécia *Graéciae* f. Greece
graecus *graeca graecum* Greek
gramen *gráminis* n. grass
grammática *grammáticae* f. grammar 102
grammáticus *grammátici* m. grammarian, scholar
grandis *grandis grande* big
granum *grani* n. grain, seed
grátia *grátiae* f. thanks, grace 80
gratus *grata gratum* agreeable, pleasing
gravis *gravis grave* heavy
grávitas *gravitátis* f. solemn demeanour, seriousness
gressus *gressus* m. step, way
grex *gregis* m. herd, flock
gusto *gustávi gustátus gustáre* taste (vb.)
gustus *gustus* m. taste (noun)
gutta *guttae* f. drop

hábeo *húbui hábitus habére* have
hábito *habitávi habitátus habitáre* inhabit
hábitus *hábitus* m. posture, appearance, dress
haec this (from *hic 1*)
haeréticus *haerétici* m. heretic
haud not
herba *herbae* f. grass, green crops
heres *herédis* m. heir
hic 1 *haec hoc* this (Table 8) 195
hic 2 here
história *históriae* f. history, narrative
hoc this (see *hic*)
homicída *homicídae* m., f. murderer, murderess
homo *hóminis* m. man
honéstus *honésta honéstum* honorable, respected
honor *honóris* m. honour
hora *horae* f. hour
horror *horróris* m. trembling, dread
hortor *hortátus hortári* encourage 199

hortus   *horti* m. garden
horum   of these (from *hic*)
hospes   *hóspitis* m., f. host, guest
hospitále   *hospitális* n. guest house
hostis   *hostis* m. enemy
humánus   *humána humánum* human
humánior   *humánior humánius* more human
húmilis   *húmilis húmile* lowly, humble
humor   *humóris* m. liquid, fluid 150
humus   *humi* f. earth, soil

iáceo   *iácui iacére* lie
iácio   *ieci iactus iácere* throw
iactátus   *iactátus* m. tossing
iacto   *iactávi iactátus iactáre* throw, toss
iactus   *iacta iactum* thrown
iáculor   *iaculátus iaculári* throw, hurl
iam   now, already, soon
iánua   *iánuae* f. door
ibam   I went (from *eo*)
ibi   there
ibídem   in the same place (abbreviated as '*ibid.*')
id   that (from *is*)
idem   *éadem idem* same 197
Idus   *Íduum* f. the Ides (the thirteenth or fifteenth day of the month) 44
ígitur   therefore
ignárus   *ignára ignárum* ignorant of
ignis   *ignis* m. fire
ignóro   *ignorávi ignorátus ignoráre* not know
ille   *illa illud* that (Table 9) 196
illústro   *illustrávi illustrátus illustráre* illustrate 214
imágo   *imáginis* f. picture
ímitor   *imitátus imitári* imitate
imménsus   *imménsa imménsum* immeasurable, immense, vast
immíneo   *immínui imminére* hang over
immoderátus   *immoderáta immoderátum* immoderate, immeasurable

immortális   *immortális immortále* immortal
impéndo   *impéndi impénsus impéndere* expend
impénsius   more expensively
imperátor   *imperatóris* m. commander, emperor 39
impérito   *imperitávi imperitátum imperitáre* rule
impérium   *impérii* n. command; power; empire 39, 90
ímpero   *imperávi imperátus imperáre* command, be in command 39
ímpius   *ímpia ímpium* impious, wicked
impóno   *impósui impósitus impónere* put, lay upon; impose
impórto   *importávi importátus importáre* bring in, import 171
ímprimo   *impréssi impréssus imprímere* print, stamp
ímprobus   *ímproba ímprobum* bad; enormous, excessive
impúlsus   *impúlsus* m. push, influence, impulse
impúne   with impunity
impunítus   *impuníta impunítum* unpunished
in   in, into, to
incéndium   *incéndii* n. fire
incértus   *incérta incértum* uncertain
incípio   *incépi incéptus incípere* begin
inclúdo   *inclúsi inclúsus inclúdere* enclose, include
íncoho   *incohávi incohátus incoháre* begin
íncolo   *incólui incólere* inhabit, cultivate
incunábula   *incunabulórum* n. cradle
índico   *indicávi indicátus indicáre* indicate, make known
indigéstus   *indigésta indigéstum* unarranged, without order
indignátio   *indignatiónis* f. displeasure, indignation
indúco   *indúxi indúctus indúcere* lead or bring in, persuade
inféctus 1   *inféctu inféctum* unmade, undone
inféctus 2   *infécta inféctum* infected
inférnus   *inférna inférnum* belonging to the underworld, infernal
ínfero   *íntuli illátus inférre* introduce, infer
ínfimus   *ínfima ínfimum* lowest
infinítus   *infiníta infinítum* unlimited
influéntia   *influéntiae* f. influence
infórmo   *informávi informátus informáre* form, shape, imagine,
   inform 173
infra   under, beneath; below, later on (in a book or writing)
ingénium   *ingénii* n. character, genius

ingens   gen. *ingéntis* huge
inhumánus   *inhumána inhumánum* inhuman
início   *iniéci iniéctus inícere* throw in
inítium   *inítii* n. beginning
iniúria   *iniúriae* f. injustice
iniústus   *iniústa iniústum* unjust
ínnocens   gen. *innocéntis* innocent
innócue   innocently
inquam   I say
inquinátus   *inquináta inquinátum* filthy, polluted
insánio   *insanívi insaníre* be mad
insígnis   *insígnis insígne* distinguished
insolens   gen. *insoléntis* unusual, excessive
inspício   *inspéxi inspéctus inspícere* examine, look into, inspect
instítuo   *instítui institútus instítuere* institute, found, determine
institútio   *institutiónis* f. instruction, principle
instruméntum   *instruménti* n. equipment, tool, instrument
ínstruo   *instrúxi instrúctus instrúere* equip, construct
insufficiéntia   *insufficiéntiae* f. insufficiency, weakness
ínsula   *ínsulae* f. island
ínteger   *íntegra íntegrum* whole, complete
intelléctus   *intelléctus* m. understanding, intelligence 114
intélligo   *intelléxi intelléctus intellígere* understand
inténdo   *inténdi inténtus inténdere* stretch out, point
inter   between, among
interdíco   *interdíxi interdíctus interdícere* forbid
interfício   *interféci interféctus interfícere* kill, destroy
interiéctio   *interiectiónis* f. interjection 104
ínterim   meanwhile
intérimo   *interémi interémptus interímere* kill
intérrogo   *interrogávi interrogátus interrogáre* ask
intra   within, inside
intro   *intrávi intrátum intráre* enter
invénio   *invéni invéntus inveníre* find, invent
invéntio   *inventiónis* f. invention, inventing 34
invíto   *invitávi invitátus invitáre* invite
invítus   *invíta invítum* unwilling, reluctant
iocus   *ioci* m. joke

Iovis   see *Iupiter*
ipse   *ipsa ipsum* self 197
ira   *irae* f. anger
irreparábilis   *irreparábilis irreparábile* irreparable, irretrievable
irrevocábilis   *irrevocábilis irrevocábile* irrevocable
is   *ea id* that (Table 7)
iste   *ista istud* that (near or concerning you)
istuc   thither, towards you 67
ita   so, thus, in this way
item   likewise, also
iter   *itíneris* n. journey
itur   one goes (from *eo 1*)
iucúndus   *iucúnda iucúndum* pleasant, agreeable
iudex   *iúdicis* m. judge
iudícium   *iudícii* n. judgement
Iuno   *Iunonis* m. Juno
Iúpiter   *Iovis* m. Jupiter
iuro   *iurávi iurátus iuráre* swear (on something)
ius   *iuris* n. right, law 71–2
iússio   *iussiónis* f. order, command
iustítia   *iustítiae* f. justice 114
iustus   *iusta iustum* just 17
iúvenis   *iúvenis* m. young man
iuvo   *iuvi iutus iuváre* help
iuxta   next to, beside

Kaléndae   *Kalendárum* f. the Kalends (the first day of the month) 44

labor 1   *labóris* m. labour, pain, trouble
labor 2   *lapsus labi* sink, slide
labóro   *laborávi laborátus laboráre* work, strive
lac   *lactis* n. milk
lacésso   *lacessivi lacessitus lacessere* tease, provoke
lácrima   *lácrimae* f. tear
lacrimósus   *lacrimósa lacrimósum* tearful
lacus   *lacus* m. lake
laedo   *laesi laesus laédere* injure, hurt, damage
laetus   *laeta laetum* glad

Basic vocabulary

lapis *lápidis* m. stone
lapsus *lapsus* m. chance, mistake
laqueátus *laqueáta laqueátum* panelled
largus *larga largum* liberal, generous
lassus *lassa lassum* tired
latínus *latína latínum* Latin 3, 92
Látium *Látii* n. Latium 7, 52–3
latus *láteris* n. side
laudátor *laudatóris* m. praiser
laudo *laudávi laudátus laudáre* praise
laúrea *laúreae* f. laurel tree, garland of laurel leaves
laus *laudis* f. praise
lavo *lavi lautus laváre* wash
lector *lectóris* m. reader
lectus *lecti* m. bed 108
legátus *legáti* m. ambassador, legate
légio *legiónis* f. legion
lego *legi lectus légere* read
lenis *lenis lene* soft, smooth, gentle
lente slowly
lentus *lenta lentum* slow
leo *leónis* m. lion 157
letum *leti* n. death
levis *levis leve* light
lex *legis* f. law
libéllus *libélli* m. small book
liber 1 *libri* m. book 28
liber 2 *líbera líberum* free
liberális *liberális liberále* free, generous
libértas *libertátis* f. freedom
libet *líbuit libére* please
libído *libídinis* f. desire, lust
líbitum *líbiti* n. pleasure
licet *lícuit licére* it is permitted
lictor *lictóris* m. lictor (official attendant of a magistrate and bearer of a bundle of rods surrounding an axe)
lignum *ligni* n. wood, timber
lílium *lílii* n. lily

limen   *líminis* n. threshold
línea   *líneae* f. line
lingua   *linguae* f. language, tongue 3, 36, 92
liquet   *liquére* be clear
líquidus   *líquida líquidum* liquid
lis   *litis* f. quarrel
líttera   *lítterae* f. letter, character
lítterae   *litterárum* f. letters, literature
litus   *lítoris* n. shore
locus   *loci* m. place
longínquus   *longínqua longínquum* remote
longus   *longa longum* long
loquax   gen. *loquácis* talkative
loquor   *locútus loqui* speak
lúcidus   *lúcida lúcidum* light, shining, bright
lumen   *lúminis* n. light
luna   *lunae* f. moon
lupus   *lupi* m. wolf
lusus   *lusus* m. game, play
lux   *lucis* f. light

máchina   *máchinae* f. machine
mágicus   *mágica mágicum* concerning wizards, magic 161
magis   more
magíster   *magístri* m. teacher
magistérium   *magistérii* n. mastery
magistra   *magístrae* f. woman teacher
magistrátus   *magistrátus* m. magistrate
magnitúdo   *magnitúdinis* f. size 24
magnus   *magna magnum* big
magus   *magi* m. wizard
maior   *maior maius* bigger
maióres   *maiórum* m., f. ancestors, forefathers
male   badly, wickedly
maléfica   *maléficae* f. witch, enchantress
malléolus   *malléoli* m. small hammer
malo   *málui malle* prefer
malum 1   *mali* n. apple

malum 2   *mali* n. evil (noun)
malus   *mala malum* evil (adj.)
mando   *mandávi mandátus mandáre* entrust, command
máneo   *mánsi manére* stay
manes   *mánium* m. the souls of the dead
mánsio   *mansiónis* f. dwelling
manus   *manus* f. hand
mare   *maris* n. sea 45
Mars   *Martis* m. Mars (god of war)
masculínus   *masculína masculínum* masculine 188
mater   *matris* f. mother 11
matéria   *matériae* f. matter, subject, material
matértera   *matérterae* f. maternal aunt 129
mathemática   *mathemáticae* f. mathematics 105
mathemáticus   *mathemática mathemáticum* mathematical
matrimónium   *matrimónii* n. marriage
matúrus   *matúra matúrum* ripe, mature
máximus   *máxima máximum* biggest
me   me
mecástor   by Castor (an oath)
mecum   with me
Medi   *Medórum* m. the Medes, Persians
médicus   *médici* m. doctor
mediócritas   *mediocritátis* f. mediocrity, moderation, mean
méditor   *meditátus meditári* consider, meditate (upon)
médius   *média médium* middle
mel   *mellis* n. honey
mélior   *mélior mélius* better
membrum   *membri* n. limb, member
meménto   remember! (from *mémini*)
mémini   *meminísse* remember
memor   gen. *mémoris* that remembers, possessed of a good memory
memória   *memóriae* f. memory 34
mendax   gen. *mendácis* lying, mendacious
mens   *mentis* f. mind, soul
mensa   *mensae* f. table
mensis   *mensis* m. month 42
méreo   *mérui méritus merére* deserve, merit

mergo   *mersi mersus mérgere* sink, engulf
merídies   *meridiéi* m. midday, noon, the south
meto   *métere* reap
métuo   *métui metúere* be afraid (of), fear
meus   *mea meum* my, mine
mi   my (from *meus*); to me (from *ego*)
mihi   to me
miles   *mílitis* m. soldier 13
milítia   *milítiae* f. military service 13
mille   thousand
mínimus   *mínima mínimum* smallest
miníster   *minístri* m. servant, waiter
minor   *minor minus* smaller
minus   less
mirábilis   *mirábilis mirábile* wonderful
mirus   *mira mirum* extraordinary
mísceo   *míscui mixtus miscére* mix, mingle
miser   *mísera míserum* wretched 53
miséreor   *miséritus miseréri* feel pity, have compassion or mercy
miséricors   gen. *misericórdis* merciful
mitto   *misi missus míttere* send 207, 213
móbilis   *móbilis móbile* movable 167
modo   just, only; now
modus   *modi* m. way, manner
moénia   *moénium* n. wall(s), ramparts
molécula   *moléculae* f. small mass 168
moles   *molis* f. mass
mónachus   *mónachi* m. monk
monastérium   *monastérii* n. monastery
móneo   *mónui mónitus monére* admonish
monéta   *monétae* f. coin
mons   *montis* m. mountain
monstro   *monstrávi monstrátus monstráre* show
monuméntum   *monuménti* n. memorial, monument
mora   *morae* f. delay
morbósus   *morbósa morbósum* sick, ill
morbus   *morbi* m. sickness, disease
mória   *móriae* f. madness, folly

Basic vocabulary

mórior   *mórtuus mori* die
moritúrus   *moritúra moritúrum* about to die (adj.)
mors   *mortis* f. death
mortális   *mortális mortále* mortal, deadly 53
mórtuus   *mórtua mórtuum* dead
mos   *moris* m. custom, habit
motacílla   *motacíllae* f. wagtail 155
motus   *motus* m. movement
móveo   *movi motus movére* move
muliébris   *muliébris muliébre* pertaining to women
múlier   *mulíeris* f. woman
multi   *multae multa* many
multus   *multa multum* much
mundus   *mundi* m. world
múnio   *munívi munítus muníre* fortify
munitíssimus   *munitíssima munitíssimum* very well supplied, armed
munítus   *muníta munítum* supplied, armed
murmur   *múrmuris* n. murmur
murus   *muri* m. wall
mus   *muris* m. mouse 11
música   *músicae* f. music 102
mutábilis   *mutábilis mutábile* changeable, mutable
mutátio   *mutatiónis* m. change
mutátus   *mutáta mutátum* changed
muto   *mutávi mutátus mutáre* change
mutus   *muta mutum* dumb

nam   for, but now
narro   *narrávi narrátus narráre* tell, narrate
nascor   *natus nasci* be born
nasus   *nasi* m. nose
nátio   *natiónis* f. nation 113, 190
natúra   *natúrae* f. nature
naturális   *naturális naturále* natural, having to do with
    nature 65, 71
natus   *nata natum* born 152
nauta   *nautae* m. sailor
návigo   *navigávi navigátus navigáre* sail

navis   *navis* f. ship
ne   not, that not
nec   and not, but not, nor
necésse   necessary
necéssitas   *necessitátis* f. necessity
négligo   *negléxi negléctus neglígere* neglect
nego   *negávi negátus negáre* deny, say no
negótium   *negótii* n. occupation
nemo   *nullíus* m., f. no one
nemorósus   *nemorósa nemorósum* of or belonging
  to a grove 155
nemus   *némoris* n. grove
nepos   *nepótis* m. grandson
neque   and not, but not, nor
nervus   *nervi* m. nerve 150
néscio   *néscii nescíre* not know
néuter   *néutra néutrum* neuter 180
nexus   *nexus* m. tying together, obligation
niger   *nigra nigrum* black
nihil, nil   n. nothing 32
nimis   too much
nímium   too much
nisi   unless
nix   *nivis* f. snow
nóbilis   *nóbilis nóbile* noble, superior
nobis   to, with us
nócens   gen. *nocéntis* guilty
nóceo   *nócui nocére* harm, hurt, injure
noctúrnus   *noctúrna noctúrnum* nocturnal 170
noli   Do not! (from *nolo*)
nolo   *nólui nolle* not to want
nomen   *nóminis* n. name 40, 104
non   not
Nonae   *Nonárum* f. the Nones (the fifth or seventh day
  of the month) 44
nonus   *nona nonum* ninth
norma   *normae* f. precept, rule
nos   we, us (Table 6)

Basic vocabulary

nosco   *novi notus nóscere* know
noster   *nostra nostrum* our 45
nota   *notae* f. mark
notábilis   *notábilis notábile* noteworthy, notable
noto   *notávi notátus notáre* mark, observe
notus   *nota notum* known (from *nosco*)
novem   nine 44
novus   *nova novum* new
nox   *noctis* f. night 170
nubes   *nubis* f. cloud
nubo   *nupsi nupta núbere* get married (of a woman)
nudus   *nuda nudum* naked
nuga   *nugae* f. joke, trifle
nullus   *nulla nullum* none, no
numen   *núminis* n. divine power
númerus   *númeri* m. number
nummus   *nummi* m. coin
numquam   never
nunc   now
núntius   *núntii* m. messenger
nupta   *nuptae* f. married woman
nútrio   *nutrívi nutrítus nutríre* nourish, feed

ob   in front of, on account of
obdúro   *obdurávi obduráre* hold out
óbeo   *obii obíre* go against; die
obício   *obiéci obiéctus obícere* throw, put before
obiéctum   *obiécti* n. something put in the way, object
obligátio   *obligatiónis* f. binding, obligation
obscúrus   *obscúra obscúrum* dark, obscure
obsto   *óbstiti obstáre* stand in the way, obstruct
obtíneo   *obtínui obténtus obtinére* acquire, obtain
occásio   *occasiónis* f. occasion, opportunity
occásus   *occásus* m. going down, setting
óccidens   *occidéntis* m. the west (where the sun sets)
óccido   *óccidi occídere* go down
óccupo   *occupávi occupátus occupáre* occupy
octo   eight 44

óculus   *óculi* m. eye
odi   *odísse* hate
odiósus   *odiósa odiósum* hateful
ódium   *ódii* n. hatred
odor   *odóris* m. smell (noun)
óffero   *óbtuli oblátus offérre* offer
offícium   *offícii* n. duty, service, favour
óleo   *ólui olére* smell (vb.)
óleum   *ólei* n. oil
olim   at some time (either in the past or the future)
olíva   *olívae* f. olive
omítto   *omísi omíssus omíttere* omit, neglect, pass over
omnis   *omnis omne* all, every
ómnia   *ómnium* n. everything (n. pl. of *omnis*)
onus   *óneris* n. burden
ópera   *óperae* f. work (n.)
opórtet   *opórtuit oportére* ought, must
óppeto   *oppetívi oppétere* meet
opportúnus   *opportúnu opportúnum* suitable, convenient,
   opportune
ópprimo   *oppréssi oppréssus opprímere* press down, suppress
óptimas   *optimátis* m. supporters of the aristocratic party 22
óptimus   *óptima óptimum* best
opto   *optávi optátus optáre* choose, wish
opus   *óperis* n. work (of literature, music, etc.)
ora 1   *orae* f. coast, region
ora 2   n. faces, mouths (pl. of *os*)
orátio   *oratiónis* f. speech, prayer 80
orátor   *oratóris* m. speaker, orator 33, 190
oratórius   *oratória oratórium* having to do with
   public speaking 33
orbis   *orbis* m. ring, world
ordo   *órdinis* m. order; class 154
organízo   *organizávi organizátus organizáre* organize
óriens   *oriéntis* m. the east (where the sun rises)
orígo   *oríginis* f. origin
órior   *ortus oríri* rise, get up
orno   *ornávi ornátus ornáre* decorate

Basic vocabulary

oro   *orávi orátus oráre* plead; pray 33, 80
os   *oris* n. face, mouth
osténdo   *osténdi osténdere* show
ótium   *ótii* n. leisure, free time, rest
ovum   *ovi* n. egg

paenúltimus   *paenúltima paenúltimum* next to last, penultimate 180
Paetus   *Paeti* m. Paetus
Palátium   *Palátii* n. Palatine (the hill in Rome where the emperors lived)
pállidus   *pállida pállidum* pale
panis   *panis* m. bread
par   gen. *paris* equal, alike
parco   *pepérci parsum párcere* spare
parens   *paréntis* m., f. parent
pário   *péperi partus párere* give birth, acquire
paro   *parávi parátus paráre* prepare
pars   *partis* f. part, region 36, 104
particípium   *particípii* n. participle 104
partum   *parti* n. possession
partúrio   *parturíre* be in labour, give birth
parvus   *parva parvum* small
passim   everywhere; (of allusions or references in a published work) to be found at various places throughout the text
pássio   *passiónis* f. suffering, passion
passus   see *patior*
pastor   *pastóris* m. herdsman
páteo   *pátui patére* lie or be open, clear, evident
pater   *patris* m. father 11, 13, 170
paternális   *paternális paternále* paternal
patiéntia   *patiéntiae* f. patience, endurance
pátior   *passus pati* suffer
patres   *patrum* m. fathers, senators 13
pátria   *pátriae* f. fatherland
patrícius   *patrícii* m. member of the upper class, patrician 13
pátrius   *pátria pátrium* belonging to, having to do with a father 58
pátruus   *pátrui* m. paternal uncle 129

pauper gen. *paúperis* poor
pax *pacis* f. peace 111, 190
peccátor *peccatóris* m. sinner
peccátum *peccáti* n. sin (noun)
pecco *peccávi peccátum peccáre* sin (vb.)
pectus *péctoris* n. chest
pecúnia *pecúniae* f. money 22
pecus *pécoris* n. livestock
pedúclus *pedúcli* m. louse
pello *pépuli pulsus péllere* drive out, away
péndeo *pepéndi pendére* hang
pendo *pepéndi pensus péndere* hang up, weigh, pay
pénetro *penetrávi penetrátus penetráre* enter, penetrate
penis *penis* m. tail, penis
penna *pennae* f. feather; pen
per through
pérago *perégi peráctus perágere* carry through
percípio *percépi percéptus percípere* perceive
perdo *pérdidi pérditus pérdere* lose
perénnis *perénnis perénne* everlasting
péreo *périi períre* disappear, perish
pérfero *pértuli perlátus perferre* carry through; endure
perfício *perféci perféctus perfícere* achieve
perículum *perículi* n. danger
perínde just as
perítus *períta perítum* experienced, expert
permítto *permísi permíssus permíttere* allow 173
perpétuus *perpétua perpétuum* perpetual
pérsequor *persecútus pérsequi* pursue
persóna *persónae* f. mask, role, person 12
persuádeo *persuási persuásus persuadére* persuade
pervénio *pervéni pervéntum perveníre* arrive at, reach
pes *pedis* m. foot
pestiléntia *pestiléntiae* f. pestilence
pestis *pestis* f. plague, pest
peto *petívi petítus pétere* seek, request
pháretra *pháretrae* f. quiver
philosophía *philosophíae* f. philosophy

❚lósophus   *philósophi* m. philosopher
❚ctúra   *pictúrae* f. painting, picture
pila   *pilae* f. ball
pingo   *pinxi pictus píngere* paint
piscis   *piscis* m. fish 11
pius   *pia pium* pious, dutiful
pláceo   *plácui plácitus placére* please
planus   *plana planum* even, flat
plátea   *pláteae* f. boulevard, square
plaúsus   *plaúsus* m. applause
plebéius   *plebéii* m. plebeian, of the (common) people 14
plebs   *plebis* f. the (common) people, the masses
plenus   *plena plenum* full
plostrum   *plostri* n. cart, wagon
plurális   *plurális plurále* concerning more than one 185
plures   *plúrium* more
plúrimi   *plurimórum* most, very many
plus   *pluris* n. more 185
póculum   *póculi* n. cup, goblet
poéna   *poénae* f. punishment 126
poénus   *poéni* m. Punic, a Carthaginian 14
poésis   *poésis* f. poetry
poéta   *poétae* m., f. poet
pol   by Pollux (an oath) 67
polus   *poli* m. pole
pomum   *pomi* n. fruit
pondus   *pónderis* n. weight
pono   *pósui pósitus pónere* put
pons   *pontis* m. bridge
populáris   *populáris populáre* of the people, popular 22
pópulus   *pópuli* m. people 8
porta   *portae* m. gate, entrance
porto   *portávi portátus portáre* carry
portus   *portus* m. harbour, haven
posco   *popósci póscere* beg, demand
possídeo   *possédi posséssus possidére* own, possess
possum   *pótui posse* can, be able
póssumus   we can (from *possum*)

póssunt they can (from *possum*)
post after
postérior *postérior postérius* next, following
póstero the next day, morrow
pósterus *póstera pósterum* next, future
postrémus *postréma postrémum* last
potens gen. *poténtis* powerful
poténtia *poténtiae* f. power
potest he/she/it can (from *possum*)
potéstas *potestátis* f. power
potior more capable
potis able, capable
pótius rather
potus *potus* m. drink
prae before
praecéptum *praecépti* n. rule, precept
praecíse in short, bricfly
praédico *pracdicávi praedicátus praedicáre* proclaim, preach
praéfero *praétuli praelátus praeférre* place before, prefer
praefício *praeféci praeféctus praefícere* place in authority
praémium *praémii* n. booty, profit 114
praemónitus *praemónita praemónitum* forewarned
praenómen *praenóminis* n. forename 40
praéparo *praeparávi praeparátus praeparáre* prepare
praepositío *praepositiónis* f. preposition 104
praesens *praeséntis* present
praesentátio *praesentatiónis* f. exhibition, presentation
praeséntia *praeséntiae* f. presence
praesértim especially
praesídium *praesídii* n. defence, garrison
praeter except
praetérea moreover
pratum *prati* n. meadow
precor *precátus precári* pray
prehéndo *prehéndi, prehénsus, prehéndere* seize
premo *pressi pressus prémere* press
présbyter *presbýteri* m. priest
prétium *prétii* n. price

Basic vocabulary

primus *prima primum* first
princeps *príncipis* m. the first, most distinguished person
princípium *princípii* n. beginning, principle
prior *prior prius* first, earlier
prius former, first
privátus *priváta privátum* private
pro for
probábilis *probábilis probábile* commendable, probable
próbitas *probitátis* f. honesty
probo *probávi probátus probáre* try, approve
procédo *procéssi procéssum procédere* go forth, advance
procul far away
procurátor *procuratóris* m. manager, tax collector
profánus *profána profánum* unholy, uninitiated, uneducated
prófugus *prófuga prófugum* fleeing, fugitive
profúndus *profúnda profúndum* deep
proício *proiéci proiéctus proícere* throw out
promissor *promissoris* m. promiser 72
promítto *promísi promíssus promíttere* promise
pronómen *pronóminis* n. pronoun 104
pronuntiátio *pronuntiatiónis* f. proclamation, expression, pronunciation 34
propóno *propósui propósitus propónere* set out, propose
próprius *própria próprium* distinctive, characteristic
propter on account of
prósperus *próspera prósperum* fortunate
prosum *prófui prodésse* be of advantage
província *provínciae* f. province
próximus *próxima próximum* nearest
prudens gen. *prudéntis* skilled, practised
prudéntia *prudéntiae* f. good sense
públicus *pública públicum* belonging to the people, public 8
pudor *pudóris* m. shame
puélla *puéllae* f. girl 17
puer *púeri* m. boy, child 17
puerílis *puerílis pueríle* childish, youthful 211
puls *pultis* f. porridge 15
pulso *pulsávi pulsátus pulsáre* strike, push

répeto   *repetívi repetítus repétere* repeat
réprimo   *représsi représsus reprímere* keep back, restrain, repress
réquies   *requiétis* f. rest
requiésco   *requiévi requiéscere* rest
requíro   *requisívi requisítus requírere* ask for, require
rerum   of things (from *res*)
res   *rei* f. thing 8,22
res pública   *rei públicae* f. republic, state 8
resído   *resédi reséssum resídere* sit down, settle
resísto   *réstiti resístere* resist
respício   *respéxi respéctus respícere* consider, respect
respóndeo   *respóndi respónsum respondére* answer
restítuo   *restítui restitútus restitúere* restore, return, give back
retíneo   *retínui reténtus retinére* hold or keep back
retro   backwards, behind
reveréntia   *reveréntiae* f. worship, respect
revértor   *revérsus revérti* return, revert to
rex   *regis* m. king, the reigning King (after a name or in the titles of
   lawsuits, e.g. *Rex. v. Jones*, 'the Crown versus Jones') 7, 190
rhetórica   *rhetóricae* f. rhetoric 33, 102
rhetóricus   *rhetórica rhetóricum* which has to do with speech,
   rhetorical
rícinus   *rícini* m. tick
rídeo   *risi risus ridére* laugh
ridículus   *ridícula ridículum* funny, ridiculous
rigor   *rigóris* m. stiffness
robur   *róboris* n. hardness, strength
rogo   *rogávi rogátus rogáre* ask
Roma   *Romae* f. Rome 5
románus 1   *románi* m. a Roman 15
románus 2   *romána románum* Roman 90, 92
roro   *rorávi roráre* drop, drip
rosa   *rosae* f. rose
rota   *rotae* f. wheel
roto   *rotávi rotátus rotáre* turn or roll round
rubricátus   *rubricáta rubricátum* headlined
rudis   *rudis rude* raw, rough
ruína   *ruínae* f. ruin

Basic vocabulary

rumor   *rumóris* m. rumour, reputation
rus   *ruris* n. the countryside
rústicus   *rústica rústicum* rustic 92

sacer   *sacra sacrum* holy 7
saéculum   *saéculi* n. lifetime, century
saevus   *saeva saevum* fierce, savage
sal   *salis* m. salt
salínus   *salína salínus* salty, of salt
salto   *saltávi saltátus saltáre* dance
saltus   *saltus* m. jump
salus   *salútis* f. safety, welfare
salúto   *salutávi salutátus salutáre* greet
salve   Hello!
salveo   *salvére* be in good health, greet, say hello
salvo   *salvávi salvátus salváre* save
salvus   *salva salvum* safe, unharmed
sanctus   *sancta sanctum* holy, sacred
sanguis   *sánguinis* m. blood 150
sanus   *sana sanum* healthy
sápiens   gen. *sapiéntis* wise
sapiéntia   *sapiéntiae* f. wisdom
sat   enough
satélles   *satéllitis* m. attendant 165
satis   enough
sátius   more satisfactory
sátura   *sáturae* f. satire
scelus   *scéleris* n. crime
schola   *scholae* f. school
sciéntia   *sciéntiae* f. skill, knowledge, science
scio   *scii scitus scire* know
scópulus   *scópuli* m. crag
scribo   *scripsi scriptus scríbere* write
scriptórium   *scriptórii* n. writing room 118
sculpo   *sculpsi sculptus scúlpere* sculpt
se   himself, herself, themselves
secrétus   *secréta secrétum* secret
secúndus   *secúnda secúndum* second, following

secúrus   *secúra secúrum* safe, sure
sed   but
sédeo   *sedi sedére* sit
semel   once
semen   *séminis* n. seed
seméntis   *seméntis* f. sowing
semper   always
senátus   *senátus* m. the Senate 8–9
senéctus   *senectútis* f. old age
senex 1   *senis* m., f. old man, old woman 9
senex 2   gen. *senis* old
senílis   *senílis seníle* concerning old age 149
sensus   *sensus* m. sense, feeling
senténtia   *senténtiae* f. opinion
séntio   *sensi sensum sentíre* feel, hear
septem   seven 44
sepúlchrum   *sepúlchri* n. grave
sepultúra   *sepultúrae* f. burial
sequor   *secútus sum sequi* follow
seréno   *serenávi serenátus serenáre* make clear or bright, light up
sermo   *sermónis* m. speech, language, talk
sero 1   *sevi satus sérere* sow
sero 2   late
sérpens   *serpéntis* f., m. snake
serva   *servae* f. female slave 17
servílis   *servílis servíle* of a slave, servile
sérvio   *seruíui cornítus servíre* be a slave
servo   *servávi servátus serváre* save
servus   *servi* m. slave 17
sese   himself, herself, themselves
sevérus   *sevéra sevérum* stern, serious
sex   six
sextus   *sexta sextum* sixth 44
si   if
sic   thus, so
sidus   *síderis* n. star, constellation
signum   *signi* f. sign

siléntium   *siléntii* f. silence
síleo   *sílui silére* be silent
silva   *silvae* f. wood
silvéstris   *silvéstris silvéstre* wood-, relating to a
   wood or forest 155
símilis   *símilis símile* like
simíllimus   *simíllima simíllimum* most like, very like
simplex   gen. *símplicis* simple
simplícitas   *simplicitátis* f. simplicity
simul   at the same time; as soon as
símulo   *simulávi simulátus simuláre* simulate
sine   without
singuláris   *singuláris singuláre* one by one, singular 185
síngulus   *síngula síngulum* single, one at a time 185
siníster   *sinístra sinístrum* left; inauspicious
sinus   *sinus* m. curve, bay
sit   is, may be (from *sum*)
situs   *situs* m. situation
sóbrius   *sóbria sóbrium* sober, temperate
socíetas   *societátis* f. fellowship, community, union, society
sócius   *sócii* m. fellow, comrade, companion
sol   *solis* m. sun
sóleo   *sólitus solére* be used to
solitúdo   *solitúdinis* f. loneliness, solitude, desert, wilderness
sollémnis   *sollémnis sollémne* solemn
solus   *sola solum* only
solvo   *solvi solútus sólvere* loosen, release, set free, solve
somnus   *somni* m. sleep
sonus   *soni* m. sound 134
sórdidus   *sórdida, sórdidum* dirty
soror   *soróris* f. sister
spargo   *sparsi sparsus spárgere* spread
spátium   *spátii* n. space, room
spécies   *speciéi* f. sight, appearance; species
spectátor   *spectatóris* m. member of the audience, spectator
specto   *spectávi spectátus spectáre* look at, regard
spero   *sperávi sperátus speráre* hope (vb.)
spes   *spei* f. hope (noun)

spíritus   *spíritus* m. breath, spirit
spiro   *spirávi spiráre* breathe
spléndeo   *spléndui splendére* shine
stabulárius   *stabulárii* m. landlord, innkeeper
státua   *státuae* f. statue
statúra   *statúrae* f. height, stature 96
status   *status* m. state, posture
stella   *stellae* f. star
stilus   *stili* m. stylus (for wax tablets); pen
stipulátio   *stipulationis* f. oral contract 72
sto   *steti stare* stand
strabus   *straba strabum* cross-eyed, one-eyed
stratum   *strati* n. cover, saddle
stricte   strictly
stúdeo   *stúdui studére* pursue, study
stúdium   *stúdii* n. eagerness; study; zeal
stultus   *stulta stultum* stupid
suádeo   *suási suásus suadére* persuade
suávis   *suávis suáve* mild, gentle
suáviter   gently
sub   under
subício   *subiéci subiéctus subícere* submit, subject
subiéctus   *subiécta subiéctum* lying near, subjected
sublímis   *sublímis sublíme* high, lofty, sublime
substantívus   *substantíva substantívum* substantive 104
succúrro   *succúrri succúrrere* help
suggíllo   *suggillávi suggillátus suggilláre* injure (eyes, etc.)
sum   *fui esse* be (Table 14)
summa   *summae* f. top, sum, main point 113
summóveo   *summóvi summótus summovére* drive off, banish
summus   *summa summum* highest, greatest 39
sumo   *sumpsi sumptus súmere* take
sumus   we are (from *sum*)
sunt   they are (from *sum*)
super   above
supérbus   *supérba supérbum* proud, arrogant
supérior   *supérior supérius* higher, upper, former
superstítio   *superstitiónis* f. superstition 77

supérsum   *supérfui superésse* be left, survive
súperus   *súpera súperum* upper
supplícium   *supplícii* n. penalty
supra   over, above; earlier on (in a book or writing)
suprémus   *supréma suprémum* highest, last
suscípio   *suscépi suscéptus suscípere* take up, support
suspéctior   *suspéctior suspéctius* more suspect
suspéctus   *suspécta suspéctum* suspect
suspéndo   *suspéndi suspénsus suspéndere* hang up, suspend
suspício   *suspiciónis* f. suspicion
sustíneo   *sustínui sustinére* hold up, support
suus   *sua suum* his, her, their (referring to the subject of the sentence)
sýllaba   *sýllabae* f. syllable 180

tábula   *tábulae* f. board, table, slate
táceo   *tácui tácitus tacére* bc silent
talis   *talis tale* such
tam   so
tamen   however
tamquam   like, as if
tandem   at length, finally
tango   *tétigi tactus tángere* touch
tantum   so much; only
tantus   *tanta tantum* so big
tardus   *tarda tardum* slow
taurus   *tauri* m. bull
te   you (singular)
tecum   with you (singular)
tego   *texi tectus tégere* cover, shelter, hide
tégula   *tégulae* f. tile
tellus   *tellúris* f. the earth
témperans   gen. *temperántis* moderate, temperate
templum   *templi* f. temple
tempus   *témporis* n. time
tendo   *teténdi tensus téndere* stretch
téneo   *ténui tenére* hold, keep
tento   *tentávi tentátus tentáre* feel, try
ténuis   *ténuis ténue* thin

ter three times
tergum *tergi* n. back
términus *términi* m. boundary
terra *terrae* f. earth, land
térreo *térrui térritus terrére* frighten
terror *terróris* m. dread
tértius *tértia tértium* third 36
testaméntum *testaménti* n. will
testis *testis* m. witness
theología *theologíae* f. theology 143
thesaúrus *thesaúri* m. treasure, wealth 126
Thrace *Thraces* f. Thrace
thronus *throni* m. throne
tibi to, for you (sg.)
tímeo *tímui timére* fear
timor *timóris* m. fear
titíllo *titillávi titillátus titilláre* tickle, tease
títulus *títuli* m. title
toga *togae* f. toga
tollo *sústuli sublátus tóllere* lift up, take away
tot so many
totus *tota totum* whole, all (Table 10) 197
trado *trádidi tráditus trádere* hand over, betray
traho *traxi tractus tráhere* drag
trans across
tránseo *tránsii transíre* go across, cross
tránsfero *tránstuli translátus transférre* carry over, translate
transmarínus *transmarína transmarínum* across the sea
transmítto *transmisi transmíssus transmíttere* send across
tremor *tremóris* m. shaking, earthquake
tres *tres tria* three
trigéminus *trigémini* m. triplet 150
trilínguis *trilínguis trilíngue* trilingual 78
tristis *tristis triste* sad
triúmphus *triúmphi* m. triumph
trívium *trívii* f. 'three ways' (the three basic disciplines of the *artes liberales*) 103
tu you (singular) (Table 6) 5

Basic vocabulary

tuba   *tubae* f. tuba
tuli   see *fero*
tum   then
tumultus   *tumultus* m. uproar
turbo   *turbávi turbátus turbáre* disturb, agitate
turris   *turris* f. tower
tutus   *tuta tutum* safe
tuus   *tua tuum* your (singular)

ubi   where
ubíque   everywhere
ultérior   *ultérior ultérius* further
últimus   *última últimum* furthest, last
ultra   beyond
umbra   *umbrae* f. shadow
unde   whence
unguis   *unguis* m. nail (of finger or toe)
únicus   *única únicum* only; unique 139
univérsus   *univérsa univérsum* whole, universal
unus   *una unum* one (Table 10) 36
urbs   *urbis* f. city
úrgeo   *urgére* drive on, urge
urna   *urnae* f. urn 114
uro   *ussi ustus úrere* burn, scorch
ursus   *ursi* m. bear 155
usque   right up to, as far as
usus   *usus* m. use
ut   as, like; in order to; that
utérque   *útraque utrúmque* both, each
útilis   *útilis útile* useful
utor   *usus uti* use 199
utrum   whether

vaco   *vacávi vacáre* be empty
vácuus   *vácua vácuum* empty
vado   *vádere* go
vae   woe!
vagans   gen. *vagántis* wandering

vagína   *vagínae* f. sheath, vagina
vale   Goodbye! (from *váleo*)
váleo   *válui valére* be worthy, be healthy
válidus   *válida válidum* strong, powerful
vallis   *vallis* f. valley
vánitas   *vanitátis* f.emptiness, vanity
vanus   *vana vanum* empty, vain
variátio   *variatiónis* f. variety
várius   *vária várium* varying, fickle
véhemens   gen. *veheméntis* violent
veho   *vexi vectus véhere* carry
velox   gen. *velócis* quick
velum   *veli* n. veil, sail
venális   *venális venúle* adj. to do with selling
venerábilis   *venerábilis venerábile* venerable 94
véneror   *venerátus venerári* worship
vénia   *véniae* f. kindness, foregiveness, permission
vénio   *veni ventum veníre* come
venter   *ventris* m. stomach, belly
ventúrus   *ventúra ventúrum* coming
ventus   *venti* m. wind
ver   *veris* n. spring
verbátim   word for word
verbum   *verbi* n. word 104, 119–20
véritas   *veritátis* f. truth
vérsio   *versiónis* f. translation
versus 1   *versus* m. line (of poetry)
versus 2   *versa versum* turned
verus   *vera verum* true
vesper   *vesperi* m. evening, evensong
vester   *vestra vestrum* your (plural)
vestígium   *vestígii* n. footprint
vestis   *vestis* f. clothes
veto   *vétui vétitus vetáre* forbid
vetus   gen. *véteris* old
via   *viae* f. way 7
vice   (abl.) f. change
vicínus   *vicíni* m. neighbouring, nearby

Basic vocabulary

victor   *victóris* m. winner (male); victorious (masc.)
victória   *victóriae* f. victory
victrix   *victrícis* f. winner (female); victorious (fem.)
vidélicet   namely
vídeo   *vidi visus vidére* see; in the passive seem
vigília   *vigíliae* f. watch, wakefulness
vigor   *vigóris* m. strength, energy
vilis   *vilis vile* cheap
villa   *villae* f. villa 114
vinco   *vici victus víncere* win, conquer
vínculum   *vínculi* n. bond
vinum   *vini* n. wine
víolo   *violávi violátus violáre* do violence to, violate
vir   *viri* m. man 16
vires   *vírium* f. forces (from *vis 1*)
virgo   *vírginis* f. maiden, virgin
víridis   *víridis víride* green
virílis   *virílis viríle* of a man, manly 211
virtus   *virtútis* f. excellence, virtue 16, 111
virus   *viri* n. slime, poisonous liquid 149
vis 1   f. strength, force
vis 2   you (sing.) want (from *volo*)
vísio   *visiónis* f. sight 165
viso   *vísere* view, stare at
vita   *vitae* f. life
vitiósus   *vitiósa vitiósum* wicked, depraved
vivo   *vixi vívere* live 11
vivus   *viva vivum* alive, living
vobis   to, for, by you (plural)
vobíscum   with you (plural)
voco   *vocávi vocátus vocáre* call
volo 1   *vólui velle* want
volo 2   *volávi voláre* fly
volúntas   *voluntátis* f. will
volúptas   *voluptátis* f. pleasure, delight
volvo   *volvi volútus vólvere* roll
vos   you (pl.) 194
votum   *voti* n. vow

vox   *vocis* f. voice
vulgáris   *vulgáris vulgáre* of the people, common 69
vulgátus   *vulgáta vulgátum* widespread
vulgus   *vulgi* n. people 69
vult   he/she/it wants (from *volo*)
vultus   *vultus* m. face, expression

Part V

Common Phrases and Expressions

Common Phrases and Expressions

a fortióri   for a stronger, more compelling reason 110

a posterióri   from after, said of knowledge which depends on experience

a prióri   from before, said of knowledge which is prior to experience 110

a tergo   from behind

ab incunábulis   from the cradle, from childhood

ab inítio   from the beginning

ab Iove princípium   things begin with Jupiter (Virgil)

ab ovo   from the very beginning

ab ovo usque ad mala   from the egg to the apples (i.e. for the whole meal) (Horace)

ab urbe cóndita   from the founding of the city (the title of Livy's history of Rome) 37

Ábeunt stúdia in mores   Study builds character

absit omen   may what is threatened not happen

Abúsus non tollit usum   Misuse does not preclude (proper) use

ad acta   to the files

ad finem   at or near or to the end

ad hoc   for this specific reason (e.g. 'an ad hoc measure')

ad hóminem   relating to a particular person

ad infinítum   without limit, for ever

ad interim   meanwhile

ad Kaléndas Giaccao   on the Greek kalends (i.e. never)

ad líb(itum)   at will, freely; improvised

ad maiórem Dei glóriam   to the greater glory of God (the motto of the Jesuits)

ad naúseam   to an excessive or disgusting degree

ad notam   for guidance

ad persónam   to the person, personally

ad rem   to the point

ad unguem factus homo   an accomplished man right down to his fingertips (Horace)

Advérsus míseros . . . inhumánus est iocus   It is not right to make fun of miserable people (Quintilian)

Aequam meménto rebus in árduis serváre mentem   Remember to keep an even temper when things are rough (Horace)

Aliéna nobis, nostra plus áliis placent   We prefer what belongs to others and other people prefer what belongs to us; the grass is always greener on the other side of the field (Publilius Syrus)

Aliquándo et insaníre iucúndum est   Sometimes it helps to be mad (Seneca)

alma mater   kind mother (used to refer to the university or school that one has studied at)

alter ego   the other I; a trusted friend; one's secondary or alternative personality

alter idem   another I (Cicero)

Amícus certus in re incérta cérnitur   A friend in need is a friend indeed (Ennius)

amícus humáni géneris   a friend of the human race

amor pátriae   love of one's country

anno aetátis suae . . .   in the . . . year of his/her life

anno Dómini   in the year of the Lord (i.e. dating from the birth of Christ, abbreviated as CE)

annus mirábilis   a wonderful year

ante merídiem   before noon (abbreviated as 'a.m.')

antíquus   *antíqua antíquum* old

aqua et igni interdíctus   forbidden the use of fire and water, i.e. banished

aqua vitae   the water of life

arguméntum ad hóminem   an argument relating to a particular individual (see also *ad hominem*)

Arma virúmque cano, Troiae qui primus ab oris Itáliam fato prófugus Laviniáque venit lítora   I sing of arms and of the man who, made fugitive by fate, first came from the coasts of Troy to Italy and the Lavinian shores (Virgil, the opening lines of the *Aeneid*)

arréctis aúribus   with ears pricked up

Ars est celáre artem   (True) art lies in hiding art

Arte et Marte   By art and war

Atque in perpétuum, frater, ave atque vale!   And forever, brother, greetings and farewell! (Catullus; from a poem at his brother's graveside, far from Italy)

Audiátur et áltera pars   Let the other side also be heard (Augustine; basic principle of law)

aúream quisquis mediocritátem diligit   whoever loves the golden mean (Horace)

auri sacra fames   the hateful hunger for gold (Virgil)

Ave grátia plena! Dóminus tecum   Hail, thou art highly favoured. The Lord is with thee (St Luke's Gospel; the angel's greeting to Mary at the Annunciation)

Ave, imperátor, moritúri te salútant   Hail, emperor, those who are about to die salute you (Suetonius, the gladiators' greeting to the emperor)

Beáti misericórdes   Blessed are the merciful (St Matthew's Gospel)

bellum ómnium in omnes   the war of everyone against everyone (Hobbes)

Benedíctus qui venit in nómine Dómini   Blessed is he who comes in the name of the Lord (St Matthew's Gospel)

Bibámus, moriéndum est   Let us drink for we must die (Seneca the elder)

bona fide   in good faith

bonis auspíciis   with good auspices

Brevis esse labóro, obscúrus fio   I strive to be brief and I end up being obscure (Horace)

Caelum, non ánimum, mutant qui trans mare currunt   Those who travel overseas change their sky but not their heart (Horace)

Caésarem vehis Caesarísque fortunam   You carry Caesar and Caesar's fate (Caesar)

cánticum canticórum   the Song of Songs (Latin name of the Song of Solomon)

Carpe diem, quam mínimum crédula póstero   Seize the day; trust as little as possible in the morrow (Horace)

casus belli   a justification or cause of war

cave canem   beware of the dog

cáveat emptor   let the buyer beware

cáveat lector   let the reader beware

Cedant arma togae   Let arms yield to the toga (i.e. military power should give way to civil authority) (Cicero)

chaos, rudis indigestáque moles   chaos, a raw formless mass (from which the universe was formed) (Ovid)

círculus vitiósus   vicious circle

citius altius fortius   faster higher stronger (the motto of the Olympic Games)

Cito aréscit lácrima, praesértim in aliénis malis   Tears are quickly dried, especially when they are for other people's troubles (Cicero)

Civis Románus est   He is a Roman citizen (Acts of the Apostles, concerning Paul, who thus avoided imprisonment and torture)

Cógito, ergo sum   I think, therefore I am (Descartes) 144

compos mentis   complete of mind; sane

conféssio fídei   declaration of faith

Consuetúdine quasi álteram quandam natúram éffici   Through practice it is as if things become second nature (Cicero)

Consuetúdinis magna vis est   The force of habit is great (Cicero)

contradíctio in adiécto   contradiction in terms, oxymoron

coram público   in public

cornu cópiae   horn of plenty

corpus delícti   the body in the crime (a clear proof such as a body or the murder weapon)

Credo quia absúrdum est   I believe because it is absurd

Credo ut intélligam   I believe in order that I may understand (Anselm of Canterbury)

Crescit amor nummi, quantum ipsa pecúnia crescit   Love of money grows as fast as money grows (Juvenal)

cui bono?   to whose advantage? (Cicero, a principle used in investigating crimes)

cum grano salis   with a grain of salt

Cur non ut plenus vitae convíva recédis aequo animóque capis secúram, stulte, quiétem?   Why not, like a guest at dinner, satisfied with life, take your leave, and with mind content take now, you fool, your sure rest? (Lucretius)

currículum vitae   the race of life (Cicero) (the important points in one's career, abbreviated as 'CV')

cursus honórum   sequence of honours (the steps in the career of a public official)

Da mi básia mille, deínde centum   Give me a thousand kisses and
then a hundred more (Catullus)

Da mihi castitátem et continéntiam, sed noli modo   Give me
chastity and restraint but not just now (St Augustine)

De brevitáte vitae   On the shortness of life (title of a work by Seneca)

de facto   in fact, in reality (whether by right or not)

de gústibus non est disputándum   There can be no discussion
about tastes

de íntegro   anew, once more, from the beginning

de iure   in law; rightful

De mórtuis nil nisi bonum   speak nothing but well of the dead

de novo   starting again; anew

De profúndis clamávi ad te, Dómine   Out of the depths I have cried
to you, Lord (Psalm 130; *De profundis* is the title of a work by Oscar
Wilde written when he was in prison)

Dei grátia   by the grace of God (used in royal and other titles)

... delineávit   ... drew (a formula with which an artist signed a piece
of work)

Deo favénte   with God's favour

Deo grátias   thanks be to God

Deo volénte   God willing

Deus ex máchina   god from a machine (a god who could be lowered
mechanically to resolve the plot at the end of a play, hence any
artificial device introduced at the last minute to solve a problem)

Deus vult   God wants (motto of the first crusade)

Deus, creátor ómnium   God, creator of all things (beginning of
a well-known hymn by St Ambrose)

Di nos quasi pilas hómines habent   The gods treat us humans as
their playthings (Plautus)

Dictum sapiénti sat est   A word is enough to a wise man (Plautus)

dies irae   day of wrath

Diffícile est sáturam non scríbere   It is hard not to write satire
(Juvenal)

**Diffugére nives, rédeunt iam grámina campis arboribúsque
comae**   The snow has gone; now the grass comes back to the fields
and the leaves to the trees (Horace)

Dimídium facti qui coepit habet   A job begun is a job half done
(Horace)

dira necéssitas   dire necessity (Horace)

disiécti membra poétae   the limbs of a dismembered poet (Horace, about a quotation taken out of context)

Dívide et ímpera!   Divide and rule! (Louis XI of France)

Dixi et salvávi ánimam meam   I have spoken and I have saved my soul

Docéndo díscimus   By teaching we learn

Dómine, quo vadis?   Lord, where are you going? (St John's Gospel)

Dóminus dedit, Dóminus ábstulit: sit nomen Dómini benedíctum   The Lord gave and the Lord has taken away: blessed be the name of the Lord (Job)

Dóminus vobíscum   The Lord be with you

Dulce est desípere in loco   It is sweet to relax on the right occasion (Horace)

Dum excusáre credis, accúsas   When you think you are excusing yourself you are really accusing yourself (Jerome)

e contrário   on the contrary

e plúribus unum   out of many (is made) one (motto of the United States of America)

Ecce agnus Dei qui tollit peccáta mundi   Behold the lamb of God who takes away the sins of the word (from the Catholic Mass)

Ecce homo   Behold the man (St John's Gospel: the words of Pontius Pilate when he showed Jesus to the people)

edítio princeps   the first printed edition

Ego sum alpha et ómega, princípium et finis, dicit Dóminus deus   I am the alpha and the omega, the beginning and the end, says the Lord God (The Book of Revelations; alpha and omega are respectively the first and last letters of the Greek alphabet)

Ego sum pastor bonus   I am the good shepherd (St John's Gospel)

Eheu fugáces, Póstume, Póstume, labúntur anni   Alas, Postumus, Postumus, how quickly the years slip away (Horace)

eiúsdem géneris   of the same kind

eo ipso   by that itself

Equi donáti dentes non inspiciúntur   Don't look a gift horse in the mouth (Jerome)

Erráre humánum est   To err is human (Cicero)

Esse quam vidéri bonus malébat   He preferred to be good than to
   seem good (Sallust writing about Cato the younger)

et consórtes   and friends

Et in Arcádia ego   Even I have been to Arcadia *or* I (=death) am
   present even in Arcadia

Et semel emíssum volat irrevocábile verbum   And once spoken the
   word flies off and cannot be called back (Horace)

Et tu, Brute   Even you, Brutus (Caesar) 25

Ex África semper áliquid novi   There is always something new out
   of Africa (proverb quoted by Pliny)

ex ánimo   from the heart

ex cáthedra   from the Pope's seat (and in general of anything said
   with the highest authority)

ex grátia   as a favour (rather than from obligation)

ex hypóthesi   according to the hypothesis proposed

ex libris NN   from NN's books

ex níhilo   out of nothing

ex offício   by virtue of one's office

ex post facto   with retrospective action or force

ex siléntio   by the absence of contrary evidence

ex témpore   on the spur of the moment

éxeunt omnes   all leave the stage

Éxitus ácta probat   The end crowns the work (Ovid)

Expérto crédite   Believe the person who has experience (Virgil)

Expértus dico: nemo est in amóre fidélis   I speak as an expert: no
   one is faithful in love (Propertius)

Extra ecclésiam nulla salus   There is no salvation outside the
   Church

Faber est suae quisque fortúnae   Everyone is the architect of their
   own destiny (Appius Claudius Caecus)

Faciéndi plures libros nullus est finis   Of making many books there
   is no end (Ecclesiastes)

Fácilis descénsus Avérno   The descent into Avernus (the realm of the
   dead) is easy (Virgil)

Facis de necessitáte virtútem   You make a virtue out of a necessity
   (St Jerome)

Facit indignátio versum   Indignation prompts the poem (Juvenal)

Factum est illud, fíeri inféctum non potest   It is done and cannot be undone (Plautus)

Fama crescit eúndo   Fame grows as it spreads (Virgil)

Fecísti pátriam divérsis géntibus unam, prófuit iniústis te dominánte capi   You have made a single fatherland for different peoples, it was to the advantage of the unjust to be conquered and brought under your authority (Rutilius Namatianus, writing about Rome's conquests)

... fecit   ... made (this work) (a formula with which an artist signed a piece of work)

Festína lente!   Make haste slowly! (motto of the Emperor Augustus)

... fides, spes, caritas, tria haec, maior autem horum est cáritas   ... faith, hope and love, and the greatest of these is love (First Letter to the Corinthians)

Fiat lux!   let there be light! (Genesis)

fídei defénsor   defender of the faith (one of the titles of the British monarch)

fidus Achátes   a devoted friend or follower

Finis corónat opus   The end crowns the work

flóreat   let it flower

Flúctuat nec mérgitur   It is tossed by the waves but is not driven under (motto of the city of Paris)

Forsan et haec olim meminísse iuvábit   Perhaps it will one day be a pleasure to remember even these things (Virgil)

Fortes fortúna ádiuvat   Fortune favours the brave (Terence)

fórtiter in re, suáviter in modo   strong in deed, mild in manner (Claudius Aquaviva)

Fúimus Troes, fuit Ílion   We Trojans have lived, Troy has been (i.e. Troy and the Trojans are no more) (Virgil)

Gaudeámus ígitur, iúvenes dum sumus   Let us rejoice while we are young (beginning of a Neo-Latin student song)

Glória in altíssimis Deo et in terra pax homínibus bonae voluntátis   Glory to God in the highest and on earth peace and good will to mankind (St Luke's Gospel)

Graeca sunt, non legúntur   These things are in Greek and people don't read what is written in Greek

Graécia capta ferum victórem cepit et artes íntulit agrésti Látio
Greece, which had been captured, in turn captured the savage victor
and brought culture to the farmers of Rome (Horace)

Grammátici certant et adhuc sub iúdice lis est   Scholars squabble,
and the question is still undecided (Horace)

Gutta cavat lápidem   A drop hollows out a stone (Ovid)

Hábeas corpus   You may have the body (in English law, the opening
words of a writ relating to the lawful or otherwise detention of an
individual) 110

Habent sua fata libélli   Books have their own destinies (Terentianus
Maurus)

**Haud ignárus summa scélera íncipi cum perículo, péragi cum
praémio**   He was not unaware of the fact that the greatest crimes are
risky to begin but rewarding to complete (Tacitus)

hic et nunc   here and now

hic et ubíque   here and everywhere

hic iacet . . .   here lies . . . (on gravestones)

hinc   hence, from here

Hinc illae lácrimae   Hence those tears (Terence)

História magístra vitae   History is life's teacher (Cicero)

**Hómini poténtiam quaerénti egentíssimus quisque
opportuníssimus**   To a man who seeks power the neediest is the
most useful (Sallust)

Homo   any primate of the genus *Homo*, including modern humans
and various extinct species

Homo hómini lupus   Man is a wolf to man (Hobbes)

Homo sápiens   wise man (Linnaeus' designation for the human species)

Homo sum, humáni nil a me aliénum puto   I am a human
being and I consider nothing human to be beyond my compass
(Terence)

honóris causa   for honour's sake, honorary (especially in the
expression 'doctor *honoris causa*', abbreviated 'h.c.')

horror vácui   nature abhors a vacuum (a basic principle of physics)

hortus siccus   a collection of dried plants

Humánius est deridére vitam quam deploráre   It is more worthy
of a man to scorn life than to weep over it (Seneca)

Iacta álea est   The die is cast (Caesar) 24–5

id est   that is, that means (abbreviated as *'i.e.'*)

Idem velle atque idem nolle, ea demum firma amicítia est   To want to do and to want not to do the same things, that is indeed the mark of true friendship (Sallust)

Ille mi par esse deo vidétur   That man seems to me like a God (Catullus)

Immortália ne speres   Do not hope for immortality (Horace)

imprímatur   it may be printed (originally Papal approval to publish a book)

in abséntia   in (his, her, their) absence

in absúrdum   to the point of absurdity

in aetérnum   for all eternity

In álio pedúclum vides, in te rícinum non vides   You can spot a louse on someone else but you can't see the tick on yourself (Petronius)

in córpore   in a group

in exténso   in (full) detail, in its entirety

in extrémis   at the point of death; in great difficulties

in flagránti   caught redhanded

In hoc signo vinces   In this sign you will win (words which came to the Emperor Constantine in a dream about the cross)

in infinítum   in infinity

in loco paréntis   in the place of a parent

in médias res   in the middle of events (Horace)

in natúra   in kind (i.e. paid in goods not money)

in pleno   in full

in praesénti   at present

in própria persóna   in his or her own person

in re   in the matter of

in saécula saeculórum   for centuries of centuries, for ever

in situ   in (its) (original) place

in spe   in hope

in statu pupillári   in the position of a pupil; under authority

in toto   completely

in usum Delphíni   for the use of the Dauphin (the Dauphin was the heir to the French throne and anything printed for him avoided the censors)

in útero   in the womb; before birth

in vácuo   in a vacuum

in vino véritas   in wine (is) the truth

in vitro   (of biological processes) taking place in a test-tube or other laboratory environment

in vivo   (of biological processes) taking place in a living organism

infra dignitatem   beneath one's dignity

Innócue vívito, numen adest   Live without guilt for God is near (Ovid; Linnaeus' motto)

ínteger vitae scelerísque purus   unstained in his life and innocent of crime (Horace)

inter ália   among other things

inter nos   between ourselves

Invéntas vitam iuvat excoluísse per artes   It is good to have enriched life through new discoveries (inscription on the medal presented to winners of the Nobel prize)

invíta Minérva   against the grain, against one's natural bent (lit. 'with Minerva unwilling' because, as Cicero explains, Minerva is the goddess of wisdom and nothing good is done against her wishes)

Ipse dixit   He himself has said it (Cicero; Pythagoreans speaking of Pythagoras; a statement resting merely on the speaker's authority)

ipsíssima verba   the very words

ipso facto   by that very fact or act

Ira furor brevis est   Anger is a short madness (Horace)

Iucúndi acti labóres   Labours completed are pleasant (Cicero)

iuráre in verba magístri   to swear by the teacher's words (Horace)

ius civíle   civil law

Labor ómnia vincit ímprobus   Unceasing effort conquers all (Virgil)

lácrimae rerum   the tragedy of life

lapsus cálami   slip of the pen, misprint

lapsus linguae   slip of the tongue

laudátor témporis acti   a praiser of former times (Horace)

Légio mihi nomen est, quia multi sumus   My name is legion for we are many (St Mark's Gospel) (This was the reply to Jesus by a man who was possessed by many evil spirits; Jesus sent the legion of spirits into a herd of 2,000 pigs, who rushed headlong into the sea and were drowned.)

loco citáto   in the cited place (abbreviated as *'loc. cit.'*)

Longum est iter per praecépta, breve et éfficax per exémpla   To learn by rules is a long road, by example a short and effective one (Seneca)

locus clássicus   the best-known or most authoritative passage on a subject

lóquitur   (he or she) speaks (with the speaker's name following, as a stage direction or to inform the reader)

Lusus natúrae   the whim of nature

Magna Charta   the Great Document (signed by King John in 1215 and recognizing the rights of barons and freemen)

magni nóminis umbra   the shade of a great name (Lucan)

magnum opus   important work, master piece

Maior e longínquo reveréntia   Reverence is greater from afar (Tacitus)

Male parta male dilabúntur   Ill-gotten gain is ill-spent (Naevius)

Malo hic primus quam Romae secúndus esse   I would rather be the first here than the second in Rome (Julius Caesar)

Malo quaeri cur nulla (státua) mihi sit pósita quam quare pósita   I would rather people asked why there is no statue of me than why there is one (Cato)

Manus manum lavat   One hand washes the other hand; you scratch my back and I'll scratch yours (Petronius)

Mater ártium necéssitas   Necessity is the mother of invention (Apuleius)

Mea culpa, mea culpa, mea máxima culpa   My fault, my fault, above all my fault (from the confession of sins in the Catholic Mass)

membrum viríle   the male organ, the penis

Meménto te mortálem esse   Remember that you are mortal

meménto mori   Remember death

Mendácem mémorem esse oportére   A liar needs to have a good memory (Quintilian)

mens sana in córpore sano   a healthy mind in a healthy body (Juvenal)

mirábile dictu   wonderful to tell

mirábile visu   wonderful to behold

Miserére mei, Dómine   Have mercy on me, Lord

modus operándi   way of working 110

modus vivéndi   way of living

monuméntum aere perénnius   a more eternal monument than bronze (Horace's assessment of his own poetry)

Moriéndum est   Death comes to us all

multum in parvo   a great quantity in a small space

mutátis mutándis   with the necessary changes

Mutáto nómine de te fábula narrátur   The tale is about you but the name is changed (Horace)

Natúra non facit saltus   Nature doesn't make leaps (Leibniz)

Natúram expélles furca, tamen usque recúrret   You can throw out nature with a pitchfork but it will always come back in again (Horace)

Navigáre necésse est, vívere non est necésse   It is necessary to sail but it is not necessary to live (Gnaeus Pompeius)

ne plus ultra   the furthest attainable point, the culmination, perfection

ne quid nimis   nothing in excess (Terence)

Nemo ante mortem beátus   No one (should be considered) blessed before they are dead

Nemo enim fere saltat sóbrius, nisi forte insánit   No one dances when they are sober unless they are completely mad (Cicero)

Nemo est tam senex qui se annum non putet posse vívere   No one is so old that they don't think they will live for one more year (Cicero)

Nemo me lacéssit impúne   No one provokes me with impunity (national motto of Scotland)

Nescit occásum   It knows no setting (said about the Polestar)

Nihil est ab omni parte beátum   Nothing is blessed by all sides (Horace)

Nihil obstat   There is nothing against (permission to print a book)

Nihil sub sole novum   There is nothing new under the sun (Ecclesiastes)

Nihil tam absúrde dici potest quod non dicátur ab áliquo philósopho   Nothing can be said that is so absurd that it is not said by some philosopher (Cicero)

Nil admirári   Never be astonished (Horace)

Nil desperándum   Never despair (Horace)

Nil mortálibus árdui est   Nothing is too hard for mortals (Horace)

Nil sine magno vita labóre dedit mortálibus   Life has given nothing to mortals without hard work (Horatius)

nolens volens   whether you want to or not, willy nilly

Noli me tángere   Do not touch me (St John's Gospel)

Noli turbáre círculos meos   Don't rub out my circles (Archimedes' last words, spoken to the soldier who killed him while he was drawing in the sand)

nomen est omen   the name is a sign

nomen néscio   I do not know the name (abbreviated as 'NN').

Nómina si nescis perit et cognítio rerum   If you do not know the names of things, then the knowledge of them dies too (Carl von Linné)

Nómina sunt odiósa   Names are odious; no names no pack drill

Non ignára mali míseris succúrrere disco   I who am not ignorant of evil am learning to help the wretched (Virgil)

Non liquet   It is not evident (Cicero)

Non mortem timémus, sed cogitatiónem mortis   It is not death that we fear but the thought of death (Seneca)

non multa sed multum   not many but much (advice to read few things but to read them carefully)

Non olet   It doesn't smell (the Emperor Vespasian's view of the revenue from toilet taxes)

Non ómnia póssumus omnes   We cannot all do everything (Virgil)

Non omnis móriar   Not all of me will die (Horace)

non placet   a negative vote in an assembly

non póssumus   we are unable: a statement of inability to act

non séquitur   it does not follow: an illogical conclusion

Non ut edam vivo, sed ut vivam edo   I do not live to eat but rather eat to live (Quintilian)

Non vitae sed scholae díscimus   We learn not for life but for school (Seneca the younger; usually but wrongly quoted the other way round) 63

Non, si male nunc, et olim sic erit   Even if things are bad now it will not always be so (Horace)

Nonúmque premátur in annum   Let it be suppressed until the ninth year (Horace) (advice not to publish something too hastily)

norma loquéndi   guide for speaking (Horace)

nota bene   observe what follows, take notice (usually drawing attention to a following qualification of what has preceded)

novus homo   a new man, i.e. someone not from a noble family (Cicero)

nuda véritas   the naked truth (Horace)

Nulla dies sine línea   No day without a line (working principle for writers or painters)

Nulla salus bello, pacem te póscimus omnes   There is no salvation in war, we beg you all to make peace (Virgil)

Nulli cóntigit impúne nasci   No one is born without punishment (Seneca)

númerus clausus   closed, fixed number (e.g. of students allowed to enrol for a course)

Nunc est bibéndum   Now we must drink (Horace)

o   Oh!

O jerum, jerum, jerum, o quae mutátio rerum   Oh jerum jerum jerum, Oh what a changing of things! (refrain of a student song, originally from Germany)

O témpora, o mores!   Oh times, Oh morals! (Cicero)

O terque quatérque beati quis ante ora patrum Troiae sub moénibus altis cóntigit oppétere!   Oh three and four times blessed you to whom it fell to meet your deaths under the walls of Troy and before the eyes of your parents! (Virgil)

obiit (followed by date)   died … (on gravestones)

óbiter dictum   a judge's incidental expression of opinion

Óderint, dum métuant   Let them hate, as long as they fear (Accius)

Odi et amo   I hate and I love (Catullus)

Odi profánum vulgus et árceo   I hate the uneducated masses and keep them at a distance (Horace)

Ódium numquam potest esse bonum   Hatred can never be good (Spinoza)

Omne bellum sumi fácile, ceterum aegórrume desínere   All wars are easy to begin but much harder to finish (Sallust)

Omnes eódem cógimur   We are all forced to go the same way (Horace)

Omnes una manet nox   There is but one night that awaits us all (Horace)

Ómnia mecum porto mea   I carry everything that is mine with me (Cicero)

Ómnia tempus habent   To every thing there is a season (Ecclesiastes)

Ómnia vincit amor   Love conquers all (Virgil)

Ómnium rerum princípia parva sunt   Everything has small
  beginnings (Cicero)
onus probándi   burden of proof
Óptima quaeque dies míseris mortálibus aevi prima fugit   Life's
  best days are the first to slip away from us wretched
  mortals (Virgil)
Ora et labóra   Pray and work
Ora pro nobis   Pray for us
Orátor est vir bonus dicéndi perítus   An orator is a good man,
  skilled in public speaking (Cato)
ótium cum dignitáte   leisure with honour (Cicero)
Ótium sine lítteris mors est et hóminis vivi sepultúra
  Leisure without literature is like dying and being buried alive
  (Seneca)

pace   (in stating a contrary opinion) with due deference to
  (the person named) literally: 'with the peace [of N]'
Paete, non dolet!   Paetus, it doesn't hurt! (Pliny the younger; the
  words of Paetus' wife as she stabbed herself when they committed
  suicide together)
pállida mors   pale death (Horace)
panem et circénses   bread and circuses (Juvenal)
párcere subiéctis et debelláre supérbos   to spare the humble and
  vanquish the haughty (Virgil)
Pares cum páribus facíllime congregántur   Birds of a feather flock
  together (Cicero)
pari passu   with equal speed; simultaneously
pars pro toto   the part for the whole
Partúrient montes, nascétur ridículus mus   The mountains will
  give birth and a ridiculous mouse will be born (Horace)
Pater noster qui es in caelis   Our father which art in heaven (The
  Lord's Prayer)
pater pátriae   father of the fatherland (one of the emperor's titles)
per annum   for each year
per árdua ad astra   through difficulties to the stars (motto of the
  Royal Air Force)
per cápita   per head
per se   in and for itself

Perfer et obdúra!   Be patient and hold out! (Ovid)

perículum in mora   there is danger in delay (Livy)

perínde ac si cadáver essent   just as if they were a corpse (concerning the duties of the Jesuits)

persóna grata, persóna non grata   a welcome person (especially a diplomat), an unwelcome person

petítio princípii   the logical fallacy of begging the question

... pinxit   ... painted (painter's signature)

placet   an affirmative vote in an assembly

Plus ... ibi boni mores valent quam álibi bonae leges   There good habits count for more than good laws elsewhere (Tacitus, speaking of the Germans)

pons asinórum   any difficult problem that defeats the slow-witted (literally: bridge of asses)

Possunt quia posse videntur   They can because they think they can (Virgil)

post festum   after the party

post hoc   after this

post merídiem   after noon (abbreviated as 'p.m.')

post partum   after childbirth

potior est, qui prior est   first come first served

pótius sero quam numquam   better late than never (Livy)

praemónitus praemunítus   forewarned is forearmed

Praetérea cénseo Cartháginem esse deléndam   Moreover I think that Carthage must be destroyed (Cato) 18

prima fácie   on a first impression, on the face of it

primum móbile   the main source of motion or action; in medieval astronomy, an outermost sphere believed to revolve round the earth in 24 hours and cause the inner spheres to revolve

primus inter pares   first among equals

pro et contra   for and against

pro hac vice   for this occasion only

pro memória   for memory's sake

pro pátria   for the fatherland

pro rata   in proportion

pro rege, lege et grege   for the king, the law, and the people

pro témpore   for the time being

Common phrases and expressions

Próbitas laudátur et alget Goodness is praised, but freezes (Juvenal)

Procul este, profáni Stay away, you who are uninitiated (Virgil)

Próprium humáni ingénii est odísse quem laéseris It is human nature to hate those you have wronged (Tacitus)

próxime accéssit the person who comes second in an examination (literally: '(s)he approached nearest')

Próximus sum égomet mihi I am nearest to myself (Terence)

Pulvis et umbra sumus We are dust and shadow (Horace)

Qualis ártifex péreo What an artist dies in me (Suetonius, Nero's dying words)

Qualis dóminus, talis et servus As is the master so is the slave (Petronius)

Quandóque bonus dormítat Homérus Sometimes even good Homer nods (Horace)

quantum satis as much as suffices (in recipes, often abbreviated 'q.s.')

Quem di díligunt aduléscens móritur Those whom the gods love die young (Plautus)

Qui ásinum non potest, stratum caedit He who cannot beat the ass, beats the ass's blanket (Petronius)

Qui dormit non peccat He who sleeps does not sin

Qui tacet conséntit Silence means consent

quid pro quo one thing in return for another

Quintíli Vare, legiónes redde! Quintilius Varus, give me back my legions! (Suetonius; Augustus' lament after the massacre by Arminius in the Teutoburger pass)

Quis custódiet ipsos custódes? Who will guard the guardians themselves? (Juvenal)

Quis fállere possit amántem? Who can deceive a lover? (Virgil)

Quis, quid, ubi, quibus auxíliis, cur, quómodo, quando? Who, what, where, with what, why, how, when? (guidelines for investigating a crime)

quod erat demonstrándum that which had to be shown (at the end of a geometrical proof, often abbreviated as 'QED')

quod vide (in cross-references) which see

Quos deus vult pérdere prius deméntat Those whom God wishes to destroy he first drives mad

Quos ego. . . Them I … (Virgil) (unfinished threat pronounced by
Jupiter)

Quot hómines, tot senténtiae There are as many opinions as there
are people (Terence)

rara avis in terris nigróque simíllima cycno a rare bird on the earth
and very like a black swan (Juvenal) 121

redúctio ad absúrdum a method of disproving a
premise by showing that the logical consequence is absurd

Reláta réfero I report what I have heard reported

Rem acu tetigísti You have hit the nail on the head (lit. 'you have
touched the thing with a needle')

Rem tene, verba sequéntur Hold on to the thing and the words will
follow (Cato)

Repetítio est mater studiórum Repetition is the mother
of study

Réquiem aetérnam dona eis, Dómine Give them eternal rest, Lord
(from the Catholic funeral service)

Requiéscat in pace May he/she rest in peace (from the burial service;
abbreviated on gravestones as 'RIP')

Ridéntem dícere verum quid vetat? What forbids us to tell the
truth while laughing? (Horace)

rigor mortis the stiffness of death

Roma locúta est, causa finíta est Rome has spoken, the matter
is over

rus in urbe the country in the city (used of a pleasant surburb)

Salus pópuli supréma lex esto Let the welfare of the people be the
highest law (Cicero)

Sancta simplícitas Holy innocence! (St Jerome and quoted by
Jan Hus)

**Sátius est impunítum relínqui fácinus nocéntis
quam innocéntem damnári** It is better that the crime of a
guilty man go unpunished than that an innocent man be condemned
(Ulpian)

Sciéntia potéstas est Knowledge is power (Francis Bacon)

. . . sculpsit … sculpted (sculptor's signature on a statue)

Semper avárus eget A miser is always in need (Horace)

semper fidélis   always faithful (motto of the US Marine Corps)

semper idem   always the same (Cicero)

Senéctus est natúra loquácior   Old age is by nature somewhat talkative (Cicero)

sensu stricto   in a narrow sense

Serit árbores quae saeclo prosint álteri   He plants trees which will yield a profit for a later age (Caecilius Statius)

Si monumentum requiris, circumspice   If you seek a monument, look around (epitaph for Sir Christopher Wren in St Paul's cathedral)

Si parva licet compónere magnis   If it is legitimate to put small things beside large ones (Virgil)

Si tacuísses, philósophus mansísses   If you had held your tongue you would have remained a philosopher (Boethius)

Si vis pacem, para bellum   If you want peace prepare for war (Vegetius)

Sic itur ad astra   Thus is the way to the stars (Virgil)

Sic semper tyrannis   Always thus for tyrants (allegedly uttered by Abraham Lincoln's assassin)

Sic transit glória mundi   Thus passes worldly glory (sung at the ceremony for the crowning of the Pope)

Silentes leges inter arma   The laws are silent when weapons are present (Cicero)

Símilis símili gaudet   Like rejoices in like

sine die   indefinitely (literally 'without a day')

sine ira et stúdio   without anger or favour (Tacitus) 73

sine qua non   a necessary circumstance (lit. 'without which not')

Sit tibi terra levis   May the earth lie light upon you (inscribed on ancient gravestones)

sit vénia verbo   if I may be excused for saying so

Spectatóres, fábula haec est acta, vos plausum date   Members of the audience, the play is over, applaud (Plautus)

Spectátum véniunt, véniunt specténtur ut ipsae   They come to see and be seen (Ovid about women at the theatre)

Stabat mater dolorósa iuxta crucem lacrimósa, dum pendébat fílius   The mother stood grieving and weeping beside the cross where her son was hanging (beginning of the hymn *Stabat mater*)

status quo (ante)   the state in which things were (before)

Stúdium discéndi voluntáte, quae cogi non potest, constat
Enthusiasm for learning depends on the will, which cannot be forced
(Quintilian)

sub iudice   under investigation (lit. 'under the judge')

sub rosa   in secret (because a rose was hung over the council table as a
sign of secrecy)

sub specie aeternitátis   from the viewpoint of eternity (Spinoza)

sui géneris   of its own kind, a 'one-off'

summa summárum   the sum of sums (Plautus)

summum bonum   the highest good

Summum ius, summa iniúria   The highest justice is the greatest
injustice (Cicero)

Sunt áliquid manes, letum non ómnia finit   The shades do exist,
death is not the end of everything (Propertius)

suo iure   in one's own right

suum cuique   to each his own (Cicero)

tábula rasa   empty slate

taédium vitae   weariness of life, especially as leading to suicide

Tamquam scópulum sic fúgias inaudítum atque ínsolens verbum
You should avoid new and unusual words as you would the cliff's edge
(Caesar)

Tantae molis erat Románam cóndere gentem   So much effort did it
cost to found the Roman nation (Virgil)

Tantaéne ánimis caeléstibus irae?   Why such wrath in the minds of
the gods? (Virgil)

Tantum relígio pótuit suadére malórum   Religion has caused so
many evils (Lucretius) 58

Te deum laudámus, te deum confitémur   We praise you, God, we
acknowledge you (Nicetas: the beginning of a hymn)

Témpora mutántur, nos et mutámur in illis   Times change and we
change with them (John Owen)

términus a quo   the starting-point of an argument, policy, etc.

términus ad quem   the finishing-point of an argument,
policy, etc.

términus ante quem   the time before which, i.e. the latest possible
date of an event (used by historians in establishing the date of one
event relative to another)

Common phrases and expressions

términus post quem   the time after which, i.e. the earliest possible
   date of an event
Tértium non datur   A third (alternative) is not given
Tímeo Dánaos et dona feréntes   I fear the Greeks even when they
   bear gifts (Virgil)
terra firma   solid earth
terra incógnita   unknown territory
Tolle lege, tolle lege!   Take and read, take and read! (Augustine)
tot discrímina rerum   so many setbacks (Virgil)
totis víribus   with all one's strength
Tu régere império pópulos, Románe, meménto   You, Roman,
   remember to rule the peoples with your power (Virgil)

Ubi bene, ibi pátria   The real fatherland is where you can live well
Ubi solitúdinem fáciunt, pacem appéllant   They make a desert and
   call it peace (Tacitus)
Última Thule   The furthest Thule (Virgil, a name for the extreme
   north of Europe)
**Unum bonum est quod beátae vitae causa et firmaméntum est,
   sibi fídere**   There is one good thing which is the cause and
   foundation of a happy life, to trust oneself (Seneca)
unus, sed leo   one but a lion
Urbi et orbi   to the city (Rome) and the world (Gregory X)
Urbs aetérna   the eternal city (Rome) (Tibullus)
Ut desint vires, tamen est laudánda volúntas   Even when the
   strength is lacking, the will must still be praised (Ovid)
... ut iam magnitúdine labóret sua   ... that it (the state of Rome)
   labours under the burden of its own size (Livy)
ut infra   as below
ut pictúra poésis   as in painting so in poetry (Horace)
Ut seméntem féceris, ita metes   As you sow so shall you reap (Cicero)
ut supra   as above
útile dulci   the useful with the sweet

Vade mecum   Go with me (a 'vademecum' is something one always
   has to hand)
Vade retro me, Sátana   Get thee behind me, Satan (St Matthew's
   Gospel)

Vae victis   Woe to the conquered (Livy)

vánitas vanitátum   vanity of vanities (Ecclesiastes)

Variátio deléctat   Variety is pleasing

Várium et mutábile semper fémina   A woman is always fickle and changing (Virgil)

Veni, vidi, vici   I came, I saw, I conquered (Caesar)

vénia praedicandi   permission to preach (can be given to people who are not ordained)

vérsio vulgáta   'The Vulgate' (name of St Jerome's translation of the Bible into Latin) 78–9

verso póllice   with thumb turned (Juvenal; gesture meaning that a gladiator should be killed)

Vestígia terrent   The footprints are terrifying (Horace) (because they go into the cave but there are none coming out again)

via média   a compromise

vice versa   with the order reversed

victor ludórum   a male sports champion

Victrix causa deis plácuit, sed victa Catóni   The victor's cause found favour with the gods, that of the vanquished with Cato (Lucan)

victrix ludórum   a female sports champion

vide   (as an instruction in a reference to a passage in a book etc.) see, consult

Vídeo melióra probóque, deterióra sequor   I see and esteem those things which are better and go after those that are worse (Ovid)

Víncere scis, Hánnibal, victória uti nescis   You know how to win, Hannibal, but not how to use your victory (Livy)

vínculum matrimónii   the bond of marriage

Vino péllite curas   Drown your sorrows in drink (Horace)

Virtus et summa potéstas non cóeunt   Virtue and high power do not go together (Lucan)

Vita brevis, ars longa   Life is short, art is long(-lasting)

Vitae summa brevis spem nos vetat incoháre longam   The shortness of life stops us nurturing long-lasting hopes (Horace)

vitam impéndere vero   devote one's life to the truth (Juvenal)

Vívere tota vita discéndum est   You must learn to live the whole of your life (Seneca)

Vívitur parvo bene   One can live well on a little (Horace)

Common phrases and expressions

Vos estis sal terrae You are the salt of the earth (St Matthew's Gospel)

vox clamántis in desérto a voice crying in the desert (St Matthew's Gospel)

vox pópuli public opinion

Suggested reading

The best reference work in English for things to do with Greece and Rome is *The Oxford Classical Dictionary*. The third revised edition, edited by Simon Hornblower and Antony Spawforth, contains many articles on topics covered in this book such as education, naming, and the law, as well as details of all the writers and political figures mentioned here, and each article comes with suggestions for more reading for those who want to take their interest further. Other useful works in the OUP reference series are *The Oxford Companion to Classical Literature*, *The Oxford History of the Classical World*, and *The Oxford Illustrated History of Medieval Europe*. See too *Encyclopedia of the Middle Ages*, ed. André Vauchez (Cambridge: James Clarke, 2000).

A book which discusses in depth the way we relate to Latin is Joseph Farrell's *Latin Language and Latin Culture: From Ancient to Modern Times* (Cambridge: Cambridge University Press, 2001). Very well written introductory essays on Latin literature are collected in Oliver Taplin (ed.), *Literature in the Roman World* (Oxford: Oxford University Press, 2000). A larger and bang up-to-date collection is *The Blackwell Companion to Latin Literature*, ed. S. J. Harrison (Oxford: Blackwell, 2004). The standard introduction in English to the way classical learning has been handed down over the ages is L. D. Reynolds and N. G. Wilson, *Scribes and Scholars: A Guide to the Transmission of Greek and Latin Literature, 3rd edn*, (Oxford: Clarendon Press, 1991).

A useful introduction to the history of Rome is Marcel Le Glay *et al.*, *A History of Rome* (Oxford: Blackwell, 2001). This is a topic for which it is handy to have at one's side a work like T. Cornell and J. Matthews's excellent *Atlas of the Roman World* (Oxford: Phaidon, 1982), which also has a limpid and succinct accompanying narrative.

For those who want to take their study of Latin further, a good course is *Reading Latin* (2 vols.: *Text* and *Grammar*) by Peter Jones and Keith Sidwell (Cambridge: Cambridge University Press, 1986). The authors have recently added a further volume entitled *An Independent Study Guide to* Reading Latin (2000) precisely for those who are working on their own without a teacher. If you want to take your reading beyond this, the obvious next port of call is the huge range of Latin texts with facing English translations in the Loeb Classical Library, published in the UK by Heinemann and in the United States by Harvard University Press. Some of the editions of Latin works in the Oxford World's Classics series also have the Latin text on the facing pages, whereas the many excellent translations in the Penguin Classics series come with useful notes but not the original texts.

Latin texts from medieval times and later are usually less readily available. Many are, however, translated into English, and some well-known authors are included in the series mentioned above. Still, most texts are published only in Latin, and are sometimes quite hard to come by. A good way to start is to use the text collection *Medieval Latin*, ed. K. P. Harrington, 2nd edn. (Chicago: University of Chicago Press, 1997).

Once you move on to reading texts on your own, you will also need a good basic dictionary such as *Cassell's Latin Dictionary* (now published by Continuum, London and New York) or C. T. Lewis, *Elementary Latin Dictionary* (Oxford: Oxford University Press, 1963). The latter is an abridged version of a monument of nineteenth-century scholarship, still in print, namely *A Latin Dictionary* by C. T. Lewis and Charles Short (Oxford: Oxford University Press,). There is an on-line version available via the Perseus website (see below). The most authoritative Latin–English dictionary now is, however, P. Glare's *Oxford Latin Dictionary* (Oxford: Oxford University Press, 1968–82), which draws on sources not available to Lewis and Short, but which only contains words from texts up to about 200 AD, whereas Lewis and Short also draws on later texts, incuding ecclesiastical ones and the early Latin translations of the Bible. For medieval Latin, the first place to go is

Revised Medieval Latin Word-List by R. E. Latham (Oxford: Oxford University Press, 1965).

Philip Baldi, *The Foundations of Latin* (Berlin: Mouton de Gruyter, 1999; paperback 2002) is an excellent compendium of linguistic information about the structure of Latin, its history and relations to other languages, and contains samples of various kinds of (mainly non-literary) texts. A very good small manual on the pronunciation of Latin, aimed at the general reader, is W. Sidney Allen, *Vox Latina* (Cambridge: Cambridge University Press, 1970). For information about the Latin language and Latin literature in the Middle Ages, see *Medieval Latin: An Introduction and Bibliographical Guide*, ed. F. A. C. Mantello and A. G. Rigg (Washington, DC: Catholic University of America Press, 1996). For later times still: J. Ijsewijn, *Companion to Neo-Latin Studies* (2 vols., Leuven: University Press, 1990, 1998).

For Latin animal and plant names, consult A. F. Gotch, *Latin Names Explained: A Guide to the Classification of Reptiles, Birds and Mammals* (London: Blandford/Cassell, 1995). Amazingly, the first ever English translation, by Stephen Freer, of Linnaeus' *Philosophia Botanica* has only just been published (Oxford: Oxford University Press, 2003).

One should not of course forget the worldwide web, which has a huge collection of resources for both the expert and the aspiring Latinist. Typing 'Latin language' into Google yields over two million hits, which should satisfy even the most enthusiastic browser! The principal site is probably www.perseus.tufts.edu, which has a vast repertory of texts and translations, and contains links to on-line grammars and dictionaries and other sites of interest to Latinists. It is possible to find and download most Latin texts from antiquity, and very many from later periods as well.

Index

Index

Index